"Curren knows the most important part of the solar value chain is the valued customer. In this pioneering book, he guides solar sellers out of the dark ages of snake oil salesmen, away from their need to scrounge for leads via robocalling and door-to-door knockers and into the 21st Century of Internet- and social media-based marketing. His mission? To help installers—those warriors on the front lines of the solar revolution—win back the all-important trust of prospective buyers."

– William P. Hirshman
Investigative Reporter, *pv magazine*
Former Associate Editor at Photon International

"As a journalist and marketing professional I encounter many of the hurdles—even in my own neighborhood—that solar companies must overcome to be taken more seriously by consumers. Curren explains why it's so important to deal with the presumed trust in utilities but also their motivations, along with a host of other challenges and consumer habits. He nails how best to do that whether through inbound marketing, authentic blogging, and leveraging all that data from your web site and social media. Read this before you try to sell your next rooftop system!"

– Jim Pierobon
Owner, Pierobon & Partners LLC
Co-founder of *Southeast Energy News*

"In the rapidly changing PV industry, *The Solar Sales Leap* is a must-read for anyone involved in the task of marketing solar power to residential homeowners. Curren summarizes here what many PV installers are failing to recognize when trying to capture the attention of a qualified residential solar power prospect."

– Joe Sadonis
Solar Consultant, Paradise Clean Energy

"The Solar Sales Leap offers a practical guide to building meaningful customer relationships in the age of new media. The concrete, real world examples, are an excellent road map for connecting with solar customers across a variety of media."

– Aaron Sutch
Program Director, VA Sun

"The Solar Sales Leap could not have been more timely for our company. I find myself repeating Curren's points to my colleagues without realizing it. It's as though he has collected all the thoughts I *should* have realized about marketing and put them into an easy-to-understand format."

– Joe Moore
Vice President of Operations, Altenergy Inc

THE SOLAR SALES LEAP

THE SOLAR SALES LEAP

Stop Knocking on Doors, Cold Calling, and Buying Leads and Start Using the Internet to Grow Your Solar Energy Business for the Long Term

ERIK CURREN

New Sky Books

Cover design: Lindsay Curren

Published by New Sky Books, Staunton, Virginia.

Printed in the United States of America

ISBN: 0692763074
ISBN 13: 9780692763070
Library of Congress Control Number: 2016912591
New Sky Books, Staunton, VA

CONTENTS

ACKNOWLEDGEMENTS

My biggest thanks goes to my wife Lindsay, who supported and helped me at every stage of creating this book. She liked the concept for the book, she encouraged me to write it up, she talked with me about ideas as I wrote, she edited the manuscript, and she even came up with a schedule for me to get up early every morning Monday through Friday and have an quiet hour just for writing and motivated me to keep doing it. She also designed the cover.

I also want to recognize Brian Halligan and Dharmesh Shah, whose excellent book *Inbound Marketing: Attract, Engage, and Delight Customers Online* served as a model for me to adapt the approach of online marketing they describe to the needs of the solar energy industry, and to do it in print form. Given the quantity of information online about online marketing, and given how fast things change on the Internet, it's consciously old-fashioned to write a book about Internet marketing. But just as I have found so much value in Halligan and Shah's insights that I found myself returning again and again to their book as a reference, which the tactile medium of print made pleasant and easy, so I hope that people who work in the solar industry will find some of the same value in this present volume.

Working as a marketer and sales rep for pioneering commercial solar developer Secure Futures gave me first-hand experience in promoting solar power with lessons applicable to both commercial and residential solar contractors. The firm's founder and CEO Anthony Smith has been a wise mentor on innovation and management, and especially on the intricacies of financing solar projects.

Finally, I'd like to thank the dozens of solar company owners, managers, and sales reps from across the United States and beyond who responded to my company's offer of a free 20-minute phone consultation, where they shared their challenges and hopes with me over the last few months. Intelligence that I gathered from these calls has helped to broaden my understanding of the solar marketing landscape, which has informed my writing here.

INTRODUCTION

*Great companies start because their founders want
to change the world...not make a fast buck.*

— GUY KAWASAKI

*Business has only two functions—
Marketing and innovation.*

— MILAN KUNDERA

WHO IS THIS BOOK FOR?

This book is for people who work in the solar power industry in marketing, sales, or management. I've written the text with residential solar professionals in mind, but many of the ideas here can also be applied to marketing of commercial-scale solar services.

1. SOLAR MARKETING PROFESSIONALS

If you are in marketing, this book will help you connect your planning and outreach with your company's sales goals and business objectives.

Across industries, too often company management views marketing as an expense without a clear and meaningful return. That's understandable, given how difficult it was in the past to measure the effect of traditional marketing methods such as putting out a new brochure, advertising in newspapers or magazines, or staffing a booth at a trade show. But with the advent of Internet marketing that's easy to measure, marketers can now demonstrate a return on investment for tactics such as building and maintaining a company website, reaching out through social media services, and running an email newsletter.

If you work for a solar company, this book will help you apply proven techniques of content marketing—also called inbound marketing because it's about getting potential customers to come to you instead of you reaching out to them through ads and cold calls—to marketing solar installations and related products and services. Your boss will be glad that you read this book because it will help you show him or her the value of marketing, especially when done primarily online, to reaching the company's business goals of more sales to a particular type of customer or more sales overall.

2. SOLAR SALES REPRESENTATIVES OR MANAGERS

If you work in sales, the book will help you and your colleagues close more deals by generating higher quality sales leads for solar installations. You already know that poor quality sales leads waste your time and destroy the morale of the whole sales team. Have you ever visited a house where the owner agreed to set an appointment for a home assessment but, when the time came, nobody was home? Have you ever had to make cold calls to a list of homeowners in a certain neighborhood that was supposed to be "hot" for solar, but turned out to be full of people who'd already gone with one of your competitors? Have you ever passed out cards at a home show or at a kiosk at a shopping mall and had very little to show for it at the end of the day?

Sales associates are responsible for generating many of their own leads, but unfortunately, traditional tools are proving less and less effective as the competition for selling solar heats up. So, it's getting harder and harder for solar salespeople to find high-quality sales leads. Wasting time on dead-end leads means lower commissions for the sales associate and lost revenue for the company. In the old days, the only answer might have been to get out there and hustle even more. More cold calls, more neighborhood canvassing, more home shows. But fortunately, today, there's a better way.

The Internet has made it possible for many industries to generate higher quality sales leads online. And while most solar installers continue to stick with old-school "outbound" sales methods like buying lists of leads from telemarketers or hiring appointment setters, a few leading solar companies have started to use their websites to get prospects to come to them. If you're in solar sales and you're fed up with the low-quality leads you're getting now, this book will help your company generate better sales leads online.

But let me warn you, if you want to start generating your own sales leads online, you'll need to be...online. And you'll need a website—having only a Facebook page is not good enough, as you'll see later on. To generate your own leads online, you'll need access to a website for yourself or your company that is regularly updated with content that your sales prospects would want to see.

If you're in sales representing a big company that doesn't offer you the chance to create your own presence online that's available to the public through their website, then you may have to get your own website. That's not as hard as it sounds. But having your own virtual real estate online is the best way to generate leads for yourself online. And this book will help you with that.

And if you are a manager at a big company that employs outside sales reps, denying your sales force the ability to publish on the web either through your company website or on their own website, is only going to hurt your sales in the long run. It's time to put Internet marketing at the center of all solar marketing and this book will demonstrate why.

3. COMPANY OWNERS AND MANAGERS

If you own or help run a solar energy company that sells to residential or commercial buyers, then this book will help you see how marketing, when done right, can generate more revenue while building your brand for the future.

With competition heating up in most solar markets these days, many new players have come onto the scene. For a period of time, the solar market is likely to be like the Wild West, where anything goes. But as in all boom markets, there's likely to be a shakeout where the weaker players go bust or are acquired by larger companies. If you want to be one of those companies doing the buying, or if you want to be ready to sell your company for a good price, then you'll need to build assets with value today.

And those assets go beyond your relationships with top-equipment suppliers. One key asset with a measurable financial value is your reputation as expressed through your company brand.

In a solar market confused by multiple financing models and too many fly-by-night installers, solar buyers are going to put more and more reliance on companies they can trust. Unfortunately, traditional methods of solar sales and marketing—especially outbound methods like canvassing, cold calls, and ads—don't work well anymore. But even worse, they turn off solar buyers and erode trust for solar companies. If you want to build a company with clear value, then you need to be known for putting the customer's needs first. And inbound marketing, done over the Internet, is the best way to show solar buyers that you're looking out for them throughout their whole customer lifecycle, from before they become a prospect to long after they've become a customer.

This book will show how to use the Internet to build your brand. But the book will also show you how you can make your sales and marketing operations into lean, mean, revenue-generating machines by replacing tactics with uncertain return on investment (ROI) with sales and marketing whose success you can measure through well established analytics. Using inbound marketing on the Internet, companies can get three times more sales leads for the same money, according to research across major industries.

With that kind of return, you can build the value of your operation more quickly, even in a highly competitive solar market that's just getting more and more crowded. Inbound marketing, in fact, will help you stand out from that crowd and get you noticed by investors, partners and other industry leaders.

WHAT WILL I GET OUT OF IT?

This book will help you sell more solar in a crowded and confusing market. With a Wild West atmosphere, solar sales right now certainly looks like a gold rush. As the price of equipment falls and financing gets easier, the public clamors for clean energy that's now much more affordable. So, it may seem like selling solar has got to be as easy as falling out of bed in the morning. In fact, as anybody who's been in the solar industry for more than a week can tell you, solar sales ain't easy.

Sure, there are a lot of roofing contractors who've decided that adding PV installations is a quick way to pull in some additional revenue while the solar market is booming. Given the world's need for more clean energy, solar will probably grow for decades to come. But this growth will probably not happen on a smooth upward curve, but instead, through fits and starts and periods of boom and bust. And when the latest bubble busts, many installers will drop out of the market. In the meantime, today's solar boom has created a marketplace crowded by sellers, not all of them doing things well. Experienced solar professionals may be able to spot low-quality work a block away. But the average homeowner or commercial facilities manager will be confused by all the options of solar products and financing and all the alternatives for installers and developers.

One way that companies will survive when today's bubble bursts is to get a reputation for high-quality solar installations and service. But that reputation won't come from just doing the work alone. Reputation is also built on awareness. If nobody knows anything about you, good or bad, then you won't have a strong reputation, even if you're the best solar installer in your area.

With so much noise in the solar marketplace today, to gain the awareness you'll need to develop a reputation of any kind (but especially a positive one) first. Then, you'll need to communicate with people who might care. And you'll need to reach those people in the way that they already like to communicate. And that means using the Internet to have conversations, whether on social media or through email, with your most valuable audiences. Knowing those audiences and providing them content online that they find valuable is the most effective way today to cut through the noise of a crowded marketplace for solar installers.

HOW IS THIS DIFFERENT THAN OTHER BOOKS?

Believe it or not, there haven't been that many books written on solar sales and marketing so far. The industry has been around for half a century. But it hasn't grown much until recently. So perhaps solar has flown beneath the radar of the kind of twenty-first century marketing and sales gurus who've applied their minds to the sale of products and services from real estate to financial services to healthcare, education, and consumer products. The few books out there that deal with solar energy marketing cover it briefly while talking mostly about sales.

Books on solar sales are good sources of answers to common objections that customer express about getting home solar. But since those books don't talk about the Internet much or at all, they seem to be implying that solar companies are going to keep interacting with potential customers using traditional tactics: cold calls, neighborhood canvassing, direct mail, trade shows. Since solar companies are already squeezing about as many sales as they can out of these activities, a new book about them would merely serve to describe what's already done. But such a book wouldn't give you many new ideas.

This book is all about new ideas, especially using the Internet. Of course, new ideas are not better just because they're new. If traditional marketing methods were still effective, then it would be fine to stick with door knocking and cold calls. But in today's crowded, competitive market, success requires solar companies to go beyond me-too marketing and instead do something to try to stand out from the rest.

And with the advent of social media, solar companies have a whole new box of tools that can help them reach customers more effectively than in the past. Indeed, the very existence of services like Facebook or Twitter has spoiled consumers for old-timey marketing like advertising that interrupts their favorite show or cold calls that interrupt their dinner. The Internet has given consumers higher expectations for how they communicate with marketers, including those from solar companies. The days when consumers were willing to put up with annoying marketing and sales tactics are closing fast. But the time when potential customers want to read a blog post from a solar company with helpful advice on how to get the best solar deal for their home or business is just beginning.

Finally, the ideas in this book may be new to the solar industry, but they're not new to business in general. While solar has stuck mostly with traditional marketing and sales tactics, industries from consumer products to healthcare have been using the Internet to connect with potential customers. Those pioneering industries have created a system over the last decade with a track-record of success. The system is called content marketing or inbound marketing and it consists of a series of steps that any business can apply to bring its marketing into the twenty-first century. Only a few solar companies have been able to adopt this system so far and I will discuss some good examples of those in this book. But I'll also help you do marketing and sales better than those companies by understanding and applying the whole gamut of inbound marketing techniques.

On the method of inbound marketing, you can find a few books out there—as well as a ton of information online—and I will recommend some of them to you as we go along. But this book is unique in applying the techniques of inbound marketing to the solar energy industry. I've already made the connection between inbound and solar, saving you the effort. This book is full of examples from the solar industry of what to do and what not to do, many of them pulled from the hundreds of marketing articles published on the website of my marketing agency, the Curren Media Group. So far, I don't think you'll find that anywhere else.

SUNBURN—TRADITIONAL SOLAR SALES AND MARKETING

It's fine to celebrate success but it is more important to heed the lessons of failure.

— BILL GATES

Stop selling. Start helping.

— ZIG ZIGLAR

Chapter 1

ENERGY HAS CHANGED...HAS YOUR SELLING STYLE?

If cavemen had photovoltaics back in the Ice Age, their only choice to sell solar to each other would have been to walk from cave to cave, making their pitch. By grunting, of course. "Solar. Big money. Save. Ugh!"

A lot has changed since then. Sort of.

Today, people around the globe think of solar PV as one of the world's most advanced energy sources. Ordinary people even discuss what kind of solar panels NASA uses in space, as several pages on the space agency's website show. And fortunately for today's solar installers, the Age of the Internet has brought plenty of new ways to sell solar unknown in the Ice Age—or even in the 1990s.

Yet, even with more effective online marketing tools widely available, many solar companies just can't seem to kick the habit of caveman sales. The habit, that is, of sending their salesmen out into neighborhoods to knock on doors in the blazing sun, pounding rain, and icy cold. "Ugh," indeed!

PEST CONTROL SERVICES AND SOLAR INSTALLS

Whether you call it cold walking, canvassing, or door knocking, many solar PV installers still rely on door-to-door solar sales. In hot markets for solar, it's as common to see salesmen for Vivint or a small local installer walking your neighborhood as it is to meet a grade schooler selling chocolate bars and magazine subscriptions or a college kid pushing food storage and pest control.

That's too bad, because while door-to-door solar sales may have worked well in the past, today this tactic is less and less effective. Even worse, door knocking is just one outdated marketing tactic common in the solar industry. But let's explore it a little bit since what's wrong with door-to-door sales is also what's wrong with most common tactics of selling solar today.

"For decades, many industries relied on door-to-door sales, both direct-to-consumer and business-to-business. Now, unsolicited solicitations are not only unwanted, but in some areas are illegal unless a hard-to-come-by permit is obtained. And, in light of the surge of social media and e-commerce, door-to-door sales is simply unwarranted," explains marketing expert Angela Stringfellow on American Express OpenForum.

Forbes has even listed door-to-door sales as one of the 10 Top Dead or Dying Career Paths, projecting an 18% decline in positions by 2018.

THE PAIN OF DOOR-TO-DOOR SOLAR SALES

Obviously, plenty of PV company sales managers seem to think that door-to-door solar sales still bring in business. Or maybe it's just that those sales managers came up through cold walking themselves, so they think it builds character. Or they think that the guys (it's usually guys, isn't it?) under them should have to pay their dues by knocking on doors to get started.

But door-to-door solar sales isn't just painful for the salesman. Cold walking is also a poor use of marketing resources with a low return-on-investment for a solar installer.

Case in point. Just consider this "ask me anything" discussion from an experienced door-to-door salesman found on one of the public forums on Reddit. It's a dialogue between a solar salesman with the username FireSuperiorityCompl and members of the forum who have questions about door-to-door solar sales.

"I'm a Solar Consultant (Sales Guy) and I am relatively new in the Solar Industry and started early this year. I get most of my leads from going door to door," says the salesman in his short bio.

Though he's been selling solar for less than a year, he explains that he's already worked for three companies: one of the largest solar companies in California and across the country; a small startup that served as a solar broker for different providers; and a marketing firm that worked for two different installers. So he knows the industry.

The discussion gets interesting when somebody asks the salesman about the results of door-to-door solar sales:

Q: How many residential front doors do you have to knock on to create a lead? How many leads turn into revenue in your pocket?

A: I have had to knock 50 times for each lead. Out of every ten leads, I would say one sells and turns into money in my pocket.

Q: You must have an iron will. That's a lot of rejection to deal with. Much respect for your effort.

A: Thank you!

And I'll add my own respect as well for this salesman or anybody who does door-to-door solar sales. I wish you well—and I hope your company offers you an easier way to sell solar very soon.

A story like this speaks loudly where statistics only whisper: door-to-door solar sales is a lot of hassle for very little reward. Just consider the numbers in the example. Knocking on 50 doors yields one sales lead. And it takes ten sales leads to close a deal. Do the math: 50 x 10 = 500. Yes, that's right. This salesman has to knock on a staggering 500 doors just to make a single solar sale. Ouch.

Fortunately, as they say, When God closes a door He opens a window. And today, that window is online solar marketing. We'll see how the sun is shining through that window later. But since canvassing is so popular in solar sales, let's talk first about why door-knocking doesn't work well anymore, to see if there's a chance that there might be a way to do it better.

WHY THE DOORS ARE NOW CLOSING

However effective door-to-door solar sales may have been in the past, several trends have made cold walking ineffective across industries today. Marketing expert Stringfellow quotes a real estate exec to explain why doors are now closing on door-to-door sales in his industry, which has long relied on this tactic:

> Randy Tivens, vice president of marketing and communications for Forecast Land Corporation, a land investment firm, said society no longer permits such a practice. "I like to tell my newer sales trainees, the only folks who go door-to-door anymore with any amount of success are either poor kids selling candy from a large box or general real estate folk who are giving out pads of paper with their pictures on them to remind homeowners to use them if/when they decide to sell their house," Tivens says.

Stringfellow identifies three trends that have led to the decline of door-to-door sales. And all of them apply to solar:

1. Rise in Reported Scams—The news is full these days of solar scams, especially in hot states like Arizona and California, where salesmen over-promise and under-deliver. As a result, consumers have become more and more suspicious of solar salespeople.

2. Changing Technologies—In the Age of Information Overload, consumers have less patience for being interrupted by marketers. And if consumers hate TV ads and cold calls more than in the past, today homeowners have even less patience for being interrupted by a cold canvasser at home.

3. Increase in Retail—Consumers don't need to wait for a salesman to come by their house to get steak knives or carpet cleaner. They can buy those themselves at a big box store or on Amazon. As for solar, now it's also being sold at Lowe's and other retail locations, where consumers can see if their home might be a good candidate for a solar installation and even schedule a home assessment.

STEP AWAY FROM THE DOOR

Forget for a moment that making solar salesmen knock on doors that yield so little interest may build character—if you define "character" as the ability to accept huge amounts of rejection. But for anybody with any emotional intelligence, so much rejection is going to be a real morale buster.

It's no wonder that it's hard for companies that rely heavily on door-to-door solar sales to recruit and retain good salespeople. But even if those companies don't mind the turnover in their sales teams, and the expense incurred in training, they should start to worry about the competition.

If you're competing only against cavemen, then maybe you can afford to keep going door-to-door for a few more years. But if your competitors are among the growing number of solar companies, both residential and commercial, that are seeing higher ROI through inbound marketing online, then if you keep knocking on doors to make sales, your company may be about to go the way of the Neanderthal.

Towards extinction, that is.

Perhaps it's time to evolve out of the Ice Age and into the Age of the Internet? This book will help you do just that.

Online marketing tactics such as exchanging ebooks for email addresses or nurturing prospects until they're ready to buy through automated email campaigns deliver better sales leads more cost effectively than traditional marketing and sales, according to research by marketing automation company HubSpot.

But first, a solar company has to be committed to doing marketing and not just doing sales alone. The company has to want to generate leads for its sales force, instead of putting the responsibility 100% on salespeople to find their own leads. It's clear how marketing support can help salespeople. It may not be so clear how doing extra work or spending extra money to make more sales will help a solar installer or developer. So let's go into the benefits for the company of generating leads for its sales force—and the risks of making your sales team responsible for getting all or most of their own leads.

Chapter 2

●　　●　　●

DOING SALES WITHOUT HELP FROM MARKETING

Many solar companies' marketing consists of hiring independent sales reps, handing them a box of brochures, and sending them off with a hearty handshake to go out and sell solar to anyone they can find. Most of these hard-working sales reps have to prospect their own leads with little or no help from the companies that employ them.

That may seem like a sweet deal to the management of some solar installers. It's easy to imagine what they're thinking:

Our company makes sales but we don't have to find any of our own leads! We just let the sales guys generate all their own leads however they can. It's their responsibility. If they can't find any leads, then they're the ones who suffer because they're 100% commission. If they make no sales, then we pay no commission. That's a pretty good incentive for them to get out there and hustle to sell solar, don'tcha think? We only have to pay 'em if they make a sale. Sure, that means the sales reps take all the risk, while the company gets all the reward. But guys willing to sell solar are dime-a-dozen these days. If some sales rep doesn't like it, well, there are five other guys waiting to take his place. So, for our company, what's not to like?

While this approach is hard on sales reps, it's also shortsighted for a solar installer.

Making sales reps generate all their own leads themselves creates low morale that increases turnover in the sales force, forcing a solar installer to constantly recruit and train new sales reps. And sales force turnover causes solar installers to close fewer deals than competitors who retain sales reps longer because they treat their sales force better and provide them with marketing support.

Fortunately, some solar companies give their salespeople more support. But too many of these well intentioned companies just buy leads from lead generation vendors instead of making their own leads in-house. Usually, solar companies get leads in one of two common ways:

1. They buy lists of leads and make cold calls in-house
2. They hire a telemarketing firm to make appointments for their salespeople to visit a prospect's home and offer a solar assessment

Though solar companies have been buying sales leads for years, lately this strategy has started to deliver fewer and fewer sales. Increased competition is partially to blame. There are just more solar installers today than there were five years ago. But with more interest in solar and better deals today than in the past, there are also more customers now than there used to be. So the real reason why purchased leads convert at lower and lower rates as time goes on is that public attitudes have changed over the last decade.

And you can blame the Internet for that. The Internet has changed marketing and it has changed what consumers and business customers alike expect marketing to look like.

In the past, marketing was all about interrupting consumers with ads. Ads during their favorite TV shows. Ads in their magazines and newspapers. Ads all across their radio dial.

Today, the Internet has changed marketing not just online, but everywhere.

Yes, there are still ads. Lots of solar companies still buy ads too. And when most people think of marketing, they think of advertising. But ads are no longer the star of the marketing show as they were in the days when TV meant three national broadcast networks. Today, with the spread of new media channels, from cable TV and satellite radio to the Internet, ads are now just a small portion of all the marketing out there today. So if you think that marketing is just about buying ads, then you'll be surprised to learn about all the other things that you can do on the Internet to get sales leads and new customers that are better and cheaper than buying ads.

One reason companies have started going beyond ads and other traditional marketing is because customers never liked being interrupted that much anyway. But today, in the Age of Information Overload, consumers have less patience than they ever did for companies trying to buy their way through the clutter. After so much news of exaggerated claims and other ripoffs across industries (and including solar), the public has lost trust in companies that appear too pushy and too greedy.

Instead, these days, consumers expect companies to earn their way to attention. And that means putting out not just ads explicitly promoting products and services, but also publishing content that offers helpful advice to help empower consumers to make their own buying decisions.

These days, it's not just newspapers, magazines, and popular blogs like *huffingtonpost.com* that are publishers. Every company that wants to succeed in marketing must also become a publisher, to a greater or lesser degree. In this way, companies build trust, which is what it takes to get attention in today's crowded media market.

BUILDING TRUST

Building trust is important for any company today. But trust is especially necessary for solar power companies, for a couple of reasons. And we need to explore that a little bit before talking more about why traditional solar marketing isn't working.

First, like all energy, solar power seems complicated to the average homeowner or businessperson. Sure, installing an 8 kilowatt PV array on a home roof is not the same as building the reactor for a 500 megawatt nuclear plant. But for the average American, any method of generating electricity is hard to understand and intimidating to think about. With its kilowatt hours, productivity, calculations of payback time, and rate of return, solar power has plenty of lingo to shut down the average American mind.

Second, the average homeowner or businessperson isn't used to thinking much about energy in general or about electricity in particular, aside from telling her kids to turn off the lights and close the fridge. And so far, except when their bills are too high, most Americans haven't had to think much about electric power. That's because they've been able to rely on one very trusted authority to take care of all their power needs: the local electric company.

Americans may grouse about their local utility for price gouging or bad customer service. But in the end, there are few closer relationships of trust in commercial life than the bond between a ratepayer and her electric utility. We'll discuss why that matters for the solar industry in the next chapter.

Chapter 3

* * *

YES, AMERICANS DO TRUST TRADITIONAL ENERGY PROVIDERS

You can't blame the average American for knowing little about energy in general or electricity in particular. Unless TV news is running stories about high gas prices ("pain at the pump") or a homeowner has to put this month's electric bill on his credit card because the bill was so high that he couldn't cover it from his paycheck, then energy doesn't seem like a problem to most people.

When everything's working the way it's supposed to work, then energy is easy for the average person to ignore. As you flick a switch to turn on the lights or push a button a few times to turn up the heat at home, you can now just press a button to start your car—as long as you fill up the tank once in a while. And with historically low oil and gas prices, filling up that tank has gotten cheaper and easier than ever. The gas lines of the 1970s are becoming a dim memory as is the big blackout that hit Northeastern states in 2003.

Electricity has also gotten cheaper and more reliable, with electricity bills at their lowest in 10 years and customer satisfaction with utility performance on the rise. As JD Power's 2016 Electric Utility Residential Customer Satisfaction Study reports:

The average frequency of brief power interruptions (outages of 5 minutes or less) reported by customers has continued to decline since 2010. Further, 41% of customers experience "perfect power," or no brief or long interruptions, up from 37% in 2010. While lengthy interruptions have remained fairly constant, the length of the longest outage has fallen to an average of 6.4 hours in 2016 from 7.0 hours in 2015.

To be fair, consumers may like the utility industry today better than they used to, but the industry is still nobody's favorite. JD Power ranks their customer satisfaction below such industries as auto insurance, banking, and the universally despised airline industry.

They may not like electric utilities, especially investor-owned ones, but when it come to trust, consumers give utilities high marks. And that's just how the traditional energy companies, whether electric utilities or oil companies, like it. They want energy to be something that ordinary people don't have to think about. And they've done a pretty good job at it. Despite a few famous disasters—the Exxon Valdez, the Deepwater Horizon, Three Mile Island, and Fukushima—oil and gas drillers, coal miners and especially nuclear plant operators have done an excellent job staying out of the news. They've kept a low profile by doing what they promised, which is to safely deliver reliable energy at an affordable price.

And those traditional energy providers have served industrial society well. Because energy has kept such a low profile, it doesn't get the credit it deserves for the many benefits that modern people enjoy. From warm baths in winter to cold beer in summer, energy has enabled the technology that has given the average citizen of an industrial society comfort and convenience that King Louis XIV or even Queen Victoria could hardly have imagined. As they like to say in the coal industry, "coal keeps the lights on" and without cheap, reliable energy, we'd all be "shivering in the dark."

So, even if you work in clean energy and are especially well prepared to see the problems of fossil fuels and nuclear power, you can't help but marvel at the monumental achievement of traditional energy companies.

Over just a couple of centuries, they've managed to steal fire from Olympus and grant humans godlike powers over time and distance and over all the raw materials of the earth.

Today, in a world threatened by climate change and resource depletion (yes, someday the world will run out of cheap oil, but nobody knows when it will happen), renewable energy must step in to replace fossil fuels. And don't get me started on the topic of nuclear power, which, aside from its obvious danger to present and future generations, was never too-cheap-to-meter and never will be.

That said, if you're working in the solar industry, you probably agree with me that traditional energy sources can no longer safely and economically meet the power needs of today's global industrial society. So by spreading solar, you probably feel like you're part of an important movement with a goal so lofty that it's come to sound like hype. Saving the world, that is.

But it's true, at least in part. And that's why anybody who helps spread solar should be proud. As long as they're trying to spread solar in a way that's ethical and effective, that gives consumers the reliable energy they've come to expect while simultaneously helping the whole industry to thrive now and in the future, then anybody developing, installing, or promoting solar power should hold their head high. As ordinary Americans get more eco-aware, and more interested in solar power, I hope they will also start to see the vital importance of the solar industry to the future of our country and our planet.

Thanks to former Vice President Al Gore and his PowerPoint deck that became the documentary *An Inconvenient Truth,* Americans have known about climate change for at least a decade. Despite the millions spent by Big Oil paying climate skeptics and other professional liars to spread doubt that burning fossil fuels is the main problem, surveys show that most Americans want to get the economy off of oil and coal. And while some people see both natural gas and nuclear power as part of the solution, it seems that everybody except the Koch Brothers and the utility lobby wants more solar power.

Yet, most people still leave issues about electricity to their local utility, which they may resent but which they still trust.

Who doesn't grouse about paying their electric bill? But we all have confidence that the electric company will keep the lights on, as they have done for as long as any of us can remember. And if the rare blackout should occur, we will complain if our area is hit and we'll wait impatiently for the power to be restored. But in most cases, on the news we'll also hear that the utility has dispatched an army of workers to restore the power as quickly as possible. The utility serving the area where I live in Virginia, for example, has an "all hands on deck" policy to restore power after a serious outage. This means that everyone from the CEO and executive suite on down puts on a hardhat and pitches in to help the line workers fix equipment on any serious power outage, as they are able.

Indeed, electric utilities are the ones who deserve thanks for providing the reliable and affordable power to urban and rural areas alike in the late nineteenth and early twentieth centuries. This effort helped electricity grow from a fad to become a staple of civilized life. Today, we can't imagine a world without 24/7 electric power. Or, if we can imagine such a world, it would be some kind of science-fiction dystopia, its ruined cities dark after World War III, a takeover by the apes, or the arrival of the zombies.

As our view of a world without electricity seems like a hell on earth, it's hard for most of us to imagine electricity without the electric company. Most people know that you can produce your own power with solar. But many Americans wonder if it's practical on a large scale for homes and offices to unplug from the grid. And if something really goes wrong, you need the electric company there to fix it, right?

Let's look at this idea in the next chapter.

Chapter 4

WHY SOLAR COMPANIES NEED TO BUILD TRUST

It's hard to imagine a more trusted relationship between a company and consumers than that between electricity customers and their local utility.

And that puts the solar industry in the difficult position of questioning that old, comfortable relationship between consumers and their electric company. Anyone who thinks it's going to be easy to break up this marriage, no matter how unhappy it may look from the outside, should think again. If you work in solar in any capacity, from home installer to marketing to the accounting department, then you're essentially asking ordinary people to trust a solar company to deliver some or all of the electric power that the customer has always gotten from their utility. I'm not sure that everyone in the solar industry appreciates just how big a request this is.

It's a big challenge. And it impacts solar sales because many homeowners and businesspeople aren't ready yet to make the leap. To gain enough credibility to make the sale, the solar industry needs to build up the kind of trust that utilities have already won and have cemented over a century or more. And as the solar industry grows, I hope it can build that same kind of trust without also generating the resentment that consumers feel towards utility monopolies.

The better solar companies have done a good job building trust, establishing a long-term relationship with a homeowner or business that goes beyond installing PV panels on the roof and doing the occasional warranty maintenance. These solar companies have successfully presented themselves as trusted providers of energy and advisors on anything energy-related, from power reliability to cost savings to the energy efficiency of the customer's whole home or operation and not just the solar part.

But too many solar installers still act like home-improvement contractors. They sell solar panels, not renewable energy. They're just like companies that install a new roof, gutters, or aluminum siding. Once they're done putting the racks and the array on your roof, then the installers are outta there until something breaks. And unforunately in some cases, solar contractors are hard to find when something does break.

The biggest risk to solar spreading around America—and the biggest barrier to solar companies making more sales—is not big monopoly utilities or cheap natural gas.

It's the solar industry's own reputation. The good news is that reputation is largely under the industry's control. The bad news is that the industry hasn't done much so far to protect the reputation of high quality installers from installers who don't do good work but do have pushy marketing.

With all the stories recently in the news in hot solar markets like California, Arizona, or Massachusetts about solar sales problems of one sort or another, there's a risk that the industry will start to get branded as untrustworthy. In a worst case scenario, the public could start to compare solar companies to used car salesmen or the kind of aluminum siding scammers depicted in the movie *Tin Men*.

If you still don't think the solar industry has a problem with its reputation, just take a sampling of customer comments about major solar installers on review sites such as Consumer Affairs. For example, here are some customer complaints from April, 2016:

It turned out that my rates were higher than my provider and I only noticed that now, as I started receiving higher bills due to longer sun hours.

...

Two weeks after installation, I now have water coming in my front entrance and [the solar company] will NOT take responsibility. I am extremely disappointed in the customer service dept for what appears to be a professional establishment.

...

The system has stopped working 3 different times in the term of 10 months. I pay a fixed rate of $153.00 per month to [the solar company], however when the system is not working they expect me to pay the monthly rate regardless. I am actually paying more in electric having solar than when I just used [my utility].

It should be clear by now that the industry needs to rebuild trust among the public in the most desirable solar markets. Of course, that means dealing with customer service problems like those listed above.

But building trust doesn't start after PV panels are installed on a rooftop. Building trust really starts at the beginning, with a solar company's marketing. And unfortunately, even solar installers with a reputation for doing good work and offering good value often do marketing that makes them look pushy at best and sleazy at worst.

Ironically, as the price of solar panels has dropped over the last couple decades, the cost of marketing and selling solar power systems has remained steady or even increased in some cases. This means that, over time, marketing costs have grown to a larger and larger piece of any solar sale. Since it can cost about $3,000 to close a new customer for an average size residential solar installation (that's 49 cents a watt for a 6 kilowatt rooftop array), according to GTM Research, it's no wonder that installers are looking for more affordable ways to get solar leads and convert prospects to solar customers. We'll examine the most common method that solar installers use to cut acquire customers in the next chapter.

Chapter 5

TELEMARKETERS, SCAMMERS, AND ELECTRIC UTILITIES

To meet the need for a more affordable way to make sales, in the last few years third-party solar lead generation companies have stepped in. These companies promise to generate more leads for residential solar installers at lower cost than the company's in-house sales force. Lead vendors tout the quality of their data-crunching abilities to produce qualified leads that meet the needs of any solar installer. As the PV Solar Report explains:

> They employ the whole gamut of marketing techniques, then sort leads into different levels of quality using "filters." Filters include credit scores, annual electric usage, whether both spouses are in the house at the same time, and roof shading. Installers can set their own thresholds for the filters, paying a premium for stricter requirements.

Though lead generation vendors connect with homeowners both by phone and online, many lead companies have come to solar power after telemarketing for industries including real estate and financial services.

And unfortunately, a few bad solar telemarketers have given the residential solar business a black eye in hot states such as California and Arizona.

RETURN OF THE TIN MEN

Former *Photon* magazine writer William P. Hirshman, who has made an in-depth examination of solar telemarketers for *pv magazine* as its investigative reporter, as well as in his blog PV and ME, has exposed some of their more shocking phone pitch scripts to public scrutiny. Solar cold callers and door knockers, he notes, are no better than the deceptive aluminum siding salesmen depicted in the movie *Tin Men*.

In that movie, two salesmen run a con on a target by visiting her house. They set up cameras on tripods on the sidewalk outside to look like they're preparing to take shots of the lady's home. This gets her attention, and she comes outside to inquire. The salesmen claim to be doing a piece on the effects of aluminum siding on improving the look of a home for *Life* magazine. They tell the homeowner that her home will be the "before" shot. Of course this disclosure achieves its intended effect, and the lady asks what it would take for her home to become the example of "after," a home beautified by aluminum siding. Well, since you, ask...

And with this lie, the Tin Men have made a sale.

As Hirshman puts it in *Renewable Energy World* magazine,

> In reality, aluminum siding is actually not a bad option for a house that has seen better facade days. But rip-off artists, seeing an ocean of easy money to be made, jumped into the water and caught the wave to push a product they hardly knew. The only quality they cared about was the legibility of the signature on the contract and the fancy cars their high commission-percentages could buy.

Hirshman's research showed solar installers using similar ethically challenged sales tactics. A quick web search for "solar scams" confirms that solar bad boys are still alive and well.

Let's take the especially bad example of a solar telemarketing company in Phoenix, AZ. The firm, known as Going Green Solar, would call senior citizens and tell them that their electric bills were going to increase from $200 a month to $1,500 a month unless they bought a solar PV system. The obvious problem was that the whole pitch was based on a lie. But the telemarketers shouldn't have been calling these consumers in the first place, since their names were listed on the National Do Not Call Registry.

Both of those problems turned out to be one big challenge for Going Green Solar. After angry consumers made numerous complaints to law enforcement, the Arizona Attorney General's office filed a suit against the telemarketer for consumer fraud. In 2015, the company settled with the state, and agreed to pay $111,000 to customers and another $120,000 in fines along with $17,000 in attorney's fees.

In this case, the solar telemarketer fraudulently presented itself as a clean energy company or even an electricity supplier, according to a story in the Arizona Republic:

> Sales representatives claimed to be calling from the "utility savings program" without mentioning they were calling from Going Green. They used "misleading and deceptive graphs, worksheets and pictures" to make false promises, according to the settlement.

Some seniors not only didn't get the savings promised, but their energy costs actually went up after purchasing the Going Green systems. Solar power that's more expensive than grid power? Now that really hurts. And it doesn't just hurt the unfortunate homeowner. Once word gets around about this kind of swindle, the term "solar scam" will become a common keyword on Google or a hashtag on Twitter, and then the whole residential solar industry will begin to look shady. Electric utilities are already pushing stories of solar scams to try to discredit the industry.

Unfortunately, there are plenty of stories like this to go around. Going Green was the second solar telemarketing company during

February of 2015 alone to settle claims with the attorney general in Arizona for fraud. In a "remarkably similar" case, as the Arizona Republic put it, "Stealth Solar owners Fred and Sandra Richie acknowledged the company illegally advertised services through deceptive telemarketing, bogus mailers, and untrue promises of savings and government subsidies."

Several other companies were also targeted by the state for deceptive telemarketing. Indeed, solar telemarketing had gotten so bad in Arizona that later in 2015, the state legislature passed a consumer protection bill intended to rein in marketers of "distributed energy"—aka, residential solar PV.

SOLAR INSTALLER PUNISHED FOR THE SINS OF ITS LEAD GENERATOR

Though Going Green Solar represented itself as a solar equipment provider and installer, part of the fraud was that the company was merely a telemarketer. More troubling for the industry, and for solar installers who buy solar leads instead of generating their own, is that the misdeeds of a vendor who gets leads from telemarketing can be traced back to the client who buys the leads.

It's not hard for the public to locate the companies who buy leads from solar telemarketers. For example, back in Arizona, Glendale resident Ben Richardson responded to an invitation from a local TV station to consumers who had received calls from Go Green Solar to tell their stories of problems with the company. Richardson worked with the station's consumer advocate on a plan to trace telemarketing calls from Go Green by taking the telemarketer's bait:

> Richardson set an appointment. The next day he says a man showed up at his home from Discover Energy Solutions. The company is based at 2400 Central Avenue in Phoenix. Richardson says the rep told him the "Go Green" campaign telemarketers work for Discover Energy Solutions.

"I think inside I was doing a little happy dance because I finally had a business card and he admitted it was his company that was doing this," Richardson said.

Not surprisingly, but very disappointing when confronted with the telemarketer's misdeeds, the solar installer distanced itself from the solar telemarketing firm:

> Discover Energy Solutions (DES) said they are not responsible for the calls to Richardson. DES says their telemarketers don't use the words "Go Green campaign" in their sales pitch as many other Phoenix-area telemarketers do. However, according to Richardson, the rep for DES confirmed for him that the "Go Green" verbiage is used by DES.

Yikes. For a solar installer to be caught lying in public is embarrassing and certainly won't help that company establish a reputation for trust. And passing the buck doesn't reassure the consumers who are annoyed by solar telemarketers. Because consumers rightly blame the solar company more than they blame the lead generator, the story is serious bad news for the brand of the solar installer. And it reflects poorly on the solar industry as a whole. It may not be fair to all the reputable installers out there, but for the general public, when it comes to the reputation of solar companies, it only takes a few bad apples to make the whole barrel look rotten.

SELLING SOLAR TO A MAN WITHOUT A ROOF

Take another example from Southern California, one of the nation's hottest markets for solar, described in the Orange County Register also in 2015:

> Eric Penner doesn't own a home nor is he planning to invest in solar equipment anytime soon. But those facts didn't deter one solar panel sales company from hammering the Laguna Niguel resident for months with robocalls.

The 30-year-old social worker said he got an average of four auto-mated phone calls a day from National Renewable Energy Center during the first half of the year.

"I was trying to get honest answers out of them," Penner said. "And as soon as my questions would deviate from the script, they would terminate the call."

Bugging homeowners with robocalls is bad enough. But when you learn what telemarketers actually say when trying to sell solar, it's no wonder that many people who live in active markets for residential solar are turned off by the whole industry. Take this script, for example, that researcher and author Hirshman found at the website CashSaver.com, from a tele-marketer with a call center in the Philippines that specializes in offering vacations as incentives to consumers in order to generate sales leads for solar installers:

Appointment Setting Pitch for Solar Companies

Hello, is this Mr./Mrs._____? This is _____ from _____.

I understand your time is very important. Therefore, if you would allow me just 2 minutes to share with you something of interest to all homeowners in (____City/ Area____), our company will reward you - with a free vacation voucher - for 3 days and 2 nights accommodations at a major hotel Casino on the strip in Las Vegas or 50 other resort cities.

Apparently, solar companies find this approach appealing, or else this tele-marketer wouldn't advertise it so openly on its website. But, as Hirshman does, I find this kind pitch appalling. Not only does the free vacation offer insult the intelligence of the potential buyer, it makes solar sound like just another phone scam for timeshares. To be fair, the pitch does go on to make perfectly fine points about solar money savings. But by that point, the damage has already been done, and the caller will sound sleazy no matter what else he or she has to say.

Commercial solar installers take note here. All the examples of solar scams we've discussed so far have been for residential solar. Since the volume of commercial solar installations is much smaller than the number of arrays put on home rooftops so far, it may be harder to find stories of solar scams on businesses. But I'm sure that those stories are out there somewhere. The B2B sales process tends to be more in-depth and takes place over a longer period, but the potential for abuse remains nonetheless. Commercial solar installers should jealously guard their reputations for high quality work by making sure that their marketing has integrity.

THE THREAT OF THE SOLAR SCAMMER

It's already hard enough for solar installers to build up enough trust to convince homeowners and businesspeople to move away from the local utility they've known for years or decades or even for their whole lives to try some solar company they might only have known about for a few weeks. When scammy installers use bullying marketing tactics, it makes selling solar harder for everybody.

The shady solar installer that I call the Solar Scammer is the enemy of every reputable home solar installer because he's polluting the customer pool. Across the country, but especially in the most competitive solar states, the Solar Scammer is causing homeowners to get suspicious of solar installers and skeptical about the value of rooftop solar.

Disreputable home solar installers create bad news for the whole industry. From the buyer's point of view, these bad apples spoil the whole barrel, casting doubt on all solar contractors. Solar Scammers make it hard for even the most highly rated home solar installers to reach new customers.

And consumer advocates are warning consumers to shop around.

"The biggest tip," advises a reporter in a 2016 Atlanta TV news report about PV installers who take customers' money but never install solar panels, "Don't just hire the first company that comes to your house...Be careful with the sweet talk you hear from these people."

So, the next time one of your sales reps knocks on a door, who knows if it will be slammed in his face?

UTILITIES ARE LOVIN' IT

Every industry has its bad apples. When you think of aluminum siding, you think of the Tin Men, right? And let's not even start on the topic of used cars. Perhaps solar scammers are getting more attention in the news today because solar is booming in many places.

But certainly, the utility industry is doing its part to make a bigger deal out of solar scams. Indeed, the Solar Scammer is like a downpour of pennies from heaven for the utility lobby. If the Solar Scammer didn't already exist, utilities would have to create him. Because the Solar Scammer gives utilities an excuse to call for government action to regulate the solar industry.

And as we all know, that kind of regulation is sure to slow solar down by adding red tape and raising soft costs, which already account for 64% of the average home solar installation according to the US Department of Energy.

Now, utilities are urging the Federal Trade Commission to crack down on the whole home solar industry, using consumer protection as the rationale. For example, in the spring of 2016 and ahead of an FTC workshop on protection for solar consumers, the Edison Electric Institute—the utility lobby—circulated a letter for members of Congress to sign claiming that rooftop solar deals are a threat to consumers.

The letter, actually signed by at least one hapless Congresswoman, Rep. Yvette Clarke from New York, called on the FTC to impose more oversight on home solar installers: "We believe the FTC should commit resources towards establishing a regulatory framework that will ensure consumers are afforded minimum standards of protections and full contract disclosures."

As Cleantech Media reports:

> The letter singles out third-party-offered leases and power-pur-chase agreements as risks, drawing a comparison to the 2008 housing crisis. "The consumer takes all of the financial risks in-herent in these long-term deals, risks that electricity prices and rate structures may change, that subsidies may go away and the like," the letter states. "The imposition of risks on the customer enables the developer to package and resell these leases to large fi-nancial interest, just as mortgage sellers packaged high-risk mort-gages a decade ago."

The letter also cites aggressive sales tactics and claims there has been a "dramatic increase in consumer complaints about abusive or deceptive acts and practices in solar sales, marketing, and financing."

While the utility claims here may be exaggerated, with all the stories of solar scams in the media, you have to recognize that the letter contains a certain amount of truth.

Fortunately, the Solar Energy Industries Association (SEIA) is taking the industry's reputation seriously.

In response to criticisms of the industry's marketing practices and in an effort to head off more regulation, SEIA has proposed that the indus-try start to regulate itself more effectively. As a start, the trade group has created an online Consumer Protection Portal with resources for both homeowners and solar contractors. The latter include helpful forms that installers can use with consumers.

Solar installers who use these resources can show that they're worthy of consumers' trust. And solar contractors who are are able to cut through the skepticism of consumers will make more sales.

So, to safeguard their reputation in a market where the Solar Scammer is getting too much media attention these days, solar companies can do three things to protect their reputations and help demonstrate that they are trustworthy.

1. USE CLEAR, INDUSTRY-STANDARD DISCLOSURE FORMS AND CONTRACTS

SEIA has released standardized disclosure statements covering the most common residential transactions. The SEIA Solar Power Purchase Agreement Disclosure statement and the revised SEIA Solar Lease Disclosure are simple summary documents that make it easier for consumers to compare solar offers from competitors and understand the terms of a proposal before entering an agreement.

"We strive to make the process of going solar as straightforward and transparent for customers as possible, and these new forms help achieve that," said Tom Kimbis, SEIA's interim president in a news release. "These disclosure forms are a big step forward toward creating a marketplace of consumers who are fully informed and educated in choosing solar."

2. DEVELOP A SALES STYLE THAT'S LESS PUSHY AND MORE LIKE CONSULTING

Solar installers should examine their sales messages. Are they accurate? Or do they promise too much? Solar sales managers should also rethink pushy sales tactics like door-knocking and telemarketing. This includes buying leads from telemarketers and using telemarketing firms to set appointments with homeowners. All of these tactics are widely hated by consumers, who have less patience than ever for being interrupted with a sales pitch in person or over the phone.

Instead of sleazy sales types, solar reps should present themselves as trusted advisors who want to help a homeowner make his or her own best decision about home solar. And the best way to do that these days is for their companies to create and publish educational content, such as blog posts and ebooks, that solar buyers want to read. This is also a great way to generate high quality, exclusive sales leads for your solar company too.

3. BUILD A LONG-TERM RELATIONSHIP WITH PROSPECTS AND CUSTOMERS

The relationship with a homeowner doesn't begin with the free home solar assessment. Nor does that relationship end when a rooftop array is switched on. Since consumers make more than half of their buying decision before they ever speak to a salesperson, solar companies should be working to become part of a potential buyer's life months or even years before a purchase.

Likewise, after an installation is done, customer reviews and word-of-mouth in person and on social media can boost—or bust—a solar contractor's reputation. That's why installers should check in with customers regularly right after an installation is done to make sure the customer is delighted and see if anything needs to be fixed.

And even if little or no service is required on a rooftop array, the installer should still keep in touch with former customers. You never know if the customer can offer a referral. Or, if the customer has a question or concern, no matter how vague, the company can address it to make sure that the customer remains delighted and continues to spread good news about the company.

Chapter 6

* * *

SALES TACTICS THAT MAKE SOLAR LOOK SLEAZY

Serious products or services are not sold over the phone by offering tawdry bribes for listening to a sales pitch. Nor are homeowners used to their energy provider using such low-class promotions to introduce a new offering.

Can you imagine a major investor-owned electric utility such as PG&E, Con Edison, or Washington Gas and Electric pushing three days and two nights on the Las Vegas strip to entice homeowners into the green energy or energy efficiency programs that they offer? If solar companies want to become as trusted to provide power as electric utilities, then solar contractors are going to have to stop treating their potential customers as fools. No fair letting their lead generation vendors do it for them, either.

And solar companies need to start taking responsibility for the telemarketers that they hire as well. Both legally and ethically, a solar installer that buys leads from a telemarketer can't distance itself from fraudulent phone sales tactics by saying that "we didn't make the calls." If you paid for the calls, or bought leads generated by the calls, then you're responsible for how the calls were made.

I hope your lawyers will tell you that. But more importantly, your marketers should tell you that too. The blowback from bad telemarketing can be worse for the marketing department than for legal counsel. A company that gets in trouble for illegal solar marketing can settle with state authorities and pay a fine. Legally the company may be able to move on with its business. But a solar installer may never be able to clear its name with consumers once it is associated with shady telemarketing. And it doesn't matter to the public whether the phones were located in the solar company's office in Arizona or California or in a telemarketer's office in India or the Philippines. Either way, the buck stops with the solar company.

WASTING MONEY ON COLD LEADS

Overall, residential installers have found that you get what you pay for when you buy from solar lead generation firms. Cheap leads are worth little because they produce few sales. And, because aggressive telemarketers annoy both the customer and your sales force, the cheapest leads may in fact be worth less than zero. Worse, they could be eating up budget that's better spent on more effective and less expensive lead generation.

For example, a sales manager with a large residential installer based out West shared this story with me. His company hired an offshore solar lead generation vendor to use telemarketing to book home appointments for the solar installer's salespeople. But it wasn't working out so well.

The job of the phone reps is to book as many appointments for the solar installer as possible. The telemarketers only get a commission if they can set an appointment. So, naturally, the phone reps are all about making the close and about getting to "yes" as soon as they can. That means the telemarketers don't take the time to build a good rapport with a homeowner. Instead, the reps just push, push, push. They get results using the approach of a whiny six-year-old—good old persistence. They just won't take "no" for an answer. So, just to get the annoying telemarketer off the phone, the homeowner agrees to book an appointment for someone from the company to visit and provide a solar assessment.

But then, when the salesperson arrives at the house...surprise. Nobody's home.

The end result? No sale. An annoyed homeowner who will tell his neighbors to avoid the solar company. And a salesperson who's just wasted a morning and knows he won't be earning a commission. In this case, a cheap sales lead turned out to be quite expensive. Cheap solar leads can damage a solar installer's brand and make sales more difficult in the future. But even worse, cheap solar leads can kill the morale of an installer's salesforce, morale which is hard enough to keep up in the first place.

Overall, abusive telemarketing is starting to give residential solar sales in many areas, from Arizona and California to Vermont, a bad name. By now, bad solar telemarketers have become such a cliché that annoyed homeowners have started posting videos where they torment the callers. Just go to YouTube and search for "solar telemarketing" to find titles including "Stubborn Solar Telemarketer gets OWNED" and "COLD CALL: Solar Telemarketer Loses His Cool!" or even "Angry Solar."

TELEMARKETING MAY NOT BE PRETTY—BUT IT STILL WORKS, RIGHT?

"Nobody wants to be cold called—even sales reps who cold call don't want to be cold called," explains sales trainer and consultant Steli Efti. "I'm more receptive than most to cold calls because I'm a sales aficionado. I appreciate good salesmanship but even I don't look forward to being pitched."

You don't need me to tell you that consumers have always hated being cold called and that they always will hate cold calls. But too many solar companies don't think about the effect that bad telemarketers might be having on potential solar customers. Instead, the companies just shrug it off, telling themselves that everybody does it this way because there's no other way to make a lot of solar sales besides telemarketing. And if telemarketing or buying leads from telemarketers works to make sales, then it's worth doing.

What sales coach Efti says about outbound sales in general applies to telemarketing in particular:

> Outbound is probably the least trendy, hip, cool, awesome, amazing thing a startup can do to grow the business. But you're not in business to get admiration from your peers and the press; it's not a popularity contest. Business is about the bottom line. The only thing that matters is: Does outbound sales make your business more successful or not?

I personally disagree that the means justify the ends in this case. Even if I could get filthy rich running a solar company on telemarketing, I'd still feel dirty because I was chasing a goal that's good (being successful) by doing something bad (annoying people).

But the real question here for Efti as for many solar installers, is, if buying leads and telemarketing works, then isn't that a good enough reason to do it? Let's answer the question, focusing on the time frame that most salespeople care about most. Not tomorrow, but today.

It would be difficult for me to get up in the morning and go to work every day knowing that I was using bad means to reach a good end, for example, by annoying homeowners (a bad thing) to sell more solar (a good thing). But that's just me. A solar marketer should judge any marketing tactic, as long as it's legal and ethical, by how well it works.

By annoying consumers, in the long run, even the best telemarketing can harm your company's reputation and hurt your sales in the future. But research shows that telemarketing is failing to bring home the bacon even in the short term. As we've seen, the average cost to acquire a new residential solar customer is $3,000, according to GTM Research. Customer acquisition cost has remained stable or even gone up even as the cost of PV panels and other equipment has fallen. That imbalance has helped make soft costs rise to 64% of the price of an average residential installation, according to the US Department of Energy.

If telemarketing and other outbound sales tactics were working, it would be getting cheaper for a solar company to get a new customer. But that's not the case. Steady or rising customer acquisition costs alone show that traditional solar sales tactics, the biggest of which is telemarketing, are less effective today than they used to be. And they're about to get even less effective in the future.

THE INTERNET HAS SPOILED CONSUMERS FOR TELEMARKETING

It's not just that consumers have always disliked telemarketing. It's that today, with the advent of the Internet, consumers hate telemarketing even more than they used to. Because of information overload, these days consumers have less tolerance for interruptive marketing than they had ten or twenty years ago.

Even if a potential buyer loves solar and wants to get some for himself, he doesn't want to hear about it from your salesperson—or lead generation vendor—during dinner. Instead, since the Internet makes it possible for him to do most of his research on his own and at his own pace, the buyer wants to talk to you *on his own time and only when he's ready*. And if you got his number via shady telemarketing, a pro-solar consumer may not really want to hear from you at all and, being fed up with your tactics, just might go to your competition instead.

These days, consumers don't need or want to talk to your salespeople until they're ready to buy. It wasn't always that way, of course. Before the Internet came along, consumers had few sources of information about products and services. Aside from ads, consumers got most of their information about what to buy from company salespeople. Today, the situation is different. Now, a consumer will surf the web to compare product features and prices and see which company appears more trustworthy. By the time a buyer talks to a salesperson, that buyer may have made up 70% of his decision already.

This means more power is on the consumer's side—and less power is on the telemarketer's side. And that means that it's getting less effective every year to call potential buyers at home and try to badger them into booking an appointment for solar. Ultimately, I hope solar companies will dump telemarketing altogether and put their marketing budgets to work in a smarter, more reputable way. Cold calling is getting less and less effective all the time. And it makes the industry look bad.

Those of us with the privilege to work in clean energy should remind ourselves of the awesome responsibility that we have towards America and towards the world. People today, as well as generations yet unborn, rely on us to get the energy transition right—and to do it soon. If society fails to move to clean energy fast enough, the consequences will be dire in terms of runaway climate change that could lay waste to the world's great coastal cities and energy depletion that could bring the global economy to its knees. But if we succeed in moving the world to clean, renewable electrons that come from the sun, then we'll change history. It's not exaggerating to say that the success of solar will help make a viable future possible for industrial society.

Will solar workers be the heroes of school kids in the year 2100? Why not?

For me, and I hope you agree, solar is not just another home improvement product like gutters or granite countertops. Solar has a noble mission to help move our civilization beyond fossil fuels and empower people to produce their own clean energy. For such an honorable calling, our methods should be as admirable as our goal.

No matter how ashamed solar installers may be to use telemarketing leads, if cold calls were the only way to sell residential solar, then solar companies and their lead vendors would just have to smile and dial and put up with it as best as they could. But fortunately, cold calling is not the only way to sell solar.

There is another way of marketing that your company and its salespeople can be proud of—a way that's also more effective to make sales than cold calling. That's what this whole book is about and the next chapter will dive right in.

For now, I understand that not every solar company is ready to fire their telemarketers. But every solar company should assess its telemarketing vendors as soon as possible.

1. First, make sure you know what they're doing. Don't just assume that because "everybody does it that way" that it's OK. Your callers may in fact be exposing your company to both legal liability and consumer disgust.
2. Then, make sure your telemarketers are not doing anything really bad. Make sure what they're saying is true and that the way they say it represents your company well.
3. Finally, start developing an alternative to telemarketing leads. The best place to start with that is online.

Chapter 7

MARKETING WITH THE CUSTOMER'S PERMISSION

A more up-to-date approach to solar lead generation has gone beyond the nineteenth century technology of the telephone ("Operator, can you get me Pettiworth 425 please?") to make use of the Internet. Since even the most ethical and respectful telemarketing will still be, well, telemarketing—which solar buyers will never welcome—online solar lead generation promises leads that are much higher quality. It would be good enough that the potential customer didn't start their relationship with your company by being annoyed. But there are many other reasons why online leads are better than cold call leads.

The Internet can provide leads to solar companies directly and also to lead generation vendors. Since the vendor model is so popular in the industry, let's start with an example of how a lead generation vendor would attract and convert leads online instead of through cold calling:

1. A lead generation vendor sets up a website to serve homeowners interested in solar.
2. The vendor attracts visitors to its site through online ads on Google, Facebook and other popular websites.

3. Once they get to the site, visitors can fill out a form such as a solar-savings calculator or a form to get quotes from various solar installers.

4. From the form, the site collects the potential customer's contact information so that solar installers can contact him about home solar.

5. The best lead generation companies, such as EnergySage, offer visitors an option of contact methods. The visitor can either give their phone number to get a call from a solar salesperson or they can provide an email address instead to hear back online.

The last point is key. Solar installers should only buy leads from solar lead generators that provide both the phone number and the email option, but never just the phone option. Visitors to a lead generation vendor's website or a solar installer's website should not be required to give their phone number at all just to get information. An email address is sufficient and a phone number should usually be optional.

Why? It's all about what marketing guru Seth Godin has called "permission marketing," which has become the ethos of the Age of the Internet, where we all suffer from information overload:

> Permission marketing is the privilege (not the right) of delivering anticipated, personal and relevant messages to people who actually want to get them. It recognizes the new power of the best consumers to ignore marketing. It realizes that treating people with respect is the best way to earn their attention.

Unfortunately, some solar lead generation companies don't play by the rules of permission marketing. And that makes their sales leads lower quality. When these solar lead generators convert visitors to prospects online, their websites don't give the option for the buyer to withhold his phone number and continue the conversation by email. Instead, once a homeowner fills out the site's solar savings calculator form, the site requires the visitor to provide his phone number. Otherwise, he can't get the form's results.

For example, take this website from a solar lead generation vendor that advertises regularly on a leading online clean energy publication. I've blacked out the name to protect the not-so-innocent:

It's a clear, simple form with a happy lady who wants to get solar on her home. What could be so bad about it?

First, the site offers a tempting online form, offering a homeowner information about solar in his area in exchange for his address and other info. So far so good. Done right, it could be a great way to get good residential solar leads. However, once the web visitor has spent a few minutes filling in his details, then he faces a final hurdle to get the promised report. Before he can hit "Submit" he has to give his phone number. Email-only communication is not an option. That's bad.

Second, and even worse, not only does the site require a phone number, but also it forces the visitor to consent to essentially receive *telemarketing calls from an unlimited number of companies from now until the end of time.*

* No time limit is placed on the telemarketing consent, so it's valid indefinitely.
* No subject limit is set either, so companies can call the consumer not just about solar but to sell other stuff too.
* The consumer is agreeing to receive calls not just from the company but also from "its partners," in this case, a list of a hundred or more solar companies listed in small print.
* And the consumer is agreeing to get calls from human telemarketers but also to get robocalls.
* And not just calls but texts too!

For the homeowner considering solar, this is means opening himself up to an awful lot of contact by phone for the foreseeable future just to get a little solar report for his home now. Is it worth it? For consumers worried about their privacy, probably not. For consumers who don't like being annoyed, definitely not!

But is the lead generation company doing anything wrong? After all, they do explain their policies about cold calls on the website, again, in small print:

> This website is compliant with the Telephone Consumer Protection Act as implemented by the FCC. By checking the submit button above, you agree to the Privacy Policy and you authorize [Company Name] and its partners to contact you at the telephone number you entered using automated telephone technology including auto-dialers and text messages, even if your telephone or mobile number is currently listed on any state, federal, or corporate "Do Not Call" list, and you are not required to give your consent as a condition of purchase.

This language shows how the lead generation vendor is so many kinds of wrong. Forcing a visitor to let this company and other companies contact him by phone forever in multiple ways even after he's bothered to put his name on the Do Not Call List?

That's terrible. And using as your excuse "it's not illegal?" That's even worse.

Yes, what this website is doing may be legal. And this company may even think it's ethical, since they have offered their disclosure statement. The visitor does have a choice, right? But even if the buyer bothers to read the small print, this can never be good business.

Of course, many visitors will abandon the form at this point, as I did, rather than provide their phone number willingly to telemarketers and their friends for the indefinite future. That loses this site a sales lead while gaining them a frustrated buyer. "I filled out all that information for nothing?" the visitor will ask, if he doesn't want to give his phone number. If he has the chance, he'll certainly spread the word about how frustrating this website is, which will hurt their marketing.

But even those visitors who do agree to give their phone number may be doing so resentfully. Yes, sometimes a homeowner is so gung-ho for solar that they want a phone call from an installer in the next few minutes. But despite the widespread belief in the solar industry that the first company to get to a potential buyer will make the sale, usually a visitor to a website is not yet ready to buy. Indeed, research shows that 96% of visitors to a typical business website are just looking around. And it's the same in solar. Most potential solar customers would rather have the chance to communicate by email over a few days or weeks, at least at first, just to build trust, before having to talk to the company.

Only when the buyer is ready will she want to talk to a salesperson. And that will be on her timeline. Not on yours. So, unless you want to lose the sale, you'll need to be patient. In the Age of the Internet, the seller is no longer in control of the conversation, as in the old days when consumers had few other sources of information on a potential purchase besides the company doing the selling. Today, when the buyer can empower herself with knowledge online, and especially can read reviews by other consumers, the buyer is actually in control of the conversation.

But being patient is not the same as being passive. It's just being emotionally intelligent and savvy about current business practices and consumer trends." There are other ways to help encourage buyers to consider your offering that don't put on the high pressure. I'll talk about those later on. For now, since we've just seen what a bad online lead generator looks like, let's check out a good one. I'll analyze screenshots as we go along.

EYE-CATCHING FIRST CONTACT

I first encountered EnergySage through an ad they were running on Facebook.

I'm not always a big fan of Facebook ads for solar installers. Unless they're done right, it's easy for ads to get lost in the clutter or just burn through a solar company's ad budget by racking up paid clicks for a lot of unqualified leads. But EnergySage's ad caught my eye because of its attractive graphic and clear message for the potential solar buyer. That message is a powerful one: going through their marketplace with many installers competing for my business could save a homeowner a lot of money over going directly to a solar installer.

I also liked their ad copy, which offers a clear benefit backed up by documented money savings:

Don't Overpay For Solar

Register your property today to receive multiple quotes from different solar installers, then compare prices and make the right decision. You can save 20% or more as a result!

NO TELEMARKETING REQUIRED

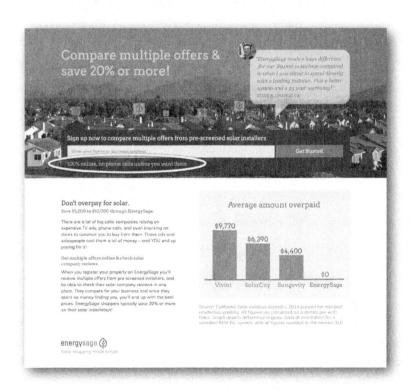

Unlike the first lead generation website we looked at, EnergySage offers to communicate with potential solar buyers 100% online, as you can see in the screenshot.

Of course, some salespeople can't understand why you wouldn't require a phone number. Top closers fresh from the used car lot (sorry—"preowned vehicle showroom") or straight out of the movie *Glengarry Glen Ross* (as sales manager Alec Baldwin urges his real estate salesmen "ABC—Always Be Closing") will find it wimpy that EnergySage doesn't actually require a phone number. Because everybody knows that real salesmen are all about hitting the phones and hitting them hard, right? After all, how are you going to sell any solar if you can't get the chump—er, customer—on the phone and pressure him—I mean, persuade him—again, with apologies to *Glengarry,* "to sign on the line which is dotted?"

Well, all I can say is that any solar installer with this approach to sales will find plenty of telemarketers from Calcutta to Manilla eager to take that solar company's money in exchange for more or less worthless leads. But solar companies that actually want to make sales will see how EnergySage's approach is superior. Right from the start, EnergySage shows respect for the buyer by making it clear that the site won't pressure him to provide a phone number, unlike the sleazy lead generator that required the visitor to agree to phone calls even if he's on the Do Not Call Registry. Compare EnergySage's approach, which is so awesome because it's the exact opposite: "100% online, no phone calls unless you want them."

Nice. Just for this alone, EnergySage deserves some kind of Solar Marketing Nobel Prize for raising the standard for all solar lead-generators.

This approach also makes good business sense with the rise of permission marketing, when buyers have less patience to be interrupted by marketers but instead want to choose how and when they deal with companies. Residential solar installers working with EnergySage can be more sure that their leads are truly hot and the prospects are interested, because the site has started from the very beginning by building trust with their solar buyers.

KEEPING THE PROMISE, BUILDING TRUST

As the visitor goes through the process, creating her profile, EnergySage proves to be as good as its word. The homeowner can enter a phone number, but it's not required. Instead, the visitor can choose to enter only his email address and then communicate with EnergySage online only. And just because they don't require a phone number, doesn't mean EnergySage is weak on marketing. Actually, it's the opposite. This is what makes EnergySage stronger on marketing than the phone-required site. Making the phone number optional and allowing the buyer to continue the process by email builds valuable rapport with the visitor.

That's how it was for me when I went through their sign-up process. Because they let me complete my profile offering email only, I now have given them my complete trust. And as they guide any potential solar buyer through their process, EnergySage only increases that trust with their attractive user interface and non-hyped sales copy. When they talk about my expected savings by going solar, which is substantial compared to doing nothing, they have something to base it on. In my case, it was the electric bill that I uploaded to their site.

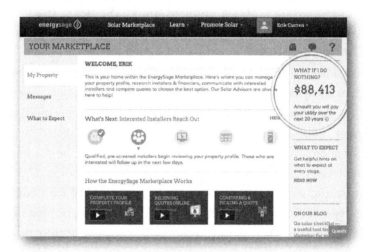

Finally, at the bottom of this same page, EnergySage helps move me along the solar buyer's journey without pressure. They help me go at my own pace by offering educational links that help empower me to make a better decision on solar.

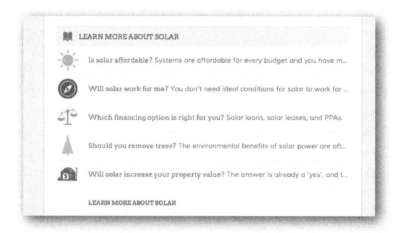

I love how these questions are phrased in ordinary English without solar industry jargon. Again, that's another sign of respect by EnergySage for the buyer.

EMAIL FOLLOW-UP FOR A HAPPY ENDING

For an old-school cold-call closer, following up with leads might mean calling back the buyer every few days to try to wear down their resistance to booking an appointment for a solar home assessment. And if Closer Guy can put down his phone long enough to send an email, you know it'll be written in all caps. THIS DEAL IS ABOUT TO GO AWAY. DO YOU WANT IT OR NOT?

But for EnergySage, follow-up is more civilized—and more effective. As it turned out, because I live in an area without many solar installers nearby yet, or solar installers who aren't registered with EnergySage, EnergySage wasn't able to send me any quotes to get solar on my home. But they didn't just ignore me. Instead, they sent a nice email with the subject line "Solar for Your Home with Energy Sage—Plan B" to explain the situation and offer me the option to get some help from them to explore other options:

Hi Erik,

We hope you're excited about going solar!

It looks that there isn't much activity from solar installers on your EnergySage account for [XX Street Address]. We wanted to touch base by phone and brainstorm ideas for finding some options for your solar installation.

We could chat via phone or email, whatever works for you! Let us know when you're free and how we can help.

I still haven't gotten around to going to their site to do an online chat with an EnergySage rep, but I'm confident it would be a positive experience.

I probably won't be buying solar through EnergySage now, mainly because I live in an historic district that unfortunately prohibits solar on roofs that is visible from the street. Darn! But in the future, I'm sure they'll be high on my list, especially if they do a good job keeping in touch by email in the coming months. Meanwhile, I'll take every chance I can to recommend them to my friends when the topic of where to get home solar comes up in conversation.

Since residential Power Purchase Agreements (PPAs) aren't available in my area, I don't know if EnergySage offers them in places where they are available, or if the company only helps homeowners to purchase solar systems outright. So if you offer PPAs, solar leases or other financing arrangements for homeowners besides selling solar panels, then the site may not be for you. But for installers seeking better leads for cash purchases, EnergySage is worth checking out.

DOWNSIDE OF A MARKETPLACE SITE FOR SOLAR INSTALLERS

As long as they can find installers in a homeowner's local area, then EnergySage might be the most price-competitive option for a consumer to get home solar. As the company claims, their marketplace can save a buyer 20% on solar through comparison shopping among their stable of installers.

But for the installers, any kind of marketplace hosting multiple solar companies is always a mixed bag. On the one hand, a service like EnergySage can get you more leads. On the other, since they're essentially pitting installers against each other to compete on price, the process is set up to favor the lowest-price bid. And that's a recipe for driving solar prices down. Again, that will benefit the homeowner, as long as the lowest priced bid still offers a high quality solar installation. But it's never a great business model for companies to get pulled into a race to the bottom on price.

This applies to solar as it applies to any industry. Once your product or service becomes a commodity, then its sole selling point will be how cheap you can make it.

If, carried to its logical extreme, the same provider always wins on price in a particular solar market, eventually everybody else will go broke. If you want your solar company to be profitable into the future, it's much better to distinguish yourself now on quality or service rather than getting caught in a price war and trying to get the reputation as the cheapest solar company in the area. Instead, seeking a reputation for value through high quality and good service rather than a reputation for low prices will allow you to charge more. Your reputation for quality and service can also help you develop a long-term relationship with your customer that may allow you to do more business with them and their friends in the future.

Overall, in spite of the downside of competing on price alone, solar installers that need better leads in the short term would be well advised to check out EnergySage or similar solar lead generation vendors that understand permission marketing and deal respectfully with the potential customer. Their leads are likely to be higher quality.

But in the long term, solar companies will be in a stronger position if they develop relationships with homeowners directly. Skipping the marketplace will save money on the commission for EnergySage or any other solar lead generation vendor. More importantly, connecting directly with a homeowner allows a solar installer to talk to a buyer without other solar companies trying to butt in. It allows an installer to sell more on quality, reputation, and service instead of just on price. And it builds a brand for that solar contractor, which is an asset that possesses financial value—value for today's business, and future value if the contractor or installer ever wants to sell the business.

Why not use a combination of a trustworthy solar lead-generation vendor and your own website to get leads now and in the future? You can get good leads quickly from a high quality lead vendor like EnergySage. Then, set yourself up for long-term success by starting to generate leads on your own website with inbound marketing on the Internet.

To sum it up, traditional solar sales and marketing tactics like tele-marketing and knocking on doors have big problems.

*   These tactics are starting to show diminishing returns and are raising the cost of customer acquisition.
*   News of solar marketing scams has eroded customer trust.
*   Regulators are starting to step in to clamp down on deceptive solar marketing.
*   As traditional tactics produce limp results, sales force morale declines and turnover increases.
*   The whole industry has been tarnished by the actions of a few bad apples, who are getting more attention in the media.

Problems with residential solar marketing may even spill over into commercial solar sales as aggressive solar installers try to pressure or trick businesses into the same kind of bad solar deals that homeowners have been complaining about for the last few years.

And as we've seen, retrograde utilities have already started to use negative public perception of solar scammers as a way to attack the solar industry in an effort to cast doubt on rooftop solar and hold onto their ratepayers. Remember the story of the Solar Scammer and how utilities were lovin' it?

Coordinating with each other through their trade association, the Edison Electric Institute, utilities around the United States have called for more regulations on rooftop solar installers in the name of consumer protection. Using stories of solar scammers, utilities have also built support among legislatures and utility regulators to roll back net metering and other public policy necessary for solar to continue to grow. This isn't just about consumer protection—it's about beating back competition from solar and protecting traditional energy company's territories. The last thing solar needs is more opposition from the well-funded, influential, and coordinated energy industry and its ties to government at all levels.

PLAY IT SAFE WHEN BUYING SOLAR LEADS

If you're going to buy lists of solar leads from third-party vendors, especially telemarketers, make sure that you know how those leads were generated.

Ask basic questions to make sure the vendor is doing things legally and ethically:

1. How do you generate leads?
2. If you get leads from telemarketing, how do you get the lists of people to call? Where are your callers located? Do you offer a vacation or some other incentive for the buyer to agree to book an appointment with a representative from the solar company? Can I review your phone script?
3. If you get leads online, what's the website address? Does a visitor have to give you their phone number or can they communicate with you only by email?
4. Has your company ever been the subject of an investigation by law enforcement or any kind of sanction from government regulators?

But in the long term, no matter how fastidious the lead-generation vendor is, leads you buy from someone else are never as good as solar leads you generate yourself. Your own leads are fresher, they're yours alone, and, most importantly, if you've followed the principles of inbound marketing, you know that your own prospects are really interested in solar. You know that the homeowner hasn't been tricked into getting your solar pitch by vacation offers or other deceptive marketing.

As solar telemarketing scams become more widely known, solar companies that generate their own leads will develop a competitive advantage. These companies will earn the trust of the public and get more business. And, in the future, if the solar telemarketing industry should start to collapse under the weight of its own bad reputation and attacks from government regulators, solar companies who've weaned themselves off of telemarketing vendors will be better prepared to continue to make sales in a post-telemarketing world.

The way to do it is with inbound marketing and I'll talk about why it works so well and suggest some ways for solar companies to get started with it soon. But first, we need to understand why inbound marketing should be happening now. And for that, we need to know how the Internet has changed marketing in general.

Section 2

RISING SUN—MARKETING ON THE INTERNET

There is never going to be a substitute for face-to-face communication, but we have seen since the alphabet, to the telephone, and now the Internet, that whenever people find a new way to communicate, they will flock to it.

— HOWARD RHEINGOLD

Chapter 8

ONLINE MARKETING IS MORE THAN JUST BUYING GOOGLE ADS

Solar may be an advanced power source, but we've already seen how solar marketing is about as old fashioned as you can get. Well, okay, solar companies don't paint charts of home energy savings on the walls of caves. Neither do they chisel into stone tablets their holiday special offer of 20% Off A Rooftop Solar System with 90 Days Same As Cash.

But the marketing that many residential solar installers rely on today isn't much more advanced. Making cold calls, driving out to the neighborhood of one of your customers and knocking on neighbors' doors, staffing booths at home improvement shows, and of course, buying ads, is straight out of the 1960s era of the Mad Men—or the *Tin Men* mentioned earlier.

Coincidentally, the 1960s were when NASA was helping develop modern solar PV to provide electric power to space missions. This suggests an interesting contrast between what solar energy does on the one hand and how companies sell solar to homeowners on the other. Can you imagine selling solar door-to-door just like the guy who sticks his foot in your door, dumps coffee on your shag rug, and then washes it up with the carpet cleaning fluid that he's peddling—the one you can't buy in stores but can only get from his company?

Of course, residential solar is not just about door-to-door sales. When I talk with solar marketers today about how they generate leads and fill the top of their sales funnel, most list other traditional marketing tactics: trade shows, their own promotional events, email blasts to lists that they've bought, in-house cold calling, outsourced telemarketing, and advertising.

If these marketing tactics still worked well, then it wouldn't matter how old-school they were. If it ain't broke, don't fix it, right?

Since the 1970s, the solar industry has relied for decades on tactics of "outbound" marketing, none so much as telemarketing. Overall, outbound marketing is when a company pushes its messages out to its potential customers. Before the Internet came along and made two-way conversations possible, outbound marketing was the *only* kind of marketing out there. "We talk and you listen." Outbound marketing is an interruptive, one-way conversation that can happen in a cold call or in an advertisement.

In the solar industry, we've already seen how, all too often, telemarketing has given residential installers a black eye. The media has documented hundreds of cases of telemarketers for solar companies not merely annoying consumers but also misleading them. It's no wonder that complaints about solar marketing have been on the rise over the last few years and that law enforcement, regulators, and legislators have started to respond.

Though solar may provide a particularly striking example, across all industries, telemarketing and other outbound marketing tactics have gotten less and less effective as the Internet has been on the rise. Researchers say that's because consumers have a different mindset today. In the old days, consumers had more tolerance for outbound marketing. In some cases, buyers actually benefited from ads or even telemarketing calls, and so the consumers were willing to put up with the interruption in their lives that outbound tactics require.

In a simpler world of three or four channels of TV, a landline phone, and a couple daily newspapers, advertising succeeded in building huge consumer brands for products ranging from Lucky Strike cigarettes to General Motors. Sales calls, whether by phone or in person, were as good a way to sell products for the home like Electrolux vacuum cleaners as they were to sell industrial products for businesses such as a new kind of punch press.

Fast forward to today, and most solar marketers have an inkling that they should be doing more marketing on the Internet. Online marketing costs less and, since it can be measured, you can also track that you're getting a better return-on-investment. But when most solar companies take their first baby steps online, what they usually start doing on the Internet is an electronic version of what they're used to doing offline. That is, some form of outbound marketing where you try to interrupt your audience and catch their eye so that they'll drop what they're doing and consider buying solar from you.

After they put up a basic website—or maybe just a Facebook page—many solar companies dip their toe in the water of online marketing by buying a few pay-per-click (PPC) ads on Google. It sounds appealing. Advertising is what solar companies understand, since they've done it offline for years. You buy ads, and you get customers, right?

To sweeten the deal, Internet advertising comes with an attractive feature that offline ads don't: you can pay only for people who interact with your ad. That means you don't have to pay for all those people who may see the ad but aren't interested in solar, unlike what happens when you pay upfront for an expensive newspaper or magazine ad. As the name pay-per-click indicates, the advertiser only pays if a Google or Facebook user clicks on their ad. And an advertiser can limit its budget to a set amount per day, such as $10 or $20, so there's no risk of spending more than you can afford if you happen to get a lot of interest.

It sounds great. But buying ads online doesn't always work out so well for solar companies. Sadly, after a few months and thousands of dollars in click fees but few new customers or even website visitors to show for their investment, a lot of solar companies decide that PPC ads are a waste of money.

For example, the owner of a local residential installer on Long Island told me that five years ago he used to be able to buy ads on Google that would get him to the top of search listings for "Long Island solar panels" for less than a dollar per click. But since then, his market has gotten more crowded, with national installers moving in and more local guys starting up. And they've all started buying Google ads, whose prices are determined by auction bidding. That is, if you want to buy an ad for that term that appears in a good position in Google—preferably on page one of search results for the term—you have to pay more for it than the previous advertiser. Then, the next advertiser has to pay more than you. And so on, until the price of the search term gets more and more expensive for everybody. This system works great for Google. But it can get very expensive for advertisers to get prominent ads for popular search terms.

To return to the example of "solar panels Long Island," as a result of heavy competition for the term, when the owner talked to me, he was faced with paying nearly $20 per click for the very same ads that used to cost him less than a dollar each.

An experience like this may give solar marketers the idea that Internet marketing doesn't work well for solar. So then it's back to making cold calls, knocking on doors, and doing other old-timey marketing and sales tactics straight out of the movies *Tin Men* and *Glengarry Glen Ross.* That's a shame. Because the Internet is definitely the future for solar marketing, as you can see from the amount of effort that big national solar installers like SolarCity and Vivint put into their websites, social media, and other online outreach.

So, if you haven't had success with PPC ads, the problem may not be with Internet marketing. The problem may be that ads, whether online or off, are just not very effective anymore. And regardless of whether PPC ads work well or not to market solar, there's a lot more you can do to market your company on the Internet besides buying ads. In fact, if you're not doing anything else online besides buying ads, then you can expect to start falling behind the competition very soon.

We'll talk about the other things that you should be doing online to market your solar business later. But for now, let's talk a little more about buying ads, since that's the online marketing tactic that's most familiar to solar companies. Online ads are often a waste of money for solar companies, but you can make them work in limited situations with a few tips.

THE CASE FOR SOLAR PPC ADS

You probably already know how search engine ads work on Google. You open an AdWords account, specify what search terms you want your ad to come up for, and then pay anywhere from a few cents to a few dollars per click, depending on how competitive your terms are. Then, your ads come up at the top of the page for the search terms you've chosen, above the organic or free listings. The appeal of pay-per-click ads is clear:

* You only get charged for your ad when somebody clicks on your ad, which means you're paying for results
* You can measure how many clicks you get, which means you can track ROI
* And you can get instant traffic to your website, which means, hopefully, that you can speed up the sales process

But you'll only get value out of search engine ads if you do them right.

ROOKIE MISTAKES TO AVOID

Too many solar companies waste their investment in PPC ads by making typical beginner's mistakes. Online ad buyer Eric Siu in Entrepreneur magazine outlines five PPC mistakes that can cost you money, and I apply them to solar companies here based on my experience:

1. **Sending visitors to your home page.** For example, if your PPC text offers residential solar in Southern California, then unless

that's all you do, your company's homepage is not the best destination for people who click on an ad. If they arrive on your homepage, your visitors will have have to click past your other products and other geographies to get to the page about home solar in their area, whether LA., Orange County, or San Diego.

2. **Sending visitors to your contact page.** This may violate the rules of PPC sites, as Siu explains: "If you're advertising through Google AdWords, for example, be aware that requiring visitors to fill out contact forms in exchange for something free goes against the search giant's guidelines." But it's also not effective. Many first-time visitors to your site are not ready to hear from a salesperson or even join an email list. They just want to poke around for a bit on their own. If you push them too fast, they may just leave your site.

3. **Failing to split-test your ad text.** Before finalizing any PPC ad campaign, try out a couple different versions of your text to see which one gets more clicks. Then, select your text accordingly.

4. **Relying entirely on "broad match" keyword ads.** Broad match ads will match any of the search terms you specify, which will get you more traffic, but maybe at the expense of irrelevant clicks. For example, "solar installation" may come up for searches on "solar batteries" or "art installation," which are probably not clicks you want to pay for.

5. **Not taking advantage of negative keywords.** Negative keywords scare a lot of people doing PPC ads. Why would you want to NOT come up in a search? But they're actually a good way to increase relevance and target your ad budget to get higher quality traffic. Thus, in the search above, you might want to exclude the words "batteries" and "art" so you won't have to pay for clicks from people who aren't really looking for a grid-tied solar array on their roof.

I'd add that, unless you already have a website that's optimized to convert visitors into sales leads with effective landing pages as destinations for your PPC ads, an essential tool that we'll discuss later on, then you're wasting money on Google ads.

THE VALUE OF ADS IS SHORT LIVED

In the long run, no matter how good your solar PPC ad campaign, ultimately, search engine advertising is a strategy with diminishing returns. On the one hand, the keywords you really want are going to be bid up by competitors, costing you more per click over time. On the other hand, up to 80% of people ignore Google-sponsored ads. So, that means PPC ads are getting more expensive but less effective. That hurts!

Of course, Google is not the only place to buy PPC ads. Alternatives like Facebook, Twitter, or LinkedIn may offer better value. Ads on social media services are generally cheaper than ads on Google. In addition, social media ads target customers more specifically, they're easier for companies to set up, and there's more interest from users. But any PPC ads, whether on Google or Facebook, will never by themselves be a successful solar marketing program. That's because, in today's world of the social web, any kind of ads are less effective than they used to be. Today, people have lots of options to block ads. And even when they can't block all advertising, people are more used to ignoring ads today than they were in the past.

Most importantly, getting traffic from ads is just renting an audience. As soon as you stop paying for the ads, the flow of traffic stops. If you rely too heavily on ads without doing any other online marketing, you can get addicted to the traffic that ads provide. Then, you'll have no other choice to keep that traffic flowing but to keep buying ads, even as they get more expensive and less effective over time.

The best solar marketing will do much more than renting an audience by buying ads. It will connect with a long-term audience by building relationships.

For a prospect to get the the point where he's ready to make the commitment to a solar company, that company needs to earn the prospect's trust. At most, PPC ads should take up 5%-10% of your online market-ing budget. The rest you should spend on creating and distributing con-tent that will add valuable search engine optimization (SEO) to your own website and build your brand in the long term and nurture your website as an asset.

Chapter 9

●　　●　　●

INTERNET MARKETING HAS CHANGED ALL MARKETING

Any business that wants to succeed online has to build trust with its customers. And the Internet is one of the best places to establish long-term relationships of trust with potential customers today.

For high value products and services, building trust is even more important. If you're selling a rooftop solar array for $15,000, you need to build much more trust with a buyer than if you're selling a big screen TV for $400 or a T shirt for $19.

For homeowners, buying solar is a big deal—much bigger than getting new gutters or landscaping.

A home solar array is either a lot of money up front for a purchase or a long-term commitment to a lease or PPA. And if a customer wants his solar off the grid, then the level of trust must be even higher. A homeowner or business owner needs to trust a solar company to make that deep a commitment. But with all the stories of solar scams out in the news media these days, building trust with solar buyers takes more work than ever.

Solar PPC ads don't build relationships—they merely get attention.

What it takes to build relationships is content marketing, where a solar company puts out stuff on their website and social media profiles that solar buyers really want to see, such as blog posts, infographics, and ebooks. With content marketing, solar companies can build authority and trust with solar buyers that will fill their online sales funnel with web visitors, leads and ultimately, new customers.

Content marketing is better than buying ads in the long run because it fills an online solar sales funnel for years to come. But content marketing *does* take time to start working. So, to get web visitors quickly, it may make sense to buy a few well-tested and smartly targeted PPC ads, as long as you already have a great solar website to send visitors to.

However, you should never make PPC ads the star of your marketing program, because they're not a good long-term investment. After all, once you stop paying for the ads, they disappear. And once they're gone, so is any benefit they provided. By contrast, when you do content marketing by publishing blog posts and other helpful stuff on your own website, it's out there for as long as your website is online, building SEO equity that will only increase over time. That SEO becomes a company asset.

Overall, in the Age of Information Overload, ads are becoming less effective. Today, where the Internet and an explosion of other media puts more than 3,000 marketing messages every day in front of the average American adult, the public's tolerance for being interrupted has nearly disappeared.

Brian Halligan, co-founder of HubSpot, explains why outbound marketing tactics don't work as well as they used to:

> I think outbound marketing techniques are getting less and less effective over time for two reasons. First, your average human today is inundated with more than 2,000 outbound marketing interruptions per day and is figuring out more and more creative ways to block them out, including caller ID, spam filtering, Tivo, and Sirius satellite radio. Second, the cost of coordination around learning about something new or shopping for something new

using the Internet (search engines, blogs, and social media) is now much lower than going to a seminar at the Marriott or flying to a trade show in Las Vegas.

The problem is that traditional outbound marketing—including buying ads, even if those ads are online rather than in a newspaper or on TV—yields weaker and weaker sales leads as time goes on. This would explain why so many solar installers complain of bad sales leads. And, since they may have to go through the process of pitching hundreds of bad leads to find a few good prospects and eventually make a single sale, it would also explain why it costs $3,000 to acquire a new residential solar customer according to GTM Research.

Just consider a few statistics that show how outbound marketing is so challenged these days, according to HubSpot:

* 200 million Americans are on the Federal Trade Commission's "Do Not Call List"
* Cold calling fails 90% of the time
* 86% of people skip television ads
* Spending on trade shows has declined 46% since 2009
* 44% of direct mail is never opened

Here's how Craig Davis, worldwide creative director of huge ad agency J. Walter Thompson put it: "Audiences everywhere are tough. They don't have time to be bored or browbeaten by orthodox, old-fashioned advertising. We need to stop interrupting what people are interested in and be what people *are* interested in."

In response to declining lead quality, some solar companies try doubling down on traditional outbound marketing. Say, knocking on more doors or buying more ads. But better than wasting more budget on things that don't work well anymore would be to employ an inbound marketing strategy done primarily on the Internet.

As tech startup guru Guy Kawasaki has quipped, "If you have more money than brains, you should focus on outbound marketing. If you have more brains than money, you should focus on inbound marketing."

So, in the next chapter, we'll see what qualifies as inbound marketing and what makes it so promising.

Chapter 10

● ● ●

WHAT IS INBOUND MARKETING AND WHY DOES IT WORK?

A more common term for inbound marketing is content marketing. Actually, which term you use is just a question of emphasis.

On the one hand, content marketing describes the main activity of this type of marketing, which is creating helpful and interesting content like blog posts, ebooks, memes for social sites, videos, etc. as a hook for people to seek your business out, instead of creating promotional messages to buy your stuff that you try to put in front of consumer. On the other hand, inbound marketing describes the *benefit* of this marketing method, which is that customers come to you to get your great content instead of you having to go to them with ads, cold calls, and unannounced home visits.

But since content marketing is still more commonly known, here I will use the two terms to mean more or less the same thing, especially when quoting from some experts. For example: "Content marketing generates three times as many leads as traditional outbound marketing, but costs 62% less," according to Demand Metric.

But whichever term you use, the benefits are the same for both content and inbound marketing, according to Rick Burnes at HubSpot:

1. **It Costs Less**—Outbound marketing means spending money - either by buying ads, buying email lists or renting huge booths at trade shows. Inbound marketing means creating content and talking about it. A blog costs nothing to start. A Twitter account is free, too. Both can draw thousands of customers to your site. The marketing ROI from inbound campaigns is higher.

2. **Better Targeting**—Techniques like cold-calling, mass mail, and email campaigns are notoriously poorly targeted. You're reaching out to individuals because of one or two attributes in a database. When you do inbound marketing, you only approach people who self-qualify themselves. They demonstrate an interest in your content, so they're likely to be interested in your product.

3. **It's an Investment, Not an Ongoing Expense**—When you buy pay-per-click advertising on search engines, its value is gone as soon as you pay for it. In order to maintain a position at the top of Google's paid results, you have to keep paying. However, if you invest your resources in creating quality content that ranks in Google's organic results, you'll be there until somebody displaces you.

The strategies of inbound marketing are new—create content online and then build audience for it through both search engine optimization and social media. But the philosophy of inbound marketing is founded on age-old principles of how people think and act. Those principles are familiarity and trust.

ROOTED IN ANCIENT PRINCIPLES OF COMMUNICATION

Throughout most of human history, people lived in small communities where they knew everyone. During her lifetime, the average person would meet no more than 150 people and travel no more than 50 miles from her place of birth. Meeting a new person, aside from a new baby or a spouse brought in from a neighboring village, was rare. So people grew up with familiarity and trust. In a small village or early human settlement, you knew what anyone's weak and strong points were and you could trust in that knowledge to make decisions on what to count on them for.

That's how life was for most people for most of human civilization. Then came agrarian civilization and the birth of the state, with its cities so big that people now interacted with strangers more frequently. Finally, history brought the industrial revolution, which added a new player: the large commercial business and the multinational corporation.

Corporations disrupted relationships among the people in communities, inserting outside marketers between people who made things and people who used those things—what we'd call the producer and the consumer. And in turn, the industrial revolution spawned the age of mass media, which allowed people to learn about happenings from outside their local area through newspapers and magazines at first and then later, through the first electronic media—movies, radio and TV. People could even communicate with others who lived far away through improved postal delivery, telegraph, and telephone. But the full promise of remote two-way communication would not be fulfilled until the Internet would come along in the late twentieth century.

In the meantime, say from the late nineteenth century through the 1970s, mass media was about one-way communication. This era saw the birth of modern advertising and public relations, paid media and earned media, respectively—the two fields which made up modern commercial marketing. Dominated by real life *Mad Men* and PR flacks, the golden age of one-way marketing saw the rise of massive consumer brands like General Motors and Coke. Companies did all the talking, consumers did all the listening, and everybody seemed okay with that.

Until the sixties and seventies, that is. Following on the Civil Rights movement, the social upheavals of the 1960s led many Americans, especially young people, to start to distrust the government and other pillars of society including the church, higher education, and, of course, big business. More nimble consumer brands tried to ride the wave of youth culture and managed to remain trusted brands even as others fell away.

Remember how Coke tied itself to peace and global understanding when it taught the world to sing in perfect harmony?

The Vietnam withdrawal, Nixon's resignation, the energy crisis, and years of inflation further eroded the trust of Americans in traditional leaders and institutions in the 1970s. By the end of that decade, Americans had gotten used to talking back to authority and they were no longer satisfied with the one-way communication of mass media.

Yet, old habits die hard, especially in business. For the next three decades, marketers continued to hammer away at the outbound tactics that had made so many sales for GM and Coke. They bought more ads, they sent out more direct mail, they made more cold calls and of course, they distributed more press releases.

So, a disconnect developed in marketing. On the one hand, consumer distrust grew. On the other, frustrated marketers shouted louder and hoped that would bridge the gap with consumers, somehow.

Fortunately, it wasn't too long until the Internet came along and, as they like to say in Silicon Valley, changed everything. Actually, at first, not that much changed with the web. From a marketing standpoint, the early web of the late 1990s and early 2000s, was just TV or a magazine with clicks. Hey, here's an ad—you can click on it to get more information! Isn't that neat? The novelty of the same old one-way marketing applied to a world where you could now waste a whole afternoon following hyperlinks all over the place remained longer than it had any business to do so.

But after the Internet's first decade as a commercial medium, consumers started to get bored with ads. The web appeared as if it might just be another place for marketers to spend money with little to show for it but "clickthrough rate."

By the way, over the last ten years, the ROI of display advertising such as banner ads on the Internet has declined. For example, while the clickthrough rate on display ads remained flat from 2013 to 2014 at about 0.06% according to comScore and Display Benchmarks Tool, ad blocking grew 41% over the same period, according to PageFair, leading to a subsequent decline in clickthroughs.

Could ads online actually do worse than ads in traditional media?

Maybe they could, at least with young people. A January 2014 study by Adroit Digital found that 18- to 34-year-olds were far more likely to ignore online ads, such as banners and those on social media and search engines, than they were traditional TV, radio, and newspaper ads.

It took social media to really change everything and to allow the web to realize its huge potential for two-way communication. With MySpace, Facebook, Twitter, YouTube, and then all the rest, consumers finally had a way to talk back to companies and, more importantly, to talk about companies in a very public way. Now, after more than a century of companies and their marketers telling consumers what to think, the power began to shift back to consumers, who now demanded that marketers earn their trust.

In this way, the web has allowed marketing to return back to the basic principles of human communication that governed every village and town from the dawn of civilization until the Industrial Revolution. Those principles are, of course, familiarity and trust.

Obviously, there was no such thing as marketing as we know it before industrialization and mass media, though Mark Twain had fun imagining 19th century advertising plopped down into Medieval England. His novel *A Connecticut Yankee in King Arthur's Court* depicted a knight in armor wearing a sandwich board: "Persimmon's soap‹—All the Prime Donne Use It."

Before the Industrial Revolution there certainly was commerce, though in a world where households met most of their own needs, the money economy was a much smaller part of everyday life than it is today. But nonetheless, people still bought and sold things in pre-industrial civilizations, whether ancient Greece or Rome, Shakespearean England, or Colonial America. Farmers who grew more than their own families could use had to sell grain while laborers had to sell their time. On the purchasing side, even the poorest people bought wine and ale from taverns and pubs. Households in cities and towns bought firewood, olive and whale oil, and later coal from the energy providers of their day. And rich people bought spices, silks, jewelry, and silverware from traders and skilled craftsmen.

But sellers in the old days didn't reach buyers through massive advertising. Instead, they counted on the oldest form of marketing, word of mouth, to establish a reputation for high quality at a fair price. Sellers who didn't satisfy customers got negative reviews, so to speak, through the grapevine. And the increasing influence of consumer reviews today will be the subject of the next chapter.

Chapter 11

●　●　●

THE POWER OF WORD-OF-MOUTH

Fast forward to today, and you can see that social media has made possible a return to word-of-mouth marketing. Whether companies want them to do it or not, consumers are now able to spread their opinions around the Internet through review sites such as Yelp. Reviews are popular with consumers—though often less so with companies.

In the solar industry, homeowners can go to SolarReviews.com and search for residential installers by state, city, or zip code. People who've already gotten solar can rank companies on a five-star scale. Some of those companies in the one- or two-star range may not be happy with what their customers have to say about the company. For example, take these one one-star reviews from Phoenix:

Roof Leaking
01/09/2016 From the first day of installment my roof start leaking. I just remodeled inside my home and all my wall paint is ruined. Very poor installment [sic].

True Definition of Racket
06/25/15 They signed us up on a lease with out disclosing the buyout and did the e-sign to run it through. We never got a copy

or the lease in the allotted time to back out and the $27,000 unit will cost $49,000 over the life of the lease.

Later, I'll talk about how solar companies can deal with negative reviews in particular and offer a strategy for solar companies to take with review websites in general.

But for now, reviews can serve as a vivid example of how social media has turned the power relationship between sellers and buyers around. In the old days, sellers had most of the power, since they controlled most of the information about their product or service. Today, consumers have most of the power, because they can go online to get nearly all the information they need to evaluate a purchase without ever needing to talk to a company salesperson. And now they can also spread their opinions about a company far and wide on review websites and over social media.

As I discussed in the first chapter, even while the solar industry has been changing the energy landscape of the United States, the way that solar is marketed in America hasn't changed much since the seventies. Residential solar installers still rely heavily on outbound marketing tactics, especially the very worst tactic marketing ever invented, door-to-door canvassing, and the second-worst method, cold-calling. Because consumers hate them, cold walking and cold calling produce some of the lowest quality sales leads that solar companies waste their time pursuing.

Inbound marketing, on the other hand, produces perhaps the highest quality solar leads because the buyer has come to a solar installer on his own and is more likely to have realistic expectations of what he can get with home solar. No pressure, no hype.

Unlike traditional outbound marketing, inbound marketing takes place primarily online. That's why it's so important to understand how the Internet has changed marketing as a whole, both online and offline. If the web were just another channel for companies to broadcast outbound messages to their customers, then it would be nice, but not that big of a deal. And many companies still treat the web as just one way among many to do the same old outbound marketing they've done for years, adding pay-per-click ads to the traditional local TV spots and print display ads in their marketing mix.

It's not surprising then that many residential solar installers have created websites that are little more than an electronic version of their print brochure. Along with buying pay-per-click ads, a brochure-website is the most common way that solar companies treat the web as just another form of traditional media. And, as we discussed earlier, many residential solar installers buy sales leads from third-party lead-generation vendors. Some of those vendors have started generating leads online rather than through telemarketing as in the past. Again, this way of using the Internet is not much different than what marketers did in the past. Now, they're just doing it digitally instead of on paper, via the airwaves, or over the phone.

Companies who treat the Internet as just one channel among many for old-style outbound marketing are missing the point. The Internet has the potential to be much more than just another place to buy ads. The web can become a company's integrated sales and marketing team that works 24/7 all year round, never takes a sick day, and has the patience to nurture a potential customer for as long as it takes to close the sale, whether that's six months or even a couple years.

If you understand the potential of the Internet for automated, always-on marketing, you'll see that online outreach is much more than an alternative to putting up your booth at the usual home show again this year. The web is so much more powerful that it might even be able to replace some of your old marketing and sales techniques. Solar marketing on the Internet can have two advantages over traditional marketing. First, it can be much cheaper. Second, it can be much more effective. And the most effective kind of Internet marketing is inbound marketing, because it utilizes the full potential of the web for interactive communication with buyers.

How inbound marketing works is what I'll discuss in the next chapter.

Chapter 12

● ● ●

HOW INBOUND MARKETING WORKS

Imagine that a solar company has installed a small PV array outside of an elementary school. The array only has a capacity of one kilowatt, so it's just for demonstration purposes. But it's placed right outside the main entrance to the school. Not only does this entrance get a lot of foot traffic from students, teachers, and staff entering the building. But in the morning, many parents drop their kids off here. That means hundreds of people see this little solar array five days a week throughout the school year.

Next to the array is an attractively designed sign, talking about why solar power is important and how it works. This information is explained in layperson's terms using ordinary English and illustrated with a few simple graphics, so that it's easy for even elementary schoolers to understand.

The whole setup is intended to get everybody who goes in and out of the school building interested in solar power. Yet, there's no rack for brochures or business cards. The only mention of the company that sponsored the display is its name on the bottom of the sign, with a website address. This is obviously not a sales kiosk, then. It's just for education.

And here's the strange part. The solar installer who paid to put up this display didn't get any grant funding to do it. Instead, the company paid for the PV array and the sign out of its marketing budget.

The director of sales was stumped. Sure, it's a nice thing to do, to help educate little kids about solar power. But fifth graders aren't typically known as great customers for residential solar. And if there's no company brochure for them to take back to their parents, then what's the point? How is this cute display going to sell any solar?

The sales manager thought that the money could be spent better on buying more ads. After all, that's how you get leads and make sales. Tell people about the benefits of solar, assure them it's more affordable than they might think, and then offer a free home assessment. Throw in a discount offer with an expiration date to encourage them to pull the trigger now, and then it's just a question of getting them to "sign on the line which is dotted," as the sales manager played by Alec Baldwin in *Glengarry Glen Ross* says. If you want to sell solar, you've got to make the pitch, right?

The director of marketing explained that she was actually trying to sell solar. But, because ads had been getting more expensive and less effective over the last few years, she was trying a new approach. She had done her research, and she had figured out that the school served several zip codes with good prospects for the company's home solar installations. Her research revealed a few bits of useful information about the area.

First, the houses had lots of good roofs. Then, the families who lived in those houses fit the profile of one of the company's ideal customers. That is, the dads did. The school had lots of dads in their thirties and early forties who were attorneys, physicians and businesspeople, which meant they had disposable income. Since the middle school and high school serving the area were both top ranked, the chances were good that many of these families would stay in their homes for the next ten years or more. That meant they'd be likely to invest in home improvements, because their family would stay in the house long enough to enjoy them.

On the weekends, many of these dads were also gear-heads who repaired classic cars in the driveway or brewed beer in the garage. They liked gadgets. This meant that lots of them were probably also fans of solar and would enjoy the chance to start making some of their own power—and monitoring that power generation on their laptops or phone apps.

Sure, the sales director said, he knew that these neighborhoods were perfect for solar. That's why his salesforce had already called nearly every house, knocked on the doors of the rest, and set as many appointments as they could for solar home assessments. That had helped them sell a couple arrays. But these people were tougher than he'd expected. When they got somebody live on the phone, they were usually irritated. Some even complained about solar scammers and threatened to report the company's salespeople to the Federal Trade Commission or the local TV station's consumer advocate. And knocking on doors hadn't done so well either. At dinner time, nobody wanted to talk to a salesperson. And during the day, women home alone just didn't answer the door.

After their own guys had come up dry, the sales manager had hired a telemarketing company to set up appointments. They were located some-place offshore and the price was definitely right. You didn't have to pay them for all their calls. You only had to pay for calls where they were able to set up an appointment for the company's home solar consultant to come by. But the problem was that, on more than half the appointments, nobody was home. It seems like the homeowners agreed to the meetings just to get the telemarketers off the phone.

Even when they were home for the appointment, the homeowners had unrealistic ideas about how much solar it took to power their home and how much money they'd save every month on their electricity.

One guy was disappointed to hear that putting as much solar on his own roof as possible still wouldn't give him enough to sell power to his neighbor. Another one said it was silly that the solar panels wouldn't work in a blackout and he wanted batteries thrown in for free so he could go off-grid. He said that a telemarketer from another solar company said that their company didn't do any solar installations without storage these days and that the price was basically the same. Too many homeowners thought that the government had some kind of program to put free solar panels on everybody's roof, eventually.

How can our guys sell to people like this, the sales director asked? These neighborhoods are a waste of our time, he added with a wave of his hand.

But the director of marketing thought that the area had much more sales potential. She wanted to try something new, a way of selling that was more indirect, to see if it might get through where the direct pitch had failed.

And that's how she came up with the idea for the solar display at the school. She would educate instead of sell. And she would reach people who weren't the actual decision-maker but nonetheless carried a lot of influence—teachers and kids—as a more effective way of getting to the dads and moms. It was all about trust and relationships, the director of marketing explained. While the homeowners listened to company salespeople with skepticism (if they listened at all), in their role as moms and dads, homeowners listened to their own kids with love and genuine interest.

Now, if the marketing director had been doing solar education online instead of in front of a school, then she would be able to measure the results. But the principle is the same, whether online or in the physical world. The marketing director is doing inbound marketing because she's drawing potential customers to the company with educational content that they want to see rather than going "outbound" to those potential customers, interrupting them with promotional messages they don't really want to see, in media such as ads and direct mail.

And inbound marketing works best on the Internet, because there you can measure your results. So, instead of buying ads, buying email lists, or cold calling, inbound marketing focuses on creating content that's so educational or entertaining that it pulls people toward your website where they can learn more about what you sell on their own accord.

Chapter 13

THEMES OF INBOUND MARKETING

Though it relies on new technology online—websites, social media, email—inbound marketing is just a systematic way of doing good communication, using age-old principles. As such, inbound marketing has several themes which any solar company should consider in its own marketing. According to HubSpot, these themes are:

* **Content**—Instead of ads trying to get people to buy something, you create targeted content that helps solve customers' problems and then you share that content as widely as possible.
* **Lifecycle Marketing**—Instead of sending the same marketing out to everybody, you tailor your content to where the customer is now in his or her decision-making process.
* **Personalization**—As you get to know more about your potential customer, you customize your content for his or her needs and you do it for many customers at once using automation.
* **Multi-channel Presence**—Meet your customer where he or she hangs out, whether Facebook, Instagram, or LinkedIn, and then try to lead that customer to your website.
* **Measurement**—Integrate all your marketing with analytics to measure results so that you can change what isn't working and report good return on investment for what is working.

If you do marketing this way, you are more likely to gain the love and trust of a potential solar buyer, instead of annoy him or her with unwanted cold calls. And if you do it right, inbound marketing can help you outsmart rather than outspend your competitors. While those competitors are pouring money into buying more ads and wondering why their sales aren't up, because they can't measure the results, you can laugh all the way to the bank as you spend less on marketing but get more leads and make more sales.

THE RIGHT MARKETING TO THE RIGHT PEOPLE AT THE RIGHT TIME

Inbound marketing is the right **marketing** to the right **people** at the right **time.** That's nothing new. Really, it's just like effective communication anywhere in life when you're not trying to sell somebody something. It turns out that being helpful also works well in selling too. In fact, in the Age of the Internet, being helpful may work better than a traditional sales approach where you start a relationship with a prospect by asking them to buy something.

Since this principle is key to inbound marketing, let's go through each part of the phrase "marketing to the right people at the right time."

THE RIGHT MARKETING

Of course, the right marketing is content that potential customers want to see, rather than ads or cold calls that just annoy them. It's about creating useful content rather than overtly promotional messages. And since you're doing it online, your content should be optimized for search engines and social media. More on how to do that later. Just know for now that content needs to interest your ideal customer no matter what media that content uses, whether a blog post, an ebook, a photo gallery, an infographic, a podcast, or a video.

THE RIGHT PEOPLE

Of course, not every piece of content will interest everybody, which brings us to the second principle of inbound marketing, the right people. You already know that, if you're selling home solar arrays for purchase, that you shouldn't target people who live in rental apartments (though you could approach the landlord). Eliminating people who are obviously not able to buy is a start.

But target marketing must get much more specific than that, focusing on the people who are most likely to buy. So, your market research should look at where people live by zip code but also, key aspects of who these people are. For that, you can look at demographics—sex, age, income—but also psychographics such as whether they strive to practice independent living or to help protect the environment. This kind of research will help you develop an ideal customer profile for your business. Only then can you create the kind of content that this kind of person wants to see.

THE RIGHT TIME

The third requirement of content marketing is that you should try to reach your ideal target customer at the right time. Since reaching buyers at the right time offers a big opportunity for solar companies, the next chapter will cover just that topic.

Chapter 14

• • •

REACHING A SOLAR BUYER AT THE RIGHT TIME

Don't you hate it when you walk into a retail store and the salespeople are pushy, asking you every few minutes if there's anything they can do to help? Sometimes you just want to browse in peace.

Well, it's the same on the web. Most people, most of the time, are just looking around. They want to browse in peace and discover things at their own pace. This may be even more common online, since the nature of the medium is anonymous. It's awkward to ignore a salesperson trying to get your attention in a retail store at the mall. But it's perfectly normal to be able to poke around a website without somebody asking if they can help. That's why web surfers so often find those little chat windows that appear on too many websites these days ("Hi, I'm Suzi. Type your questions for me here.") almost as annoying as the pushy salespeople at the mall.

On your website, you'll get visitors at all stages of the decision-making process, but mostly at the beginning. Indeed, on average, 96% of visitors to a website are not yet ready to make a purchase, according to Spokal. Unfortunately, too many solar companies don't seem to know that. That's why they make the mistake of catering only to the 4% of web visitors who are ready to buy soon. For example, a solar company might slap a solar savings calculator on the homepage of its website and think that this will bring in tons of new sales leads because to get the information from the form, the visitor has to agree to receive a free home solar assessment.

The problem is that the form works for a certain type of website visitor, but it doesn't work for everybody. It will be attractive for a potential buyer who is so far along in his decision to get solar that he's now comparing companies and costs and might actually want a free home solar assessment. But most visitors to your website are not ready to take the big step to invite a salesperson into their home. Instead, the vast majority of people who visit your website will feel that inviting even a phone call from a salesperson—not to mention a home visit—feels like too much commitment. They'd rather just explore your website quietly for a while without being bugged by a sales rep or anybody else from your company.

To convert visitors who are not yet ready to commit to solar to your website into early-stage leads so that when they are ready to buy, they'll think of your company first, you need to understand what early-stage solar buyers want from a website. Then, you should try to provide what they want given where they are in their buying process.

To do that, let's look more deeply at the decision-making process of the average buyer to understand better what content to provide to him at what time.

HubSpot has identified three stages of what it calls the Buyer's Journey. Basically, it's the decision-making process that a potential customer goes through from initial awareness through growing interest to making a purchase.

* In the **Awareness Stage** the potential customer is starting to realize that something is wrong, but he doesn't yet know what. To reach him at this early stage, you have to help him self-diagnose his symptoms and lead him towards settling on a problem that solar could solve. For example, perhaps he's feeling stressed

about money. But maybe the problem isn't that he doesn't have a high enough income. Perhaps the problem is that his expenses are too high. And it could be that energy is one of his biggest costs.

* The **Consideration Stage** is where the buyer is able to define his problem and seek solutions. To reach him in this middle stage, you have to present your solar offering as the solution to that problem. So, if energy is a big monthly expenditure, then solar may be the best way to cut that cost.

* Finally, when the prospect is ready to buy, he enters the **Decision Stage**, when he puts together a long list of vendors, whittles it down to a short list, and then ultimately selects one of those companies to buy from. Contrary to a common industry myth, these days a homeowner is not likely to buy from the first solar company that knocks on his door. Instead, customers want time to do their research on solar. And just before making a commitment for such a big purchase as a rooftop array, the customer will most likely go with the company he trusts the most to deliver on its promises.

The most important way to put all this into practice in your marketing is to offer different types of content to people at different stages of the buyer's journey. See the chart below for examples.

Awareness Stage	Consideration Stage	Decision Stage
Customer Stories	Buyer's Guide	Customer References
News Media Coverage	Podcasts	Demos
Educational Content	Videos	Vendor Comparison
Simple Graphics	Webcasts	Live Interaction

After you know your customer well enough to deliver the content he wants to see when he wants to see it, you can then personalize your marketing for him. This means adapting your marketing to the type of person and his stage in the buyer's journey.

But to do it at scale, which means for a large number of prospects, then you have to automate the process.

Just think about it. If you were to send personalized content to potential buyers manually, such as a different email message to one of three buyer personas at three different stages of the buyer's journey—nine email messages total—that would be a lot of work and a lot to keep track of, but it might still be doable. However, if you were sending all those messages manually to dozens or hundreds of prospects daily, then you wouldn't have time to do anything else. And it would be so confusing to keep track of who gets what email and when they get it, that you'd surely start sending the wrong email messages to the wrong people at the wrong time. Then, your attempt to look personalized would just wind up looking silly.

To do personalized marketing for a large number of potential buyers, you have to automate the process. This will allow you to send different email messages or offer different ebooks to someone who's at the awareness stage and is just learning about home solar as an option on the one hand, or to someone who's ready to sign up for a 20-year PPA on the other.

Personalization can go even further, beyond tailored sequences of email messages. Some website systems allow you to create different versions of your homepage or other pages that can be served up automatically to different types of visitors. This "dynamic content" or "adaptive content" changes based on the interests or past behavior of the viewer. You've already encountered a simple version of dynamic content when you go to a website where you've already filled out a contact form. When you return to the site a second time and reach a page with a form, you may notice that your information is already partially or completely filled in and that you don't have to enter it a second time. The form may even display a message saying that it recognizes you, which always feels nice—it's just one more way to save time online.

But dynamic content can do much more than that. For example, first-time visitors may get a general version of your homepage that talks about all your offerings, including both residential and commercial solar. But once a visitor has filled out a form and clicked around your site a bit and shown that he's probably interested in home solar, then when he comes back to your website next time, the homepage will only display information for home solar buyers.

In the future, more and more websites are likely to embrace this kind of ultra-personalization not only because it gives them an advantage over the competition, but because it provides a better experience to the web visitor. There will probably come a point where most people will expect serious company websites to only offer them personalized content. At that point, websites that waste the visitor's time with generic content will start to look cheap and dated.

When you target one type of ideal customer and publish content that he'll enjoy at various stages of his decision-making process, then you've covered the first three themes of inbound marketing: content, personalization, and lifecycle marketing. That basically answers the questions What (content), Who (personalization) and When (lifecycle). Now, to reach our audiences with that content, we have to answer the questions of Where and How Well It Works. And that brings in the two remaining themes of inbound marketing: multichannel presence and measurement and integration.

MULTICHANNEL PRESENCE

In the old days, if you were a TV advertiser and wanted to reach a wide audience, you could advertise on a single channel, say the local CBS station. But if you wanted to reach a wider audience, you would need to advertise on more than one channel, throwing in local affiliates for ABC, NBC, and Fox. Today, in the Age of the Internet, marketing is about much more than advertising. And the channels that marketers use go far beyond broadcast TV or even cable TV.

For inbound marketing, when we're talking about channels, we mostly mean online media or services. "Multichannel" then would mean using your website together with the appropriate social media services for the audience you're trying to reach. Thus, in inbound marketing, it's not enough to share content on your website and forget about social media. It's better to share on both your website and at least one social network. But if you have time, it's worthwhile to branch out to two or three social media services and throw email in there as well.

The important thing is not how many places you post your content. What matters is whether those are the right places to reach your target customer.

So, depending on whether that customer is a homeowner or a business executive, you may use a different channel. For example, people think of LinkedIn as being all-business. And it's true that this service is indeed a good place to reach commercial solar buyers. But LinkedIn members also get information about products and services for their personal or home use. So, LinkedIn may be a good choice to reach both residential and commercial solar buyers. If they're active on the service, of course.

A more traditional place to reach homeowners is Facebook, or, if you're targeting women, a photo-centric service like Instagram or Pinterest. If you need to connect with young people, for example, to create demand for solar at a school or with their parents, then a video site like YouTube or even Vine might be a better choice.

MEASUREMENT AND INTEGRATION

Finally, the last theme of inbound marketing is measuring what you do so you can see what works and what doesn't work and then try to do more of the first and less of the second.

Measurement is perhaps the most tempting promise of online marketing and what sets it apart from traditional outbound marketing tactics like direct mail or trade shows whose results are hard or impossible to measure. When it comes to inbound marketing specifically, your analytics should be integrated with your content creation and your outreach, so that you can easily determine ROI and make changes where necessary.

Analytics, measurement, and data can be scary topics for marketers. And some people will make it worse by giving you a list of 35 data points that you must monitor every day to have any credibility as an Internet marketer. But the best inbound marketers don't get overwhelmed by data. They find a way to measure the half dozen metrics that really matter to their business and find ways to display this information that are easy to understand and easy to explain to busy executives.

So, to sum up inbound marketing in a nutshell: Market with a magnet, not a sledgehammer. You publish content that's attractive enough to your buyers and share it with them in such an effective way that they start coming to you instead of you having to go out to them.

But you really can't do any inbound marketing at all unless you have a website. You already know that the quality of PV panels can differ a great deal even though the panels might look the same to the uneducated eye, whether polycrystalline or monocrystalline, whether made in China or Germany.

Likewise, not all solar websites are created equal. The next chapter will tell you what you need in a website to get traffic and generate your own sales leads for home or commercial solar. And it will start by looking at whether you can save money building a website by just starting a Facebook page instead.

Section 3

YOUR PLACE IN THE SUN—WEB DESIGN

The problem with the Internet is that it gives you everything—reliable material and crazy material. So the problem becomes, how do you discriminate?

— UMBERTO ECO

Chapter 15

● ● ●

CAN'T YOU JUST USE FACEBOOK AS YOUR WEBSITE?

To do Internet marketing of any kind, a solar company needs a presence on the web. And to do inbound marketing, that company needs the right kind of online presence.

In the early days of the web, there were websites and that was it. But since the advent of social media, there are now lots of ways to set up a location online. Of course, you can launch a website, but unless you have the skills to do it yourself, you'll have to spend money hiring a web designer. When cash flow is tight at the beginning of your business, you may be tempted to just forgo a website to save money and instead, just create a free page on a social media service. The most popular is Facebook. Let's consider the pros and cons of this approach.

First pro—it's free. And you can put up everything you need your buyers to see: your company description and location, phone numbers, a basic list of products and even a few customer testimonials. Then, you can post updates about your new products and services and your special offers, whether it's 90-days-same-as-cash financing or your big 25% off sale on all parts and labor.

You can even build an audience by asking people to like your page and become your fans. Then, whenever you have a new product to sell or a new special offer, you can let them know about it, by posting new announcements. The more fans you recruit, the bigger your audience and the more potential buyers.

And did I mention that it's free?

If you want to spend a little money, you can reach a larger audience on Facebook through buying ads. There are even a couple of guys online who help independent solar salespeople set up a Facebook page and then get traffic through buying ads. These guys claim that they can get you six or more new solar installations each month only by using Facebook ads, which would cover the cost of hiring them.

If you are an independent solar salesman and you're only planning to do business for a few months, then building your online headquarters on Facebook might be good enough for you. For example, maybe you're just going to run a liquidation sale for last year's PV panels out in a parking lot one summer between July 4th and Labor Day. In that case, a website might be overkill. After all, you're not trying to build anything for the future. You're just trying to sell some deeply discounted solar panels for a few weeks, get your cash, and get out.

Maybe next summer you can start another Facebook page and then liquidate some other product out on the parking lot, say, Lay-Z-Boy recliners or steel-belted radial tires?

I'm being a bit snarky here, but here's my point. If you're planning to be in the solar business for the long term, it's not good enough to rely on a Facebook page as your sole or main online presence. And though it starts out free, because you have to buy ads to promote it, very quickly a Facebook page can become more expensive than building your own website, but with few of the advantages.

Facebook is pretty good for promoting one-time events. Though to get any traffic to your event, if you don't have an existing page with fans already recruited, you may need to buy ads to get in front of people. And even if you already have an audience of fans on a Facebook page, you may still have to buy ads to get visibility in your audience's Facebook news feed, since the service's algorithm may decide that your event announcement is not really relevant to everybody who's a fan of your page, and so Facebook may never show it to them.

In fact, to encourage businesses to buy more ads, at some point Facebook changed their algorithm to make it harder for businesses to get their free updates in their fans' news feeds. Their explanation was that they wanted to deliver higher quality information to their members. But downgrading free posts from businesses was also an excellent way to encourage businesses to try to get their traffic back by buying ads.

And really, you can hardly blame Facebook for trying to squeeze money out of the free service it offers to businesses who are themselves trying to use Facebook to make money. Mark Zuckerberg has to make a living too, doesn't he? And he's doing that off of selling ads to businesses on Facebook, which can also help businesses. His ads can be good value compared to ads on Google, which are generally more expensive. And they can get quick traffic to your Facebook updates and even to a website, if you have one.

But Facebook alone is lousy for building a long-term audience for a business of any kind. And it's especially lousy at creating a community of potential buyers for a residential solar installer. Of course, plenty of homeowners who might want solar someday are active on Facebook. And you might even be able to get a decent number of them to like your company's page. But remember, even if you post updates, Facebook may decide to hide them from the fans of your page. Companies don't like it. But that's tough luck, because companies don't make the rules for Facebook. Mark Zuckerberg does.

In fact, Facebook explains in their terms of use that you don't own anything you put on Facebook—they do. And what that means is that they can do what they want with your content. They can display it any way they want or they can decide not to display it at all. If they think your content is inappropriate for their service, because someone has reported it or for some other reason, they can delete that content. If they think you're not playing by their rules, they can take your page down or even ban you from Facebook. And in the future, they can change their rules any way they choose. They can even start to charge for companies to create pages on Facebook. Or they can start to charge for "premium" services like, say, posting a product update.

This all means that if you entrust your online digital storefront to Facebook, you're putting your fate into someone else's hands. The next chapter will explore the dangers of this strategy.

Chapter 16

THE DANGER OF DIGITAL SHARECROPPING

Lack of control is the problem with what writer Nicholas Carr has dubbed "digital sharecropping."

When you build your business on somebody else's service—whether Facebook or any social media site—then you're on somebody else's digital land. They own the territory, they make the rules, and they can change them anytime they want to. That means they can start charging you in the future for things that are free today, and they can evict you for whatever reason they like. They can even just shut down their whole service at some point if it's not working out for them. And if you don't agree with their actions, there's not much you can do about it except go somewhere else.

Even if social media sites keep their faith with you, those sites still get more out of the relationship than you do. You may think of Facebook as a free website. But Mark Zuckerberg thinks of pages like yours as free content that he can sell to advertisers.

When somebody creates content on a website, if it's done correctly, Google notices it. The owner of that content starts to build up credibility with search engines, which leads to more online visitors over time. That search engine mojo is valuable enough that a whole field of experts who do search engine optimization, or SEO, has arisen to help online marketers score well in Google for certain words that are popular with web searchers.

Facebook does a good job optimizing its site for search engines. And millions of Facebook members do a good job of adding new content every day to give Google something to index. That means Google is giving Facebook more and more credibility over time.

And who do you think benefits from that search engine mojo—a) a business that puts up a Facebook page? Or b) Facebook itself?

If you answered b) you are correct. If your content on Facebook is awesome, then Facebook gets the search engine juice, not you.

When everything goes well, social media sites continually build more SEO for themselves. That in turn attracts more members, which helps the site build even more SEO. It becomes a virtuous cycle that seems unstoppable. And if social media sites have good SEO, then that can bring more traffic to their members, including your solar business.

Until that cycle goes into reverse, of course.

And that's the other problem with entrusting your web presence 100% to a social media site. Just think of all the businesses that invested time into sites like Digg or MySpace. As far as I know, the services are still online. Somebody must still use them. But these social media sites have declined so much that marketers no longer take them seriously. In a world where things change so quickly online, these dusty old social media sites have become so passé that they have very little business value.

Enticing lots of ordinary web users, from teenagers to marketing managers for solar companies, is good business for the few people including Mark Zuckerberg who own social media services. As Carr puts it "by putting the means of production into the hands of the masses but withholding from those same masses any ownership over the product of their work, [social media] provides an incredibly efficient mechanism to harvest the economic value of the free labor provided by the very many and concentrate it into the hands of the very few."

This business model, which works so well for the owners of social media sites, stinks for most businesses trying to make money off of social media.

Of course, most Facebook members with a personal account don't care about making any money, since they're just using Facebook for fun. And since someone else is providing the tools to share vacation photos and cat videos with their friends for free, they don't complain, as Carr explains: "It's a sharecropping system, but the sharecroppers are generally happy because their interest lies in self-expression or socializing, not in making money." Or, put another way,

> The sharecroppers operate happily in an attention economy while their overseers operate happily in a cash economy. In this view, the attention economy does not operate separately from the cash economy; it's simply a means of creating cheap inputs for the cash economy.

The problem for a business is that its work on social media takes time, which in business, costs money. So, it's not enough to invest the time of in-house staff or outsourced social media consultants just to get attention on Facebook or Twitter for attention's sake. Exchanging cash for attention alone is not a good bargain, especially for a solar company with a rising cost of customer acquisition.

By contrast, if you can exchange cash for attention plus action—if you can use social media to help convert web audiences into solar customers—then you've made a good investment in social media outreach. But you can't just have your business on Facebook to do that. You need your own website.

Copyblogger, a company that helps businesses build their own websites and develop effective content for websites, has made it their mission to warn businesspeople about the risks of digital sharecropping. For years, *Copyblogger* has been trying to help those people free themselves from doing unpaid work that only earns them attention but doesn't get them much business benefit. As the company's Sonia Simone explains,

> Anyone can create content on sites like Facebook, but that content effectively belongs to Facebook. The more content we create for free, the more valuable Facebook becomes. We do the work, they reap the profit.

> The term sharecropping refers to the farming practices common after the US Civil War, but it's essentially the same thing as feudalism. A big landholder allows individual farmers to work their land and takes most of the profits generated from the crops.

> The landlord has all the control. If he decides to get rid of you, you lose your livelihood. If he decides to raise his fees, you go a little hungrier. You do all the work and the landlord gets most of the profit, leaving you a pittance to eke out a living on.

Simone says that social media services aren't bad for business, if you use them the right way. But don't make them a social media account your online headquarters. Instead, use social media to attract attention for marketing assets that you control. She suggests three assets—only two of them specifically in online marketing—that "you should be building today and should continue to focus on for the lifetime of your digital business":

1. A well-designed website with your own hosting
2. An opt-in email list, ideally with a high-quality autoresponder
3. A reputation for providing impeccable value

"Developing these assets are the equivalent of buying your building instead of renting it," Simone says.

So, I hope by now you understand the dangers of digital sharecropping. If your solar company is interested in doing a vigorous, growth-oriented business for years to come, then you can't get away with just a Facebook page but no website—if for no other reason than credibility. Solar is such a big commitment for a buyer that she'll only buy from a company she can trust. Lack of a website makes a company look untrustworthy—poorly funded, unprofessional, and certainly not built to last.

Chapter 17

* * *

YOUR OWN WEBSITE

Copyblogger's Simone is right that to achieve any success in marketing today you need both a website and your own email list. I'll talk about how solar companies can use an email list later. For now, let's talk about websites.

For any company or organization, a website should be its marketing hub, the center of all that organization's marketing activity not just on the Internet, but overall. That means even print materials—business cards, brochures, magazine and newspaper ads, posters—should point readers back to your website. So should traditional broadcast ads, whether on TV or radio, if you're still spending (or wasting) money on those.

You may think that you're sending people to your website to get more information. But if that's all your website does—provide information— then you're missing the point.

To succeed online, you need to do much more than provide information on your website. To generate solar leads and nurture prospects into customers online, your website needs to be built from the ground up to help move potential customers along the buyer's journey.

Few solar company websites are set up properly to offer content at each stage of the buyer's journey. Instead, most websites for solar installers are just online versions of a product brochure. Their sites offer product specs, pricing, and an easy way to contact the sales department. That's a very straightforward approach for those hot prospects who have reached the decision stage and are just trying to pick among a few options before they buy. But this approach offers little for buyers who are earlier in their buying process, either just learning about solar at the initial awareness stage or ready to dig deeper into features and benefits at the intermediate or consideration stage. And as we discussed, visitors who are not yet ready to buy make up the vast majority—more than nine out of ten—of visitors to your website.

For example, during the fall of a recent year, one solar installer in Massachusetts used the most valuable real estate on its website, the first screen on the homepage, to advertise its holiday special. On a background of snowflakes, the installer offered 20% off all home solar arrays until December 31. Unfortunately for the installer, they probably didn't get many takers on this offer, which was put in the very wrong place on their website.

The company hadn't considered who generally looks at the top of a website homepage. It's not buyers at the decision stage ready to sign on the dotted line for a home solar installation. Those buyers have already gotten into your website and are now deep inside, studying the details of your equipment and your financing. By contrast, the people looking at the top of your homepage are newcomers who are likely in the awareness stage. They're just learning about solar or about your company. They may not know the difference between a PPA and a pickled pepper from Peter Piper. But even if they know a bit about home solar, they probably know little about your company's offering, its reputation, and its value proposition versus the competition.

Someone so early in her buying process is unlikely to be moved by your 20% holiday discount or any other "Act now!" sales tactic to click on the link to start the paperwork for her new home solar array, especially in December when she's thinking about cleaning the guest room for holiday company and how to stuff everyone's stockings!

Instead, since she was really just looking around at this point, the visitor will probably just be turned off by a message of urgency because it's irrelevant to her situation. She's nowhere near ready to buy and a discount offer isn't going to change that. So, she may spend a few more minutes on your site to give you the benefit of the doubt. Or she may leave and go somewhere else right away. Maybe she'll check out your competitor—who was smart enough to save the discount offers for deeper in its website— where she's welcomed at the top of the homepage by a nice friendly video with satisfied customers glowing about how much they love their new solar systems.

Trying to get somebody to buy right away after they've come to your website for the first time is like asking someone to marry you on the first date. That's not just desperate—it's creepy. Few marriages have resulted from such a poorly timed proposal. It's more likely that the first date was also the last date.

A more effective approach to turn the general public into website visitors and then turn visitors into leads and leads into customers is to cater to the online visitor at each stage of her journey, not only when she's ready to buy. To do that, you need to make sure your website does two things. First, offer content appropriate for each stage of a buyer's decision making process. Second, organize your website experience to help the buyer comfortably find the content that's right for her at her stage.

The next chapter will talk about how to welcome early-stage solar buyers on your website's homepage.

Chapter 18

• • •

CASE STUDIES: EFFECTIVE SOLAR HOMEPAGES

The homepage is the most important page on any website, and one that should be optimized not for prospects ready to pull the trigger but instead for curious visitors just starting to learn about solar. In general, an effective homepage has seven components:

1. Clearly answers "Who I am," "What I do," and/or "What can you (the visitor) do here."
2. Resonates with the target audience
3. Communicates a compelling value-proposition
4. Looks as good on a phone or a tablet as on a laptop
5. Includes calls-to-action (CTAs)
6. Always changes offering new content

To help the solar marketer see how these apply to his or her company, below are three quick examples of brilliant solar website design—all with clean, minimalist design optimized for mobile devices, but each with different strengths. Please note that, because the web changes so quickly, these homepages were current as of the time I wrote this book, but that they have probably changed by the time you're reading this. Even so, the principles behind good solar homepage design will remain the same.

1. VIVINT SOLAR

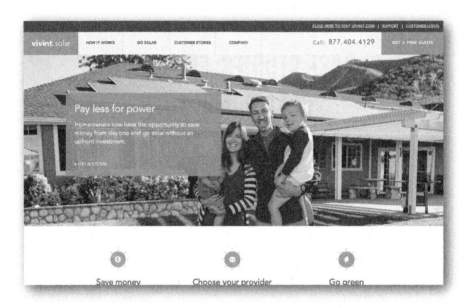

WHY IT'S BRILLIANT

It's economical. Right above the fold, the Vivint Solar homepage tells the potential customer everything he needs to know in the eight seconds that he's likely to spend before he decides to stay or go: this company does residential installations for people who look like you (young professional families with a decent-sized home) with the benefits you care about (money saving, choice, and going green).

More importantly, Vivint Solar elegantly lets its visitors know who this page is for. There are no photos of city or county managers going over blueprints with an engineer, which shows that the primary audience is not local government officials. Nor do the photos and design suggest that the site is for commercial businesses or utilities either. Instead, it's clear that

Vivint Solar's homepage is targeted at one audience only: homeowners. By making their homepage only about residential solar, they avoid intimidating ordinary people, or confusing their message with too many targets.

"Don't worry," the homepage seems to say, "our offering is not too big, too expensive, or too complicated for you, Mr. and Mrs. Homeowner. In fact, our solar solution is just the right size for your ranch house."

It also helps make the site less intimidating to web visitors that the homepage is easy to consume. At only three screens, it's quick to see everything on the homepage. If you want more, it's easy to click inside the site. By the way, that's good practice not only to make a homepage look easy to use on a desktop computer. A short, clear homepage is even better for phones and tablets. And since more and more website traffic every year comes from mobile devices, making your homepage simple now is a good investment for the future.

Finally, the Vivint homepage gives a choice of calls-to-action (CTAs) for people at each stage of the solar buyer's journey. For those just exploring, there's a video further down the page. For those visitors who are ready to decide, there's the button at the top to get a price quote.

2. SOLARCITY

WHY IT'S BRILLIANT

First, it helps visitors sort themselves by audience right away. Like Vivint Solar's homepage, SolarCity's site is friendly and won't intimidate homeowners. But unlike Vivint, it's clear that SolarCity has more than one audience and that they offer solar power not only to homeowners but also to business and government. However, the company is smart enough to know who the main audience for the site is—consumers—and to make the site most friendly to residential buyers.

Many solar companies that serve both business and consumer customers try to make their homepage equally appealing to both groups. So, for example, at some point on their homepage they may have two columns. One column displays serious text for corporate energy managers about reliability and concepts like "peak shaving" that usually apply only to commercial electricity billing. Then, the homepage will display a second column with nice friendly language for homeowners about many similar families have already gone solar. By doing it this way, the solar company homepage hopes to serve both business and residential audiences with information pertinent to them.

But the problem is that by trying to serve everybody equally, such an approach winds up serving nobody really well. On the one hand, a corporate energy manager will be turned off by photos of moms, dads, and kids posed smiling in front of their 5 kW rooftop array. In his mind, this makes the company look like they only do little home installations. He'll want to go somewhere that feels more serious to him. On the other hand, a mom or a dad looking into options for solar at home may be scared off by a photo of a 1 megawatt canopy of PV panels over a parking lot with hundreds of cars.

You can't please everybody. And so you shouldn't really try. Instead, just pick the one single main audience for your homepage and target your graphics, text, and layout towards that audience. If your company does any combination of utility, commercial, and/or government on the one hand and residential installations on the other, guess which audience should always be featured on your homepage?

That's right—it's the homeowner.

Since people who work for businesses, government agencies, and utilities who find your website are all presumably looking into solar as part of their job, they'll more likely have the patience to click through to the section of your site meant for them, as long as it's clear from the beginning where that is. But it's the homeowner who's seeking solar for his own use who will probably leave your site right away if your homepage doesn't feel welcoming enough.

You should follow the example of SolarCity when you format your homepage. The page's design and content, starting with the zip code search, appeals primarily to homeowners. But the homepage is also clear that the company has other audiences. And those audiences can get to the pages meant for them by clicking in the top navigation on the menu choice for "Business & Government." Solar City even offers information for investors, as you can also see from the navigation menu.

But again, the company is smart enough not to clutter up the look of the homepage with a shot of a guy in a shirt, tie, and suspenders reading the Wall Street Journal. That investor guy can just click on the link and get to the information he needs on an inside page of the website. You don't need to provide the same visual cues to make an investor feel welcome as you do to the average homeowner.

So, if you're a homeowner, the SolarCity site looks trustworthy. The top graphic establishes credibility right away by showing real, satisfied customers. Some of them may be business or government workers, of course. But, still, the implicit message to an unsure and welcoming potential customer is the reassurance provided by the "bandwagon effect" that we all learned about in high school English class. To use the metaphor of a swimming pool: "Come on in and join us, the water's just fine."

SolarCity's homepage invites interaction. It's hard not to enter your zip code into the little box to check availability—there's so little risk or effort required and it's always fun to get feedback right away. And once you see that you qualify, you feel like a winner, part of a select group, which encourages you to take the next step.

This homepage appeals to different audiences well. Without adding clutter that might turn off the main audience of residential solar customers, the site menu offers options for other audiences too in the first screen—business and government as well as investors.

3. SUNPOWER

WHY IT'S BRILLIANT

A big customer success story makes SunPower's homepage human. Solar is not about technology but about people. So, the picture of a smiling mom and her daughter is warm and inviting. The message: SunPower is about people too.

Smaller case studies offer something for everyone. Well, maybe not exactly everyone, but key types of target customers for residential solar, from New York to Colorado, in houses with traditional construction and modern design whether located on big yards or small yards.

The SunPower homepage makes it easy for homeowners interested in solar to take action. Even though the customer stories are halfway down the page, a fixed top navigation menu that stays on the screen even when you scroll down makes it easy to click on the well highlighted "Get Started" button.

Since SunPower's page is so good, let's spend a little more time on what makes it effective.

1. **Headline:** "Demand Better Solar." The trademarked phrase shows that the company is addressing solar-savvy homeowners who don't need to be convinced that solar is desirable and already know that there are differences between solar companies. As the solar market gets crowded, more solar installers will be adopting language like this that tries to set the company apart from the competition.

2. **Benefits:** What's in it for the visitor? The SunPower homepage elegantly supports the message from the text with an attractive and impactful background photo of a roof-mounted PV array on a clearly upscale home, an attractive target customer for residential solar.

3. **Primary calls-to-action:** SunPower puts the main CTA front and center, "See how much you can save with 30 years of innovation on your roof" and a zip code checker where nobody can miss them right on the first screen.

4. **Features:** Case studies further down the page show how the company provides the two benefits of affordable/reliable power and social values in real life, adding credibility. Just to take a single example: "SunPower solar panels are good for a New Jersey family's pocketbook."

5. **Customer proof:** These case studies, along with customer testimonials, add even more credibility. The testimonial on the homepage is especially effective because it's accompanied by a large photo of a real customer, in this case, a mom holding a young child. She's not just an anonymous customer or even a stock photo person, but Rebecca Amato, Solar Homeowner from Oakland, California. Her quote will be more impactful because

the full name with the photo lets the web visitor know that she's a real person: "The efficiency of the solar panels and seeing how much solar energy our home really did generate was the most surprising. It's exciting to get an electrical bill every month and see a zero!"

The page also contains other key elements such as effective navigation that easily guides visitors into the site and secondary calls-to-action that give visitors who aren't ready yet to hit the link to "Get Started" something else to do on the homepage. This helps the page cater to homeowners at both early and later stages of the buyer's journey.

Websites this good are not cheap. But even solar companies with smaller budgets can follow the same principles to make themselves look bigger online, as the next chapter will demonstrate.

Chapter 19

GETTING A WEBSITE TO COMPETE WITH THE BIG BOYS

One of the main selling points of web marketing is that online smaller businesses can look as good as bigger ones. In the solar industry, it's that smaller installers can use the web to effectively challenge the big established national installers. And while I'm pretty sure that the top five or ten national installers have spent tens of thousands of dollars to build and maintain their websites, you can get a comparable web presence for much less—if you're smart about it.

First of all, ask yourself if you really need to build a new website or if you can just upgrade the one you have now. Since you probably look at your own website nearly every day, you might be getting tired of the colors or the fonts. But for a visitor who comes for the first time, most solar websites done in the last 3-5 years look fine. If your site is older than that, you should consider a re-design, especially since most older sites aren't set up to look good on phones and tablets. Being mobile friendly is an absolute requirement for solar websites after Google's "Mobilegeddon" algorithm update in 2015, which rewards sites that try to look good on phones, and punishes sites that don't.

But if your website is already mobile friendly and nobody's got any specific problems with it, then you may not need an expensive redesign. Instead, you could invest that money in inbound marketing tactics that will increase your traffic and help you generate leads. This approach will likely show a much better return on investment than doing a whole new website just to get something prettier.

If your site isn't mobile friendly, if it's been online more than five years with the same look and layout, or if the site isn't optimized to generate leads online, then you should commit to redesigning your site.

DO IT YOURSELF

Of course, you don't have to spend a lot of money on a website to get a good one. If your company is small and if you're comfortable with basic computing tasks like word processing or photo management, then you may just consider an off-the-shelf Do It Yourself (DIY) website builder such as SquareSpace.

If you're willing to forgo a custom design, you'll find that such a service offers dozens of templates with a contemporary, minimalist look and a content management system that lets you get started quickly as long as you have the time and you're comfortable working on it on your own.

DIY website builders are the most affordable way to get started. Most don't charge any initial fee and monthly fees start as low as $10 per month and include hosting, which makes them even more affordable. But if you're a little more tech savvy and want to build your own site in the popular WordPress content management system, WordPress.com offers free websites with the option to add on paid features for more functionality.

GET HELP THAT'S AFFORDABLE

But if DIY isn't for you—for example, you're not comfortable teaching yourself how to build a website on your own—then you may want to consider a new kind of online service known as done-for-you or DFY.

As an alternative for attractive but affordable websites built just for the solar industry, the Curren Group started a new service in 2016 called Solar Sales Rocket (SSR).

Like SquareSpace or WordPress.com, the service offers template websites. But instead of making you figure everything out yourself, Solar Sales Rocket will take your content and set up the site for you using the principles of brilliant website design especially for solar. Then, SSR will take care of hosting, uptime, security, make routine website changes for you, and provide you with ongoing marketing advice specific to the solar industry.

INVEST IN PROFESSIONAL HELP FOR A CUSTOM WEBSITE

A larger solar company with, say, more than a few million dollars per year in sales, will not want to trust its website to a free or low-cost website building service of any kind, no matter how good it may be for smaller companies. Once you reach a certain size, you need a custom website built by a web design professional with superior software for lead tracking and generation built right in.

And in that case, you won't want to have your site built in-house by your marketing assistant who did a few WordPress sites in college. Your site needs a specific structure to generate leads online, with appealing content serving to attract visitors and help guide them through the buyer's journey so that they convert to trackable leads, prospects, and customers. People who do website design on the side are more likely to create a website as an online version of a brochure than as a lead-generation and inbound marketing hub, or even with the unique propositions of solar sales in mind. They might make something pretty, but without the principles that make solar websites work for you.

As to technology, any company beyond the very smallest home installer will require customization beyond what an off-the-shelf website can offer, including the ability to track not just website visitors but also those visitors who turn into leads. Tracking leads is a more advanced function for a website and requires a bigger investment in either website building skill or software, or both.

The cost for a custom website will range widely. Your marketing assistant might be able to build one for you for free (if you don't count the 250 hours she spent messing with code and fixing typical amateur mistakes), though you may not like the result. If you have to hire a professional web designer, then a website for a solar company can range from about $5,000 to upwards of $30,000. Whether you get your money's worth will depend largely on who builds your site. That's why you should choose your web designer carefully.

Web designers typically come from one of three different backgrounds—either software programming, graphic design, or marketing. I'm a marketer, so I may be biased, but I lean towards websites done by marketers rather than by people who are primarily either technical (programmers) or visual (graphic designers). Those skills are necessary to any successful website project and should be represented on a design team. For example, my wife Lindsay heads our in-house visual design team. But to create a website that converts visitors to leads, then you need someone who understands the psychology of sales to coordinate the programming and graphic design to produce the right result.

People with a marketing background know that the main purpose of a business website is to gain a company new customers and encourage repeat business from existing customers to generate revenue.

So, when a digital marketing agency builds a website they are more likely to have their eyes on the prize—building your business—and are less likely to get distracted by either whiz-bang technical features or a cool but complicated visual look created with design awards in mind. A good digital marketing agency will be able to draw on the skills of all three disciplines of programming, visual design, and customer outreach to produce a website that is both technically excellent and visually attractive in the service of making more sales for your company. But if a website design team is like an orchestra, and the music is the sound of the cash register, then the marketer should be the conductor.

LOCATING THE RIGHT HELP FOR A SOLAR WEBSITE

To find the right digital marketer to build an effective website for a solar company, you need a company that knows both the solar industry and the web.

If you're with a bigger solar company, your boss may think you should write up a request for proposals and send it to twenty or thirty digital agencies that build websites for solar companies. The idea is that once you put out your RFP, you'll only hear back from agencies that are interested in working with you—maybe so interested that they'll really hustle to win your business, putting in dozens of hours of staff time in a gamble to get your business. Then, you can see in detail how they think, so you can better judge which agency is the best fit. And of course you can test their ideas and see some sample work. Trying before you buy takes a lot of the risk out of committing to one agency and its work, right?

Unfortunately for companies seeking digital design agencies, putting out an RFP may not lower the risk. Just the opposite—an RFP may give you a false sense of security even as you're heading down exactly the wrong path.

Contrary to what your boss thinks, inviting marketing agencies to respond to a 25-page request for proposals won't necessarily get you the best qualified agency for your specific needs. What a big RFP will get you for certain is an agency that's sure to be expensive.

It's the bigger shops that are more likely to invest dozens or even hundreds of staff hours to compile all the RFP materials. But more and more skilled agencies these days ignore RFPs and refuse to do work on spec. That is, they don't want to invest those dozens of hours of time from copywriters, programmers, and graphic designers on a one-in-twenty chance that they'll land your big account. That's not only because it's a hassle for them. It's also because good agencies know that pulling a bunch of ideas out of thin area with little understanding of the company won't give the client a good result.

A better web agency will want to spend some time with your company and get to know your goals, your marketplace, your competitors, and what you've done so far before proposing a plan to redo your website. Indeed, in the web marketing world, the RFP may soon be a thing of the past, replaced by conversations or workshops with agencies.

There are more effective ways to create a short list of solar web marketing agencies that you may want to work with, for example:

* Ask colleagues in other solar companies to refer you to an agencies they've worked with.
* Look for marketing agencies whose writers are published in industry publications such as *Solar Power World* or *Renewable Energy World*.
* And perhaps the easiest but, ironically, the most effective method of all to find a digital agency—do a Google search for "solar marketing" or "solar websites" or even "solar lead generation." If they come up on the first page of results, it shows that an agency knows how to market itself online and suggests that it will be able to do the same for you. And if they come up in a search for lead generation but they still do websites, then it shows that the company positions its web design not as an end in itself but as a way to help your company get more business.

A marketing agency that specializes in serving solar companies is a good place to begin. Of course, you can find them at any solar trade show. They're the ones who did the booths for the solar installers. And their own booth will probably look impressive, while offering some top logo item giveaways. Don't forget to pick up stuff to take back to the kids—a few bags of mints, a smiley face solar squishy ball, or a USB multiport/ keychain/micro-mini-Mag flashlight.

But the agency with the cutest logo swag may not also be the best one to build a website that uses the latest techniques to convert online visitors to solar leads. Knowing the solar industry well is not good enough to do well on the web. To help you succeed online, a marketing agency also needs to really know the Internet. Because so many solar companies have done marketing the same old way for decades, experience with other solar installers is not enough if you want a digital-savvy agency that knows how to make your solar homepage into an active sales funnel rather than a passive online brochure. Along with knowing the solar industry, you also need your agency to know the digital world.

PUT THEM TO THE CHAMPAGNE TEST

So, to see if an agency is really a digital native or just a recent move-in from the world of print design and old-school marketing, apply what Silicon Valley executive Jo Hoppe calls the "Drink Your Own Champagne Test." That is, look at what the agency says they can do—web design, blogging, social media, etc.—and then compare that to how well this agency does all those things for themselves on their own website.

*   If their own blog hasn't been updated in months or if it contains boring news releases about awards and new clients, then they don't know how to write an effective blog that will actually get readers.

*   If their site doesn't display attractive calls-to-action and content offers that help convert visitors into leads, then the agency may not build websites that generate leads online.

*   If their portfolio is filled with trade-show banners and glossy brochures, then the agency may just view a website as another form of graphic design—pretty to look at but lacking in interactive power. That's the kind of power you need to attract visitors and then convert them to sales leads online.

*   And if the text and pictures on their site focus more on how fun and creative their account executives are than on what the agency can do for you, then the firm may not be able to deliver a good ROI on your digital marketing investment.

The signs of a promising digital marketing agency for solar are, of course, the opposite of everything in the list above. An agency shouldn't claim to be too busy helping clients to do its own online marketing. No, any decent agency will certainly drink its own champagne and will do for itself the marketing tactics that it wants to sell its clients. As evidence, the website of a solar marketing agency that knows the web will have a few key things:

* An active and interesting blog with actionable online marketing advice for solar companies.
* Attractive, clickable call-to-action graphics throughout the website promoting premium content like ebooks and checklists that online visitors can download in exchange for their email address, thus converting visitors to leads online.
* Use of Web 2.0 tools, especially active social media accounts, to build relationships with key target audiences.
* Evidence in both words and pictures that this company is focused on helping solar installers use digital media to build high quality traffic for your website that converts into qualified leads, likely prospects, and new customers.

Choosing the right digital agency can make the difference between success and failure in your web design or online marketing project. In the next chapter, I'll talk about what else you need to do to avoid flopping when you build or contract for a website.

Chapter 20

HOW TO AVOID FAILURE ON YOUR WEBSITE PROJECT

Once you find a digital marketing agency that doesn't just know the solar industry but also knows the web, then work with them to help your website project succeed. If you're a small, startup company, you may want to check out our service at Solar Sales Rocket. There, you'll see that we addressed all these questions in building the templates we offer, making it a fairly turnkey effort for our customers. But if you want to build from scratch, keep these things in mind:

1. DEVELOP CLEAR GOALS FOR YOUR SOLAR WEBSITE

That the company founder's wife thinks your website is ugly doesn't help you develop a real goal for your new site. You need real clarity on goals if you're going to design a site that helps sell more solar. Start by answering questions about your market strategy, for example: Do you want to expand out of residential installs into commercial solar? Do you want to look more credible to big utilities to start selling to them? Do you want to recruit community members as your ambassadors to do solar in a particular city? Then, build your website from the beginning to fit that audience and that purpose.

2. UNDERSTAND YOUR ONLINE AUDIENCES

Not every solar website is created equal. A website for utility executives is going to look very different than one for homeowners. Utility execs want to see evidence of expertise and good management in your solar company. It's less about sex-appeal and more about stability. Data is good, case studies are better. By contrast, homeowners want to you to wow them with coolness—especially photos. Commercial property owners or local government officials will want even different things on your website.

Don't start redesigning your website until you've created 3-5 solar buyer personas first so you can understand your ideal solar customer. You need to know their motivation to buy solar, messages that resonate with them, and where they go for solar information online. In the next chapter, I'll talk about how to research your ideal customers and then organize that research into buyer persona profiles.

3. INSIST ON A SITE YOU CAN UPDATE YOURSELF

In the bad old days of web design, say from the late 90s through about 2010, the technology to create a serious business website was so complicated that only a web designer could understand it. This meant that every time a business wanted to change a comma on its About Us page, it had pay its web designer to make the change. That was a hassle and an expense that prevented most companies from keeping their websites fresh.

Thank goodness that those days are over. Today, with a content management system (CMS) like WordPress, anybody who knows how to use Microsoft Office can figure out how to maintain their own website— maybe not to change the design and layout but certainly to edit text, swap out photos on inside pages, and add blog posts. So, if you're ready to build a new website from scratch, and the web designer you're considering tells you that he doesn't do CMS websites or that he uses his own proprietary CMS that is just too hard for clients to run themselves, then don't just walk, but run, the other direction. There's no excuse anymore for having to pay your web guy to make regular changes to the content of your website.

4. AVOID FAKE SEO

While web designers who build new sites with outdated technology are getting harder and harder to find, unfortunately SEO guys who use outdated search engine tricks are still all too common. If your company hires a vendor to do just SEO without building a new website or offering any content marketing, then I'd say that your chances are greater than 50% that the SEO vendor will be a charlatan.

Not only will he waste your money on stuff like metatags that Google doesn't care about anymore. But he may even cause you harm by doing "black hat" or deceptive SEO like buying inbound links. If Google detects that you've tried to trick their algorithms and earn a better search ranking than it thinks you deserve, there are several ways that the search engine giant can put your website over its knee that can cost you website traffic or be disastrous to your business. Penalties range from demoting you in searches for desirable keywords to banning you altogether from search results.

But even SEO guys who try to avoid black hat tactics may still be stuck on stuff that might have worked well in 2012 when Google still required websites to write text artificially phrased for search keywords but are no longer effective. Now that Google has evolved to the point where it can deal well with text written for humans—and may even prefer ordinary language to text written specifically for search engines—it's a waste of time to over-optimize your web pages for their algorithm. Today, the best SEO is to create original content on a regular basis using keywords that your customers search for in a natural, unforced way throughout your website. We'll talk more about this later when we discuss using search keywords in your writing.

5. MAKE IT INTERACTIVE

Ten years ago, all that web technology would allow is for a company to post some pictures and text and maybe a bit of multimedia about itself. Interactivity wouldn't go much beyond comments on a blog (for most company blogs there never were any comments), filling out a contact form, or clicking an email link. That's why a website in the past was just an online version of a print brochure. But today, a brochure website is behind the times. And a solar company that builds a website that's no more than an online brochure is getting a poor return on its marketing investment.

Today, customers know that websites can do so much more than display product specs and a link to contact the sales department. If a larger, multi-state solar company doesn't offer a way for homeowners to see if their zip code qualifies them for a PPA or other financing right on the home page, then they'll go to a competitor that does. Make sure that if you're investing in a fully customized from scratch new website for a larger, established solar firm, that it's truly interactive. And the best way to do that is to gauge it against the best solar websites out there today such as SolarCity or Vivint Solar that I discussed above. Smaller firms, and solar start-ups can get away with less at first, but should still strive to add interactivity through things like a simple solar savings calculator.

6. TAKE MOBILE DEVICES SERIOUSLY

I've mentioned above that, if your website isn't yet mobile friendly, then you should redesign it as soon as possible. These days, no decent solar web designer will build you a new website that will fail Google's Mobile Friendly Test. But that's not enough. Your site also needs to have a layout, font and color scheme that are all convenient to use on phones and tablets.

That may mean adopting "mobile-first" design. For example, you may want to avoid a two- or three-column homepage in favor of a single long column that makes it easy for a phone visitor to swipe straight down the page.

7. PUT CONTENT BEFORE AESTHETICS

It doesn't matter what colors your website is if all your text is stale and unappealing for your target audiences. Is the only thing new on your website in the last six months a news release announcing that you hired a new VP of sales? Then you have bigger problems than whether to choose ocean blue or bright yellow as the background for your site header.

Both humans and search engines like new content and they like lots of content, too. So, start a blog for people interested in getting solar before you worry about website colors.

8. LIMIT THE NUMBER OF COOKS IN THE KITCHEN

You've heard about the pitfalls of "designing by committee," right? Letting too many cooks into the kitchen can ruin a website as quickly as it can kill a brochure or ad design. Everybody from installers in the field to legal counsel to the 13-year-old son of the VP of product development seems to think your website will be a total flop unless you can benefit from their feedback about submenus on your draft layout. And every department wants to be represented on the home page, whether that would add value for potential customers or not.

The politics of your company may mean you can't keep all these folks out of your process entirely. And of course you need to build support inside the company for the new site. But try to keep your core group of regular in-house reviewers manageable. If you're a solar marketer, you already know that the marketing department should have primary control over a website project because you best understand how to reach out effectively to customers. Be sure to bring in sales and other departments to review a draft website design and offer targeted feedback on their area of expertise at the right time. But also gently let others in the company know that your new website is based on research, the kind of data that any good web design company will use to plan your web project.

9. EVEN AFTER IT GOES LIVE, KEEP WORKING ON YOUR WEBSITE

With a print brochure, you scramble to get all your text and pictures finalized before your graphic designer's deadline. But then, once the brochure is printed, it's done. Unless you missed an embarrassing typo or some other big problem that requires you to throw out the whole print run of your new brochure and fix the file before running it all over again, you won't be working on this brochure anymore. At least until you do the next one in five years.

By contrast, a website is never done. Obviously, pixels on a screen can be easily rearranged in a way that ink on paper cannot. Thus, because you can change a website, the best marketers will take advantage of the chance to update their content on a regular basis. At a bare minimum, you should be updating your website's text and pictures as things change in your company, to show new products and services or new personnel. But if you want anybody to see your new site besides your mom, then you'll also need to make changes to your site to build traffic.

"Build it and they will come" has become a tired joke about companies that kill their investment in perfectly good websites by failing to update and promote them properly. Once your site is live is when the real work begins: creating new content like blog posts and ebooks which you can then promote through social media, search engines, and email blasts to increase your website traffic.

10. INSTALL AN ANALYTICS SYSTEM

Once you have a modern website design that works well on both computers and phones, then the next step is to make sure that you can measure its performance. Most solar companies I talk to have no idea how many visitors to their website they get on average by day, week, or month. And unfortunately, for most companies, once I have a look at their websites, the visitor numbers turn out to be close to zero. If your website gets no traffic, then it's not doing your business much good.

But web analytics can be intimidating for the average solar business-person. So I'll talk about how to make web visitor tracking easier to implement and use in the next chapter.

Chapter 21

●   ●   ●

EASILY TRACK VISITORS TO YOUR WEBSITE

If you've already got Google Analytics set up for your website, and especially if you also use other tools such as Moz or SEMRush or even analytics from a marketing suite like HubSpot or InfusionSoft, and you regularly check-in with the data, then you may want to skip to the end of this chapter. I'll offer a few resources for power users of analytics and web measurement later on, but most of this chapter is geared towards analytics beginners. In my experience, that describes the majority of marketing staffers and salespeople in the solar industry.

So, for those of you who are new to measuring traffic on your website, this is the place for you.

And if you're scared of web statistics, don't worry. Our discussion here will keep it simple and help you get started measuring what counts online quickly and easily.

I always think it's funny when my one of my clients tells me that they have no idea how many people visit their website because that client is afraid of numbers. People in the solar industry deal with numbers all the time. Start with sales figures. If the sales management of a solar installer doesn't know how many leads they're bringing in, how many leads they're closing, and how much revenue they're bringing in for the quarter, then their company is heading for bankruptcy. But solar sales reps and marketers also have to be comfortable talking about the generation capacity of an installed solar array in kilowatts or megawatts. And then they have to be able to go into cost per watt, rate-of-return on a PPA versus a lease or equipment purchase financed by a loan, and area of a rooftop in square feet. And those are just the easy numbers. Once you get into the technical stuff with the engineers and installation staff—beyond volts and amps—the numbers can be serious.

Yet, a solar contractor who is comfortable with dozens of different figures when it comes to designing and pricing a solar system will still tell me that he's uncomfortable with numbers when it comes to how many people visited his website per day on average last month. It must be some kind of mental block. Or, perhaps some people who work in solar don't think that website statistics are important enough to bother with.

Whatever the reason, I would estimate that more than half of solar company owners and sales managers have no idea how much traffic comes to their website. That's a problem for those who want to generate their own leads online because, just like in any kind of sales or marketing funnel, lead-generation is a numbers game. Take this marketing funnel image from HubSpot.

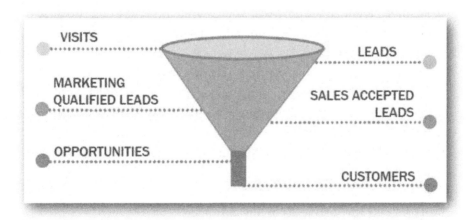

The goal of any company is to get customers. So, if you work your way back up the funnel, for every single customer you may need ten sales-accepted leads. And to get those ten leads you may need 100 marketing-qualified leads. Those in turn may require 1,000 visits to your website. So, as you can see, just to know if you're on track to get enough leads to turn into a customer, you need to know how much traffic you get on your website.

So, for those people in solar companies who are turned off by web statistics, I'd say that if there's one number you should know it's how many visitors come to your website on an average day. It would be nice to also know how this number changes by month, by season, and in connection with any special events (such as the day you publish a new blog post or start running a Facebook ad, or the day after your business sponsored a beer festival or had a booth at a local event).

Perhaps another reason that so many people who market and manage solar companies don't know their web traffic is that the most popular software used to track website traffic, Google Analytics, is intimidating. While its interface has gotten more friendly over the years, it's also added new ways to slice and dice results, which makes it more powerful, but also more complicated. So, I don't blame anyone who's not an SEO guru for being a bit wary of this tool that's mentioned everywhere and ignored nearly as often.

But don't let fear of Google Analytics stop you from getting the most basic information about how well your website is performing. Because if you don't know how your website is doing, that means it's probably not doing well.

And a website without traffic is like an order of brochures that you just leave in the boxes after they arrive from the printer. Unless you open up the boxes, take out the brochures and start distributing them at your front desk, at events, and in available literature racks at good locations, then nobody will see your brochure and it won't have a chance to reach potential customers. It's the same with a website. Unless people see it, it doesn't matter how good your website is. A website without enough traffic won't get you any sales leads or any customers.

So, to make things easier on you in the short run, if Google Analytics seems like too much at this point, then install a system to track your website visits that's easier to use. If your website is built on WordPress, then Jetpack offers a slimmed-down, no-nonsense display of page views that you can install right in your WordPress Dashboard. Jetpack offers only a small fraction of the data you'd get with Google Analytics, but it will give you the most important numbers as a start, so you can see if your site is getting visitors or not.

In the longer term, it makes sense for you or someone in your company to get comfortable enough with Google Analytics to get at least basic information. To learn what you need to get started, there are lots of guides online to Google Analytics. I'll suggest two of them here from respected authorities on search engine analysis and marketing:

1. The Absolute Beginner's Guide to Google Analytics by Moz: https://moz.com/blog/absolute-beginners-guide-to-google-analytics

The Moz guide walks you through all the steps to start your own Google Analytics account and connect it to your website. Then, it takes you through the main types of reports you can get about your website visitors and the performance of different pages on your website: Audience (everything about your visitors), Acquisition (how they found your site), Behavior (everything about the performance of your content), and Conversions (how many people are clicking on your landing pages or product pages).

The guide finishes up with advice on how to have reports emailed to you and answers frequently asked questions about Google Analytics. There you'll learn such useful things as how to share your data with someone else or find recommendations for other services that help make Google Analytics easier to use.

2. Beginner's Guide To Web Data Analysis: Ten Steps To Love & Success by Avinash Kaushik: http://www.kaushik.net/avinash/beginners-guide-web-data-analysis-ten-steps-tips-best-practices/

Kaushik's guide shows you how to use the common reports available in Google Analytics, from the Traffic Sources report, to Visitor Loyalty and Recency, to Top Landing Pages. But Kaushik goes beyond by placing analytics in context of the overall user experience. His first section is actually all about looking at your website from the visitor's point of view. As Kaushik, explains, before you even look at Google Analytics, you should check out your site as your visitor would:

> The very first thing I do, and I recommend you do, is visit the website whose data you are analyzing. See how it looks. Go to the product pages. Go to the donation pages. Go to the B2B dancing monkey video (what!). Go to the add to cart page. Go to the RSS / Email sign up page and sign up. Go read some customer reviews (if an e-commerce site) or visitor comments (if a blog). Go download the white papers. Go use site search.

Since these are the days of Big Data, as web gurus have been telling us for the last few years, you can use dozens of other services beyond Google Analytics to learn even more about the performance of your website. But unless you are already a power user of data tools, my advice is not to get seduced by the latest data analysis software to come along. Instead, focus on what you really need to know about your website, namely, the four categories covered in Google Analytics:

* How many visitors you're getting and where they're coming from
* How those visitors found your website originally
* What pages those visitors are viewing on your website and how long they're staying
* How many leads you are generating on your site and how good those leads are

The last point about lead generation is key for solar companies that are dissatisfied with the quality of leads they're getting from traditional solar marketing, whether door knocking, events, or buying lists from telemarketers.

An easy way to track your lead generation efforts is to use the free software from HubSpot called LeadIn. It's much easier to work with than Google Analytics's conversion reports, and will give you the basic information you need to see what's working and pass along qualified leads to your sales team. I'll discuss this helpful system in more detail later on.

Now that you can see what's going on with your website, you need to add some content that the potential solar customers you want to reach will want to see. And that's what I'll talk about in the chapters that make up the next section.

Section 4

SPREADING SUNSHINE— CREATING GREAT CONTENT

As marketers, we should be changing the mantra from always be closing to always be helping.

— JONATHAN LISTER

Creating good content is part habit, part education in some fundamental rules, and part giving a damn.

— ANN HANDLEY

Chapter 22

YOU HAVE TO GIVE TO GET

First, your new solar website needs content, whether text, pictures, or videos. And hopefully that content is stuff that your desired audience wants to see. Then, you need that audience to discover you, through social media and search engines. Unfortunately, that's where most American solar companies stop. And that's too bad, because it means they're leaving money on the table. Instead, what all solar companies should do is to go to the next step and make their site a lead-generating machine with clickable calls-to-action as this solar company in India did.

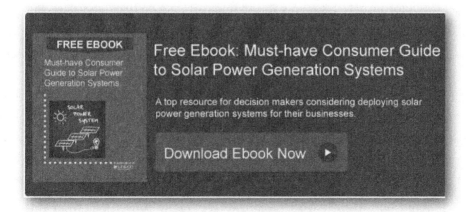

Through a graphic that looks like a banner ad, Sunipod Solar offers its Must Have Guide to Solar Power Generation Systems to help educate homeowners on their options for solar. The ebook is free but if a visitor wants it, she has to fill out and submit a form with her name and email address. In that way, Sunipod Solar converts website visitors into qualified and interested sales leads.

Sunipod Solar gets the most mileage out of this call-to-action by placing it at the bottom of each blog post and elsewhere throughout its website. After discovering Sunipod, I was able to find an American solar company, Sunpower by Infinity Solar in New York State, that had an ebook call-to-action which was very attractive:

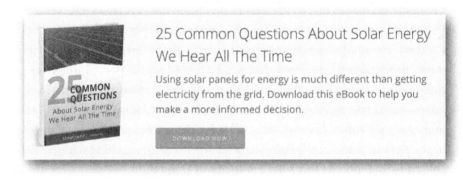

Unfortunately, I was only able to find this CTA on their homepage, but not at the bottom of their blog posts. That's a missed opportunity. On the plus side, Sunpower by Infinity Solar (that's a bit of an awkward name to repeat over and over) did place another offer at the bottom of its blog posts, a CTA to get a free solar home assessment. So at least they're doing something. Too bad it's not the right thing for their blog post audience. Readers of blog posts are generally near the beginning of the Buyer's Journey, which means that they're probably not ready to talk to a company sales rep.

Early-stage buyers still want to poke around quietly on the web and educate themselves about solar—its benefits and affordability mostly. So, I would be surprised if the company gets many conversions from this advanced CTA placed on entry-level content. It would have been better for them to offer the ebook at the bottom of their blog posts and save the free quote offer for more advanced content such as their page on government incentives for solar buyers.

This is the part of solar inbound marketing that's hard to do yourself. A smaller solar company could certainly build its own website and the site would probably be pretty good looking if done using a high quality service such as SquareSpace. Of course, someone would have to create the initial content on the site. But you can pull that from your brochure and other print materials initially and then refine it based on performance later on. So, it's very doable for a smaller company to launch its own website. A site like this won't have the backend tools to generate and track many leads, but at least it's a place for potential buyers to check you out and decide if they want to add you to their list of potential solar installers.

You can even set yourself up to get web traffic by optimizing your content for obvious search keywords while getting the word out through social media and pay-per-click ads. I'll discuss ways to attract visitors to your website in more detail later on in this chapter. But with a keyword tool, a couple of social media accounts, and an email list, you can make a good start on building audience for your new website.

But going beyond that to convert visitors to leads, prospects, and customers is more difficult to do by yourself. And perhaps that's why few solar companies do it well. Even the big national installers in the United States fail to optimize their otherwise powerful websites for lead generation.

As a marketer, that's frustrating for me to see. Large solar installers have obviously spent tens of thousands of dollars to give their websites contemporary design and to fill them with well crafted content. But they haven't gone to the next step yet, to offer the more substantial content like ebooks or private webinars in exchange for the contact information of visitors. That's what would convert those visitors to sales leads.

Why the large solar installers haven't optimized their websites for lead generation is a mystery to me. Maybe they still get enough leads through traditional outbound marketing? Maybe they're so swamped with orders that they don't need more business for the next couple years? Or maybe most of their marketing is stuck in the 1970s just as it is for most local solar installers?

National solar installers are clearly run by smart people who know the solar market today and are helping to expand that market in the future. When it comes to PV panels or roof racking, the big solar companies are obviously able to translate innovation into action. They even produce great content like customer case studies and videos. And they spread it well through social media and their own email lists.

But when it comes to the most valuable part of inbound marketing, generating leads online, most of the leading solar companies are still leaving money on the table.

With the advice I'm going to give you here, you'll be able to beat the big boys, even if you work for a small residential solar installer. You don't need a lot of money to start generating sales leads on your own website. All you need is time, effort, and the roadmap I'll give you right now.

Are you excited? I hope so.

But is it worth the trouble? Well, yes, but only if you plan on being in business for a while. If you just want to ride the solar boom for a couple of years and then cash out, you can keep knocking on doors and buying leads from cold callers. But then if you were only thinking of short-term sales, you wouldn't be reading this book, would you?

I'm guessing you want to use marketing to help your company stick around for the long-term. If you start generating your own leads on your website now, you'll be building a solar business that's built to last. You'll free yourself from relying on telemarketers, appointment-setters, and other lead-generation vendors. By cutting out those middlemen, you'll build a strong relationship with your audience that will yield potential customers and real sales for years to come.

So, this is the part of inbound marketing where you get the big payoff. But it's the part that most solar marketers don't get right. Now, you'll be able to join the small, elite group who does understand the immense power of new marketing methods applied online. If you implement your online marketing plan according to the steps below, then you can beat the competition. Ready?

By now, inbound marketing on the Internet has been boiled down to a process that any solar marketer can apply and then repeat:

1. Build 1-3 buyer personas, or fictional profiles of ideal customers for your solar offering.
2. Find out what keywords or search terms those personas enter in Google when they want info on solar.
3. Publish blog posts on your website using those solar keywords and offering content about solar power that real humans who fit those buyer personas would want to read and share. Hint: your content needs to be interesting, which rules out most of what companies usually post as news, whether new hire or new product announcements. Or worse, purchased "canned" content from the industry used as filler on many blogs.
4. Attract traffic to those solar blog posts through social media, email, and other online outreach.
5. Put a call-to-action in each blog post offering an ebook or some other content that your potential customer would want to download (eg, "The Homeowner's Guide to Rooftop Solar with No Money Down.").
6. When your web visitor wants to download the offer, ask him or her to fill out a form with their contact information.
7. Follow up by email, either manual, automated, or a combination of the two.

Voilá! Once you have a web visitor's contact info, you've now got a promising inbound inquiry—someone who's interested in solar now and who gave you their contact information by choice. Now, qualify that inquiry as a lead. Not everybody who downloads an offer from your website will be interested in buying solar. But some will. So, the marketing department can now follow up with them according to the principles of permission marketing, with an email perhaps offering another ebook or even a free phone consultation. And once an early-stage lead has been nurtured for a while by online marketing content, the person may be ready to talk to a salesperson.

SLOWER BUT BETTER

Does generating your own solar leads take longer than buying a solar lead list from a vendor? You bet it does. So if you still hire appointment-setting vendors and you want to keep your sales team busy, you may still want to keep those vendors for a while yet. But in the meantime, why not get started on generating your own, much more qualified, solar leads? If you do it right, the day may come when you can start to cut back on buying lists or paying vendors to set appointments and eventually generate all your solar leads in-house. With better leads, your conversion rate will rise and you'll sell more solar.

Don't worry if you've never generated many leads from your website before. If you've tried to generate leads online previously but it hasn't worked well, then you've probably made one of the common mistakes of online lead generation, such as sending first-time web visitors straight to a form to request a call from a salesperson.

As we saw earlier, the psychology of your buyer requires a more subtle approach that's customized for each stage of a solar buyer's journey. So, if a potential customer is still just mulling whether to get solar or not, he's not ready to talk to a salesperson. Instead, he needs help understanding the basic options for home solar. And he needs that help delivered in a low-pressure way, with no commitment. At later stages of the buyer's journey, he'll need more detailed information and he'll be ready to exchange his email address to get it.

And finally, when he's ready to decide between your company and a couple others, the buyer will want to talk to your salesperson, especially if you've given him free downloadable guides, conservation tips, and other content that shows you really care about his energy needs and are helping him to learn more. But you have to understand where the buyer is in his lifecycle to provide him with the help he needs in the way he wants to receive that help.

That's what you'll learn here. In the next few chapters I'll go through each stage of the inbound marketing process in more detail to help you get started generating solar sales leads on your own website. I'm sure you'll find it useful.

Chapter 23

FOCUS ON YOUR IDEAL CUSTOMER

To sell more solar, you need to know about your customer. You probably already know the basics:

* Possible motivation to buy solar: To save money on electricity, gain energy self-sufficiency, keep up with neighbors who already have solar, or help the environment.
* Barriers to buying solar: High upfront cost, worries about reliability.
* Incentive to buy solar now: Limited-time discounts (perhaps connected to tax credits that will expire), no-money down financing, demonstrated monthly savings over purchasing power from the local electric utility.

But this is just the start. Your competitors know all this stuff too. To beat the competition and get better solar leads that you generate yourself and that convert into customers at a higher rate, you really need to dig deeper into your most likely sales prospects. This might sound daunting. Or course, it would be impractical to research hundreds or thousands of potential solar buyers individually. But you can approximate what your best customers are like by developing a solar buyer persona.

WHAT'S A PERSONA AND WHY YOU NEED ONE

A buyer persona is a fictional version of your ideal customer. According to Kim Goodwin in *Designing for the Digital Age,*

> Personas are archetypes that describe the various goals and observed behavior patterns among your potential users and customers. Personas help everybody in a solar company—Marketing, Sales, Product Development—internalize the ideal customer that you're trying to attract, and relate to our customers as real humans.

And why is it necessary to focus on your best kind of customer to sell solar?

With the market getting more competitive, potential customers now have more choice about where to get a solar array. To stand out from the competition, you need to show that you're a better fit—in fact, that you understand your favorite kind of prospect's needs better, sympathize with their pain points, and can offer better solutions. Once you understand a prospect's style, general interests, where they get their solar information, and how they like to receive that information, then you can convert solar leads on your website who are more likely to match your ideal customer.

"Understanding your buyer persona is critical to driving content creation, product development, sales follow up, and really anything that relates to customer acquisition and retention," according to HubSpot.

HOW TO DEVELOP A SOLAR BUYER PERSONA

Fortunately, it's not that hard to develop a buyer persona for a residential or commercial solar installer. And there are a few good resources to help you develop a persona, which I'll list below. Here are the basic steps:

1. OUTLINE THE INFORMATION YOU WANT TO KNOW ABOUT YOUR PERSONA

For example, you certainly need demographics—gender, age, income, and education. But it can also be helpful to know buzzwords and mannerisms. Why? If you can use the language in your blogs and other website content that your prospect uses when searching for solar information online, your site will more likely come up high in search engine results for those terms. MakeMyPersona.com offers a simple worksheet that you can fill out online that can help you understand your ideal customer well enough to start to come up with keywords they might use in a web search for solar information.

2. DEVELOP INTERVIEW QUESTIONS

A useful buyer persona is a fictional portrait based on fact. A high quality persona profile is not built on guesswork but on real-life examples, and those come from research. The best way to find out about your ideal customer is to interview some of your real customers. Ask residential solar customers how decisions are made on big purchases in the family, what are long-term goals for the household, and even how important is the value of household self-reliance. For a business or government customer, ask about size of the organization, and the person's role there in decision-making.

3. CONDUCT INTERVIEWS

You can interview prospects, referrals, or people at trade shows, but the best information will come from your own customers who've actually bought solar from your company. Of course you don't want to annoy your customers, so offer an incentive for them to participate in a 10-15 minute persona interview—maybe a discount on future services or a $20 gift card to a local pizza place. You may not need to offer much at all. If your customers are happy with their solar installation and with your company's work, they'll want to share their positive opinion. When you contact customers, make clear that it's not a sales call. Start with 3-5 interviews and stop when you begin to hear the same answers repeated.

4. WRITE UP THE RESULTS

Here's where you take everything you've gotten and put it together in a usable form for your marketing team to use in developing search keywords, creating content that this kind of person will like, and sharing that content in the ways most likely to reach buyers who match the persona profile. But this writeup will also be helpful to Sales, Product Development, Financing, and even company management as they plan strategy for the future, perhaps targeting new markets. Below you'll find a sample buyer persona profile for residential solar.

Ranch House Ralph

Background: Owns a home that's under 40-years-old in a suburban area of a Sun Belt state like Arizona or Florida.

Demographics: Age 45-65, married, 2-3 kids either getting ready for college or already moved out, annual family income of $80,000 to $150,000.

Identifiers: Socially liberal but fiscally conservative, modestly DIY, financially responsible, not an activist but environmentally aware, likes straight-talk with little patience for hype or fluff.

Real Quote: "Every summer our electric bill spikes into the stratosphere. We've already done the energy efficiency stuff. But it gets hot here and we need to run the AC. I'm sick and tired of writing a check for $650 every August to the electric company."

Common Objections: Doesn't have cash available for large up-front payment. Needs approval for a rooftop array from the home-owner's association. Concerned that panels may break or produce less power in the future.

Marketing Messages: No-money down installation, meets common homeowners association requirements, 25-year warranty on equipment, installer offers a guarantee and support at no extra charge.

Elevator Pitch: Get solar on your roof that you own with no up-front cost through low-interest rate financing.

If you're an experienced solar marketer, you'll recognize Ranch House Ralph as a common residential solar customer type. Some of the information in this sample profile will probably apply to your target buyers as well. However, please do remember that this profile is just a sample and that you shouldn't apply it as-is to your own marketing. Instead, use it as a model to develop your own home solar buyer persona based on your own past customers, the geographic area that you serve, and other values in your community. For example, you may find that your ideal residential solar customer emphasizes religiously motivated Creation Care more than "environmental awareness," or owns a hybrid car, or that the family hikes, camps, and enjoys other outdoor adventures.

As you can see in that last example, a persona can contain information not listed in the sample profile, such as hobbies/interests, sources of information and much more. But to avoid delay, you can certainly start with the basics listed above and then expand your persona over time. As with any good planning document, your buyer persona profile should change over time, as you get better information and as your market evolves. So don't wait for your persona profiles to be completely final before you start marketing to this type of potential customer. Get good enough information and then get going. As in everything connected to inbound marketing, the Perfect is the enemy of the Good.

Once you've created your first buyer persona profile, create at least another couple more. After all, you don't want to put all your eggs in one basket. Don't count on just one type of customer to account for all your sales. Instead, try to segment your market to recognize the important differences among related types of solar buyers.

For example, the Sun Belt suburb where Ranch House Ralph is likely to be found may be located near a larger city with smaller and older homes. Though they don't have as much rooftop as Ralph's 1990s rancher placed at the center of a generous lot with no shading from nearby buildings or trees, homes closer to a downtown may also be good prospects for residential solar, especially if your company offers an off-site option such as a larger shared array or community solar. But the messages for a hip urban couple wondering if they can even qualify for solar in their densely built neighborhood will be a bit different than the marketing pitch that will appeal to suburban Ralph and his wife.

USE YOUR PERSONA TO GENERATE SOLAR LEADS

Now that you've got one or more customer personas, your marketing department can use each persona as the starting-point for a solar lead generation campaign. Using the language of that persona, a solar marketer can create blogs, ebooks, and other helpful content online with keywords that will get your website found more easily in a Google search. Once you've attracted interested visitors to your site, you can use calls-to-action, premium content offers, and forms to convert as many of your website visitors as possible to new sales leads.

Chapter 24

DEVELOP A LIST OF TARGET KEYWORDS

Once you've developed the best picture you can of your ideal customer by creating a solar buyer persona, then you're ready to find out the specific keywords that will attract people who match that persona to your website. Once on your site, you can convert those visitors to sales leads.

WHY SOLAR KEYWORDS MATTER

You've probably heard lots of talk about the importance of keywords. To get more traffic on your website, using the right keywords is essential. As the search engine tracking company Moz explains, "Keyword research is one of the most important, valuable, and high return activities in the search marketing field. Ranking for the right keywords can make or break your website."

Finding the right solar keywords will also give you valuable insight into your target customer and help you generate traffic to your site most likely to turn into qualified solar leads. In the words of Moz:

It's not always about getting visitors to your site, but about getting the right kind of visitors. The usefulness of this intelligence cannot be overstated; with keyword research you can predict shifts in demand, respond to changing market conditions, and produce the products, services, and content that web searchers are actively seeking. In the history of marketing, there has never been such a low barrier to entry in understanding the motivations of consumers in virtually any niche.

Start your keyword list with your own website. Look at Google Analytics or whatever system is installed on your website to track visitors, traffic sources, and the top pages viewed. Look at the keywords that bring visitors to your site through organic search. Are they something like "solar installers San Antonio" or "no money down solar panels"?

You may be surprised at the words your customers use. Perhaps the wording of searches is different than how you refer to things in your sales materials. If so, make a note of it—and try to use the customer's language on your website in the future.

Then, you can try to do a few Google searches on your own for those keywords or others you think your customers might use to find you.

At the bottom of the Google search results, you'll see searches related to the one you just did. These are real keywords that searchers have used in Google, so you know that they work. Pick the ones that apply to your company and add them to your keyword list.

That's a good start. Now, if you want to get more and better keywords, you'll need to use a keyword tool. Not only will such a tool help you find keyword phrasing but the tool will also help you evaluate keywords based on how popular they are, how well your website already ranks for those keywords, and how competitive it would be for you to come up in searches for those terms.

Here are a few popular keyword tools available online that you can use for free:

* Google AdWords Keyword Planner Tool
* Google Trends
* Microsoft Bing Ads Intelligence
* Wordtracker (free trial)

I've had good experience with HubSpot's keyword tool, which is part of their integrated inbound marketing software suite. The advantage of their system is that you can connect keywords to a buyer persona, allowing you to close the loop between your ideal solar customer and what solar keywords they're likely to search for.

But whichever keyword tool you use, you then need to develop a list of a few dozen organic (unpaid) keywords that your persona is searching for on a regular basis but that aren't too competitive—that is, the search terms aren't already dominated by larger competitors who it will be hard for you to organically overtake on Google without having to buy expensive pay-per-click ads for those terms.

For example, "residential solar installer" gets a lot of monthly searches. But it's not a good keyword for most solar companies that do home installations because it's too competitive. Big, well established companies like SolarCity are already taking up the top spots for this search. That means it would be difficult for your company to get on the first screen of Google (where you really want to be) for such a broad and popular term. To have a better chance of coming up near the top of your potential buyer's Google search, you need to find keywords that are more attainable.

So, the last stage in your keyword research should be to refine your general keywords into "long-tail keywords" that are more specific. These keywords have less traffic, but they are also less competitive, and thus, more likely to send traffic to your website instead of to the websites of bigger solar companies. SEO software company Wordtracker explains the benefit of long-tail keywords:

> Long-tail keywords are those three- and four-keyword phrases which are very, very specific to whatever you are selling. You see, whenever a customer uses a highly specific search phrase, they tend to be looking for exactly what they are actually going to buy. In virtually every case, such very specific searches are far more likely to convert to sales than general generic searches that tend to be geared more toward the type of research that consumers typically do prior to making a buying decision.

So, not only are long-tail keywords easier for a mid-size or small solar installer to rank well on Google searches, especially when they're location specific. But these more specific keywords will also bring you higher quality web traffic—that is, visitors who are more likely to convert into leads and customers because they *really* want what you're selling and didn't just land on your site by accident.

To make a general solar keyword into a long-tail keyword phrase, try adding your city or another term to your more popular keywords. For example, "no money down solar San Antonio" or "no money down home solar PPA." Then test the keyword phrase in your keyword tool of choice. In addition to professional tools, Search-engine optimizer Jayson DeMers offers some free ways to make your general keywords into long-tail ones:

* Use Google Suggest and related keywords found at the bottom of most Google searches.
* Your stronger competitors may have already figured out good long-tail keywords—check out a few key things on their websites such as meta tags (look at their source code), page titles, and blog post snippets.
* Forums, comment threads, and emails—as Google's own software gets better over time, Google searches recognize more natural language. Language doesn't get any more natural than the casual wording that people type into online discussions.

Once you have a list of 25 or so long-tail keywords, then you're ready to start using them to generate more qualified solar leads. And the way to do that is to put those keywords in all the content on your website, especially pages and blog posts. What you don't want to do is use keywords in an artificial way (known as "keyword stuffing"). Instead, work keywords naturally into text, focusing on the places where Google will give you the most credit, such as the headline, subheads, and "alt tags" for images. Alt tags offer text labels for vision-impaired people who are surfing the web with screen readers. Alt tags also help search engines know the content of an image. On your website, you can set alt tags through the insert image function in Wordpress or insert them directly into HTML code.

In the bad old days, to many people who worked on websites, keywords were all about search-engine optimization, and SEO was all about technical tricks to help your site come up higher in a Google search.

So, for example, webmasters would place a list of 30-40 keywords at the top of a page. The keywords weren't hyperlinked to anything. They just sat above the text in hopes that Google would somehow read them and rank your site highly for those terms, even if such a list of terms annoyed human readers. Other webmasters would try tricks to fool Google to get credit for using search terms that the website didn't deserve, such as putting a list of keywords in white-colored type on a white background. In that way, the keywords would be invisible to humans but Google could still read them and hopefully give the website credit for all those terms.

While the first type of keyword stuffing was merely annoying to website visitors, the second type was intentionally deceptive, at least in the opinion of Google's programmers. Such black hat SEO might get a website a quick bump in traffic, but it could also backfire if Google found out about it. Because Google considered such practices to be a kind of fraud, once they discovered that a website was using black hat SEO, Google might punish that site. Penalties could range from a simple demotion in such results for certain terms to totally banishment for the whole website from any Google searches.

Most web developers and web marketers know that they should stay away from black hat SEO tactics. The risk is greater than the reward. And with the improvement in Google's algorithms over the years, such tactics are less and less effective anyway. Indeed, as Google gets closer and closer to understanding natural language, technical SEO will become less effective overall. So, while your local SEO guy may still be charging you $500 a month to stuff keywords into the metatags of your website, real SEO experts with contemporary and evolving techniques advise a different approach. For example, Joost de Valk, founder of SEO company Yoast, says that technical SEO is still useful. But only if you also optimize your website in other ways, doing what he calls "holistic SEO":

> Here at Yoast we try to combat the notion that SEO is just a trick. SEO is so much more. Over the years, social media has become more important as a method for discovering new content and products. Google changes its algorithm literally hundreds of times a year. It adapts to the changing influence of social media, and with it SEO becomes more complicated.
>
> Permanently ranking well in Google demands an extensive SEO-strategy focused on every aspect of your website. The technical stuff, the user experience, the content on your website and even the security of your website all need to be in order. To keep ranking well in Google, you should develop what we call a holistic SEO approach.

So, don't let some SEO geek talk you into doing complex technical SEO that may not help and could even hurt. If you can't understand some SEO tactic, then just say no.

For example, I had a client once whose SEO guy had created a blog, separate from the client's website, as a way to get links from other websites that would signal to Google that the client's site was worthwhile. The problem was that the client hated the content on this blog so much that they didn't want any of their audiences to read it. Apparently, the blog posts had generic text that was being peddled as a "white label" offering to companies across the industry—anyone could buy the content, so it wasn't even unique. And the writing was poor quality to boot.

So, this basically became a secret blog, with no links from the company's main website. Of course, the whole idea of a blog is to be visible—to get more readers and more shares on social media. If the blog was good enough, it could hope to get some links from other websites. But it takes humans to give those links. There's no automatic software out there that just bestows links from legitimate websites on blogs, no matter how unworthy the content of those blogs. Yet, that was apparently the theory behind this SEO-only blog. How such a stealth blog could generate inbound links to the company's site remains a mystery to me.

This terrible SEO consultant did get one thing right, though. Blogging is one of the most powerful ways to do well in Google searches and get more traffic to your website. So, let's see how real blogging really works.

Chapter 25

●　　●　　●

WHAT'S ALL THE FUSS ABOUT BLOGGING?

Blogging is the third step in the inbound marketing methodology. If you do it right, your company blog will be key to building the web traffic that you need to generate sales leads from potential solar buyers.

But blogging takes time. And doing it well isn't easy. So you might wonder if blogging is really worth the trouble and whether it really leads to solar sales? It's clear how a Facebook ad promotes your business or how setting appointments with homeowners can lead to sales of home solar arrays. But writing articles about various aspects of solar power and home energy management might seem like a helpful thing to do for people without a clear connection to how that's going to get you more business.

At this point, I'd ask you to remember the strategy behind inbound marketing. You get customers to come to you, instead of you having to go out to them, by creating content (blog posts, videos, social media shares, free informative ebooks) that those customers want to see. It's definitely a different approach from running ads or making cold calls. But it's effective. Content marketing generates 54% more sales leads than traditional outbound marketing, according to research by HubSpot.

Today, the king of content is the blog. It's the place on your website where you'll add new content the most often. And blogging is the online marketing tactic that drives all other tactics, from social media outreach to email campaigns. Again, according to HubSpot, blogging is the best tactic of content marketing. While we saw above that content marketing generates more than half as many leads as outbound marketing, the average company that blogs generates 126% more leads than companies that don't blog. That makes blogging the top secret weapon for companies that want to generate their own sales leads.

They do that by doing better in SEO:

* 55% more website visitors
* 97% more inbound links
* 434% more pages indexed or listed by Google

So, if you want to generate your own solar sales leads, then blogging is certainly worth the time. I'd go even further and say that I can't imagine how you would generate your own sales leads online at all without publishing regular articles that your main buyer personas want to see.

A page listing the benefits of solar power, a couple of cute photos of sunflowers and roof arrays against a blue sky, and a contact form to see if your house has the right kind of roof and if you live in the right zip code just aren't enough to convert potential customers at early stages of the buyer's journey into sales leads. These buyers need more persuasion to get interested in your company. And if you don't offer this kind of help to your web visitors through blog posts that solar buyers want to read and that build your brand (with conservation tips, incentive and tax news, issues about climate, solar innovations, stories about other customers, and ways your company is engaging with the community in events or sponsorships) then online solar buyers will go to another solar website that does. They'll probably go to one of your competitors, in fact.

I hope you can now understand the massive benefits of blogging for a solar company. And I hope you're ready to get started either with making your company blog better, if you already have one, or launching a new blog from scratch.

Whether you write your blog in-house or hire a digital marketing agency to do it for you, there are a few things you need to help your blog generate qualified solar leads:

1. POST REGULARLY

Twice a month is better than nothing to get started for a small residential installer. Once a week is good and twice or three times a week is better. Bigger companies can even blog daily, as long as they blog on several different areas of solar for different audiences. For example, larger installers can run separate blogs about residential, commercial, and community solar. Don't worry too much about overwhelming your audience. Even if they subscribe to your blog and get every post by email, followers won't read them all. They'll just skim over the post titles to find what interests them. Over time, you'll build up a big list of email subscribers who want to see your blogs. And if you use keywords effectively in your blog texts, then you'll also get more and more traffic over time from Google searches. So, the more blog posts you publish, the more chances you have to reach new visitors searching for your carefully chosen keywords (see below).

2. WRITE ABOUT TOPICS THAT INTEREST YOUR AUDIENCE

A solar blog should be at most 20% promotional, with news and offers about your company and its services. The other 80% of your blog posts should be entertaining or helpful to your audience, the kind of things they'd want to read whether it came from your company or not. Lists and how-to's get the most clicks, according to research. But if you have the ability to produce multimedia, infographics, social media meme graphics, and videos also do well.

And by all means, please don't put company news releases on your blog.

Create a separate section on your site for the specialized audiences—news media and investors—who want information in a news release format. To come up with blog post topics go through a process where you pick a goal for the post, look at what topics have driven traffic to your website in the past, come up with new topics that are SEO-friendly, and then formulate a working title and write the text.

Let's take an example for a residential solar installer. Let's say you want to generate more leads for homeowners who are in the market for rooftop PV. That would be the goal of your blog post.

Then, review your website to see what article topics have been popular among your readers. For example, perhaps you got a lot of visits to a post on the five things that make a house's roof suitable for a solar array? This might inspire you to come up with a new

but related topic for your new blog post, such as what to do if your home's roof doesn't have all five requirements for solar.

Check and see if anybody is searching for that in Google. If so, then it's a good topic that can get you traffic. Then brainstorm the content for your post. You could start with a series of questions. For example: Can you trim nearby trees to reduce shading on the roof? Do you need to replace your 25-year-old asphalt shingles before you can put up solar?

3. OPTIMIZE FOR KEYWORDS—BUT DON'T OVER-OPTIMIZE

Once you've developed a list of a dozen or two dozen keywords for each of your buyer personas, then pick one keyword per blog post and include that keyword phrase in several crucial places in your blog text: the headline, alt text for at least one image, subheads, bulleted and numbered lists, outbound links, and post tags (hyperlinked keywords found at the bottom of a blog post). You can pick your keyword before you start writing or you can just write a great working title first and then try to optimize it for a target keyword afterwards.

But you shouldn't write just to use a keyword. Instead, keep the keyword in the back of your mind as you write, but be sure that your text is created for humans, not search engines. Then, once you've got nice text that your audience would want to read, tweak it here and there to include a few instances of the keyword. By all means, avoid the black hat SEO tactics like keyword stuffing that I mentioned earlier. Not only will your audience hate that, but as we've seen, Google could penalize you for trying to play the system by downgrading your site or even removing it from search listings.

4. INTEGRATE YOUR BLOG WITH ANALYTICS AND EMAIL MARKETING AUTOMATION

To know what's working and what's not, you need data on your blog posts. Using Google Analytics or a simpler analytics system such as the one from Jetpack, check at least once daily during the work week on page views and unique visitors to your blog posts and what percentage of those clicked on your call-to-action and converted to leads.

To get more bang for your blogging buck, connect your website to an email automation system that can send out a pre-written email response to everyone who downloads your content offer. This will help move them along the Solar Buyer's Journey and encourage them to take the next step of engagement with your company. MailChimp and other email marketing services offer both analytics and the ability to send out a series of emails automatically to a list that you select, a feature called email drip campaigns or, alternatively, workflows. Larger solar companies may be interested in an integrated marketing automation system such as the full suites offered by HubSpot, InfusionSoft, Pardot, or a half dozen other providers.

5. BUILD AUDIENCE WITH SOCIAL MEDIA AND BLOG SUBSCRIPTIONS

If you've written your blog posts around good solar keywords, eventually, your posts will start to attract traffic from Google searches. But you don't have to just sit around and wait for web searchers to find you. In the meantime, you can speed up the process by pushing your blog posts out to your audiences on social media and by offering a way to subscribe to your blog. Do that by tapping into your blog's Really Simple Syndication (RSS) feed. If your site is built in WordPress, Jetpack Subscriptions is a simple way to do RSS subscriptions. Connecting a service like MailChimp's RSS-to-Email will give you more control over your subscription, for example, by allowing you to send out a single weekly email on a certain day each week with multiple blog posts.

Sometimes solar company managers are skeptical of the value of blogging. If you follow these steps, not only will your solar blog rank higher in Google search and start to bring in qualified leads that your sales force will be glad to have. But you'll also be able to measure your success and show documented ROI for your blogging efforts. To do that effectively, you'll need a good analytics system in place to know how many people are coming to your website, how they found you, and what they're doing once they get there.

Then, you'll need to collect data showing results that go beyond how many people visited your website and what pages they clicked on but also how many of those visitors your site converted to qualified sales leads, prospects, and customers for solar. I'll talk about that in more detail later on.

Meantime, the whole next section will go more deeply into SEO, to help you get more free traffic from web searchers without having to buy ads.

CATCH THE SUN—ATTRACTING VISITORS FROM SEARCH ENGINES

If you're trying to persuade people to do something, or buy something, it seems to me you should use their language.

— DAVID OGILVY

Chapter 26

DON'T BUY GOOGLE ADS—BE ORGANIC INSTEAD

Let's open with a search engine optimization joke:

Q: Do you know the best place to hide a dead body?
A: On the second page of Google search results.

Funny, right? Well, SEO gurus do have a dry sense of humor. But the serious point here is that you'll get more traffic from web searches the higher you rank in search results. Your goal should be to get onto page one of Google results for several keyword searches that are important to your business. For example, you want to be on page one for the search "solar panels" plus your city or local area, such as "solar panels Phoenix" or "Long Island solar panels."

The reason you need to do well in Google search results is to get traffic to your website. Once you've got your shiny new solar website, then you need people to see it. That means attracting visitors. Here are some numbers from content marketing software company Spokal to show just how important it is for your website to do well in search:

* 93% of all online experiences begin with a search engine
* Search is the top source of traffic to solar websites, beating social media by more than 300%

* After you get visitors on your site, you get to look forward to a 14.6% close rate (as opposed to 1.7% close rate of outbound marketing)
* The best place to be is the first page of a Google search, since 75% of web searchers never scroll past that first page of search results

You may be tempted to buy pay-per-click ads on Google to get to the top page of search results. Please consider carefully before doing this. First, as I mentioned earlier, if you're going to buy PPC ads online, ads from Facebook may give better value. Desirable auction-based keyword terms in Google for competitive solar markets have probably already been bid up to several dollars or more per click, making their ads expensive. But since Facebook ads are priced differently, they may still be more affordable.

Second, wherever you buy ads online, you should limit your ad spending to a small portion of your overall marketing budget. Why? Because online ads don't work very well anymore. Since 70%-80% of web surfers ignore paid ads, according to SEO expert Mark Simmons who writes at the social media and digital advisement firm Business 2 Community, this means it's much more important for you to do well in organic search results than to buy ads.

Finally, even if your ads work temporarily, as I've said before, once you stop paying for them, then they stop working. Buying ads is just a way to rent an audience. No ads, no audience. But if you build ranking in organic search, then you'll have an audience for the long term, for as long as your company's website is online. In fact, length of time your website has been online is a key Google ranking indicator when paired with new content, regular blogging, and good keyword optimization.

Doing well in organic search doesn't happen by accident. It happens by optimizing your website for search engines. And these days, that means optimizing your website for people, specifically, the ideal solar customers that you profiled earlier. If you create content about the topics that your ideal customers care about, like saving money on energy bills and being a leader in their neighborhood, and talk about it using the language that they use, then you'll have a better change of coming up on Google's page 1 instead of page 21 for a search term that's important to your solar business.

SEARCH BEYOND GOOGLE

It can be a bit confusing, but when SEO experts talk about search engines, most of the time they're really talking about just one single search engine, Google.

When search engines first came out in the mid-1990s, it made sense to check your listings in Yahoo!, Alta Vista, and other search sites that have since gone bust or faded in importance. Today, though other search engines including Bing still enjoy modest market share, Google accounts for more than 60% of searches for web sites. The next biggest traditional search engine, run by Microsoft and including Bing, only hosts about 20% of web searches, with Yahoo! following at 13% and both Ask and AOL at under 2% each. So, most solar marketers will do best focusing only on Google to start.

But with the advance of technology over the last few years, traditional text-based search is only part of the story today. Other options are now offering people new, easier ways to search the web.

For example, though it's not a traditional search engine, YouTube actually hosts the second highest number of searches online each month, coming in right behind Google. That's probably why Google actually bought YouTube in 2006 and paid $1.65 billion to do it. According to Mushroom Networks, YouTube hosts more than three billion searches each month, a number that's larger than searches on Bing, Yahoo, Ask, and AOL combined. The video-sharing site reaches more Americans age 18-34 than any cable network. About half of all people on the Internet use the service on a regular basis.

For all these reasons, YouTube is sure to change the way that people search, making search more visual and hopefully, more engaging. So, if you're not doing videos now, you should think about starting to do them soon.

EAT AN APPLE, TALK TO YOUR SEARCH ENGINE

A couple other trends to keep an eye on in the world of search are Apple's search engine and voice search.

If you have a Mac or use an iPhone, then you've already used Apple's Spotlight search engine. Spotlight is what comes up on your desktop when you hit COMMAND-SPACE or on your phone when you hit "slide down" when on your home screen. You'll get results from all over the place—Wikipedia pages, App Store links, and more—but

without any ads. When I searched recently for "solar panels" on my iPhone, along with a Wikipedia article, search results included a couple of websites selling PV panels for DIY installation, a TED talk video, and a link to PV panels listed on Amazon.

Venture capital investor Jason Calacanis thinks that ad-free Spotlight could represent a serious threat to Google:

> Google has gone from unstoppable to "about to be stopped," in the minds of the smartest folks in the industry. Search ads are Google's cash cow; unfortunately, for them, it seems that Google is not advancing the platform (outside of slamming massive amounts of "paid inclusion").

By paid inclusion, Calacanis means that Google has started putting more ads on its search pages, and making those ads harder to distinguish from organic search listings. As a result, the user experience on Google is declining, Calacanis argues, and people are starting to notice—and they're starting to get annoyed. If Apple's search continues to make progress, could more and more people online defect from Google? Only time will tell. But more advanced solar marketers should think about the Spotlight experience as they do their own SEO.

Another up-and-coming search technology is voice search. As of this writing, more than half of teens and about half of adults use voice search everyday, mostly through virtual assistants on their phones such as Siri. Other virtual assistants such as the one provided by Alexa along with voice recognition technology from Shazam and SoundHound, and Google's Natural Language Processing technology will make voice search more widely available. Some experts predict that within a decade voice search will replace the computer keyboard.

To get ready for voice search, web programmers can make a few technical changes to their websites such as maximizing opportunities for Schema mark-up and using XML (this is pretty techy stuff, so ask your webmaster for help) and other readable feeds to make information online easier to find by voice searchers. But any solar marketer should make her website ready for voice search by using more common phrases and more conversational language.

For now, you can prepare for future search technologies by making your website friendly to what Google wants today. And that may be different than what organic SEO gurus were telling people to do in the past.

ON GOOGLE, NOT YOUR FATHER'S SEO

SEO isn't what it used to be. And that's a very good thing for everybody except shady SEO opportunists who make a living by peddling complicated technical tricks.

Gone are the days of writing text for computers rather than humans just to try to score well in Google. No matter what your SEO guy says, these days you should never create content aimed primarily at search engines. Instead, you should develop text and multimedia for your human audiences and then just tweak it for the search engine.

Today, after about a gazillion updates to its software algorithm, Google is now able to understand natural language almost as well as humans do. In fact, website pages written in ordinary English may do much better in search results than pages awkwardly cobbled together around repeating keyword phrases.

To attract the high quality traffic that a residential solar installer or commercial solar developer needs to turn visitors into leads and ultimately, into new customers, a solar marketer must think of search engine optimization holistically. And that means doing both on-page and off-page SEO.

Off-page SEO is sexier and so it gets more attention. Off-page SEO is when you try to get other websites, especially ones with lots of traffic and thus, lots of authority with search engines, to link to your site. As we'll discuss later, one single link from a big website like the New York Times is many times more valuable than a hundred links from websites of small local businesses.

While off-page SEO is important, solar marketers shouldn't forget about on-page SEO. And today, that should be done holistically too.

According to Stephen Murphy of Red Bamboo Marketing, there are three main pieces to SEO: Relevance, authority, and experience (emphasis mine):

Relevance is all about your content and how useful it is to a user. This includes keyword research, competitive research, writing content (not just blogs, but also product pages, location pages, graphics, tools/templates, etc.), re-optimizing existing content, and analytics.

Authority refers to links—both quantity and quality. Your company should build strong internal links first, then focus on building external links from authoritative and related sites (could be through PR, outreach, guest content, asking nicely, etc.) And don't forget low hanging fruit like citation building, especially if you're locally focused.

Finally, you should be looking at Experience, which deals with most of the technical aspects of your website and SEO program. This includes site architecture, page architecture, menus, code, site speed, sitemaps, 301 redirects, mobile friendliness, and a billion other jargony words.

Start your on-page SEO with the third point, a good user experience. That should be built into your website—fast loading, good security, mobile-friendly design, menus that are easy to follow. No amount of awesome content or inbound links from impressive websites will make up for a bad user experience. That's why it's important to have a great website, as we saw in Section 3.

Then, create great content on topics that solar buyers care about. The next chapter will show you how to do that using keywords in a strategic but natural-sounding way.

Chapter 27

USING KEYWORDS TO TARGET YOUR SOLAR BUYER

When you're confident that your website offers a good user experience, next start creating content optimized for search. And to do that, start by using keywords in your text that your target audiences are already searching for.

You should already have a keyword list from your planning and strategy process. Before that point, you should have developed 1-3 ideal solar buyer personas. Then, for each type of buyer, you should have found a dozen or so terms that real people similar to this type of person searched for on Google when looking for information about solar.

It's best to have keyword lists prepared before you start writing. Having keywords in mind in advance will help you use them naturally in whatever text you create. Keyword lists can even give you ideas for your next text, whether a blog post or an ebook. Whatever you're planning to write, you should select one main audience for the piece and then, when you create the text, be sure to use one or more of the keywords from your list for that audience. If you want to be really strategic about it, you can let the keyword list help you choose a topic in the first place. Then, write your piece around the keyword(s) you've selected.

But however you go about using keywords in developing your content, don't take it too far. Write your text for humans and not for search engines. Don't repeat keywords too often and don't use them in an awkward or artificial way. There's more on how to avoid that below.

For now, it helps to know that Google will give you more credit for your keywords if you place your most important ones within specific content elements of your web page or blog post. These on-page elements include key parts of a web page's content:

* Page Title
* Page URL
* Sub-headlines
* Image Alt Tags
* Outbound Links
* Bolded Text
* Bulleted or Numbered Lists

Some elements found behind the scenes of a blog post (what's called the "back-end" of the website) used to get special consideration in Google rankings but no longer do. For example, the meta description, which is an area on the back-end of on any web page that allows you to add a short summary of the content of that page. In the past, it was unthinkable to publish a blog post without filling the meta description with strategic keywords, whether the text made much sense to humans or not. But then, in 2009, Google announced that neither meta descriptions nor meta keywords factored into their algorithms to rank page results in web search.

Yet, meta descriptions are still important for Google to display the summary of your page that you want web searchers to see, as Moz explains:

Meta description tags, while not important to search engine rankings, are extremely important in gaining user click-through from SERPs [Search Engine Results Pages]. These short paragraphs are a webmaster's opportunity to advertise content to searchers and to let them know exactly whether the given page contains the information they're looking for.

The meta description should employ the keywords intelligently, but also create a compelling description that a searcher will want to click. Direct relevance to the page and uniqueness between each page's meta description is key. The description should optimally be between 150-160 characters.

Unfortunately, too many SEO gurus still harp on meta descriptions because they say that they'll affect your rank in Google, which we now know is not true because Google told us so. Further, reputable authorities on SEO even say that sometimes it's OK to skip the meta description. As Moz puts it,

Use the general rule that if the page is targeting between one and three heavily searched terms or phrases, go with a meta description that hits those users performing that search. If the page is targeting long-tail traffic (three or more keywords)—for example, with hundreds of articles or blog entries, or even a huge product catalog—it can sometimes be wiser to let the engines extract the relevant text, themselves. The reason is simple: When engines pull, they always display the keywords and surrounding phrases that the user has searched for. If a webmaster forces a meta description, they can detract from the relevance the engines make naturally. In some cases, they'll overrule the meta description anyway, but a webmaster can not always rely on the engines to use the more relevant text in the SERP.

Things change so quickly in search engine technology that it's hard to keep up. Even consultants who get paid to help websites do better in search engines may be giving their clients outdated advice.

Here's another example. In the past, a lot of on-page SEO focused on "keyword density." The idea was to select one or more keywords for your page, such as "Boston home solar installer" or "solar thermal payback period" and then try to use those as often as possible in the text of that page and especially in the key areas listed above such as headlines and image tags. However, today most SEO experts reject the concept of keyword density in favor of natural use of search terms.

For example, Matt Ridout of SEO Unique explains that he never calculates keyword density:

> It's like saying to an artist you have too much red on your canvas, use a calculator to work out how much more to add or subtract from the painting. If you follow simple SEO guidelines and do good keyword research you should be fine. At the end of the day it's about the user experience on your site that you should be concentrating on, and stuffing a page full of keywords will just take something away from their experience and could harm your brand.

Keyword density may be a myth. But if you believe in it, you may be doing worse than wasting time on SEO that doesn't work. You may actually be harming your SEO, for two reasons.

First, if you use the keyword too often, Google will notice it and won't like it. Google considers overuse of a keyword on a page to be "keyword stuffing" and if the search engine's crawler catches you doing that, Google may even punish you by demoting your page in search results or removing it from results altogether. Second, Google has gotten much better at understanding natural language, the way humans write it for each other and not for computers. That means you don't need to stick strictly to your keyword terms but can use synonyms or variations and still get credit for those terms with Google.

This will obviously read much more smoothly for your human audience—the only audience that really matters in SEO or anything else online. After all, search engines don't buy solar panels. Only humans do. And Google will no doubt continue to get even better at understanding natural language, so the clearer your prose, the better you'll do as Google improves.

But that doesn't mean you shouldn't be strategic about the language of your page. On-page SEO is still the crucial first step towards doing well in Google for a particular topic. And the good news is, unlike off-page SEO, which relies on attracting other websites to link to yours and can be hit-or-miss, a solar marketer has total control over on-page SEO and thus can see positive results almost right away.

It's very common that businesses will do either too little on-page optimization or too much (keyword stuffing). While it's important to include your keyword as many times as necessary within a page, you don't want to go overboard with keywords either. Here's some advice to get started doing on-page SEO right:

1. Pick a primary keyword (such as "solar power system" or "solar PPA") for each page and focus on optimizing that page for that word. If you oversaturate a page with too many keywords on one page, the page will lose its importance and authority because search engines won't have a clear idea of what the page is about. This is very common on homepages in particular, where too many keywords are used.

2. Place your primary keywords in your headline and sub-headline. These areas of content carry greater weight with search engines.

3. Include the keywords in the body content but don't use them out of context. Make sure they are relevant to the rest of your content, and that they read naturally.

4. Include keywords in the file name of images (e.g. solarfinancing. jpg or homebattery.png) as well as in the alt tag for images.

5. Include the keywords in the page URL and keep the URL clean. For example, for a page about the risks of power purchase agreements, the URL www.mysolarcompany.com/x39912.xml is not

clean. It doesn't help your reader or Google understand what your page is about. A better URL would be www.mysolarcompany. com/dangers-of-solar-PPA.

6. And lastly, as we discussed above, write for humans first and search engines second. Always prepare your content for your audience and then look to optimize it for search. Content written in the reverse order won't read naturally and your visitors will recognize it.

For a good example of effective solar SEO on-page that uses keywords but keeps the text sounding natural, I offer a post on SolarCity's blog, "Joining the Solar Movement," an invitation to join the company's Solar Ambassador program of citizen solar advocates. The word "movement" appears in the headline but also a few times throughout the text. Yet, it never sounds forced or artificial. What it does sound is inspiring. And if you care about solar power, of course you want to be part of the movement, don't you?

Speaking of movement, you'll get more movement of traffic to your site if, after you optimize your content, you then seek high quality websites to link to it. The next chapter will show you how to do that through off-page SEO.

Chapter 28

EARN MORE CREDIT WITH OFF-PAGE SEO

Every solar marketer wants his or her website to reach the #1 position in search engines for searches appropriate to the company's business, whether a residential solar installer, a commercial solar developer, or a PV manufacturer. But because there is only one top spot per keyword phrase, not everyone can make it. So, at least you want to be on the first page of results for your desired term, particularly in your service area. Of course you can buy pay-per-click ads and if you bid enough you can get on that first page. And you can stay there as long as you're still paying for the ads—and paying enough to outbid the competition.

But since most searchers skip over the ads and go directly to the organic search listings, the real question is how can you increase your chances of getting one of the ten organic slots available on that first page?

If you've already written text that you think will interest your audiences using keywords they use in a natural way, that's a good start. But it's not enough. As *Copyblogger* explains,

> Here's the deal. . .much of what determines the ranking position of any particular page is due to factors that are independent from the words on the page, in the form of links from other sites, social

sharing, and other signals. Getting those links and other signals naturally has become the hardest part of SEO, which is why we've seen the mainstream emergence of content marketing as a way to attract links with compelling content.

Put simply: If your content isn't good enough to attract good, natural links and social sharing, it doesn't matter how "optimized" the words on the page are.

So, once you've done good on-page SEO to create content that speaks directly to your readers, then off-page search engine optimization is key to increasing your ranking results. Off-page SEO is about building inbound links, essentially getting other high quality websites to link back to yours. Search engines call this "authority" or "link juice." The more inbound links you have, the more important your site will appear to Google. Thus, the more good inbound links, the higher you'll rank. As Woorank puts it,

Link juice is a colloquial term in the SEO world that refers to the power or equity passed to a site via links from external or internal sources. This power is interpreted as a vote of recommendation toward your site and is one of the most important factors in determining your site's search ranking (and PageRank).

There are many ways to earn links from the web through direct and indirect efforts. Direct effort refers to link building strategies, such as document sharing, guest posting, social media marketing, press release publishing and more...The indirect effort is gained from presenting excellent content (like guides and infographics) on your site that causes readers to share it around the web, linking the pages naturally. The link equity that passes from these sites to your site is the link juice, and this link juice differs in its authority depending on the sites linking to you.

Link building, when done right, isn't easy. Unlike adding links to your own website, which you should be able to do easily if you have a modern content management system, adding links to other websites is usually out of your control. To try to get other sites to link to your site, you will probably have to convince the management of another website that your site represents a resource that the other site's visitors will find valuable. Like almost everything online, this goes back to content. You need to create content that people who run other websites will like and then get the word out to those people.

Here are some tips to start building inbound links. Mostly, they involve you getting out to places online where you can establish your authority, help people with questions, and share information:

1. ANSWER QUESTIONS

Join a question-and-answer website such as Quora, Yahoo Answers, or a Reddit group devoted to solar power. Follow along with the conversation for a while. And then, once you feel comfortable becoming an active participant, start asking and/or answering questions. In your answers you can include a link to a post or page on your site.

2. DO GUEST POSTING

Seek out a website that publishes articles about solar power, home improvement, commercial energy management, or another topic relevant to your business. Spend some time reading the site's articles to get a sense of the tone and approach. Then, come up with a topic that you think might interest the site's readers, and propose it to the site's editor. For example, I proposed writing about solar lead generation to an editor of *Solar Power World* and he accepted the idea, which gave me a chance to write an article about the subject that the website later published.

You could target one of the national renewable energy publications or, perhaps even better, a site that caters to an audience in your local area. If the site decides to publish your article, you probably won't get paid. But you will get a backlink to your website, which could be even more valuable if the article site has a lot of authority with Google.

3. USE SOCIAL MEDIA

Since you control your own social media accounts, it might seem like posting links back to your site on Facebook or Twitter would be a shortcut to getting backlinks to your website. Well, in this case, if it sounds too good to be true, then it probably is. First, due to volume of postings, Google only crawls a small amount of social media content. Second, links from social media are so-called "no follow links" which are programmed to withhold link juice.

Google has said that they ignore such links, but there's evidence that postings on social media will have some indirect benefit to your SEO. As Channel Digital explains, "Overall, Google does use some signals from these social sites as part of their overall ranking algorithm. We recommend that you do not ignore social media and nofollow links as part of your overall ranking/link building strategy. You will be ahead of the game if you can get as many links as you can from a variety of sites, including nofollow and social media links."

4. PUBLISH SHAREABLE CONTENT

Infographics seem to be on top these days, but in the future there may be some other kind of content that people can't stop themselves from sharing around the Internet. If you publish this format of content, you can raise your chances of earning more inbound links. Do the research yourself—for example, profile the solar market in your local area—and then find a designer to put your data in visual form. Of course, once you release an infographic, you still have to get the word out through good on-page optimization and social posts. You can email websites that you think might be interested in using your infographic. And you can even submit your infographic to one of dozens of online directories, such as Reddit Infographics, Mashable Infographics, or I Love Charts.

There are dozens of other ways to earn white hat backlinks from high-quality websites that will raise your ranking in Google. For example, if you're a bit techy minded, then you can try the Moving Man Method advocated by Brian Dean at Backlinko. Using his method, you first locate sites that have changed names, shut down, or moved. Then, find other live sites that are still linking to a page on the dead site. Finally, contact those live sites, tell them that their link is dead, and offer a page or post on your site as a live substitute.

For more ideas on getting inbound links, check out Backlinko.com or read articles by respected writers on SEO. I like Joost de Valk, Rand Fishkin, Joanna Wiebe, and Neil Patel.

Does your company deal with more than one customer group, for example, both homeowners and commercial businesses? Then rinse and repeat the above for each audience.

As you're doing your SEO, make sure to avoid common mistakes. The next chapter will help you do that.

Chapter 29

STUPID SEO TRICKS: AVOID THE MOST COMMON MISTAKES

Let's talk a little more about black hat SEO. According to online ad agency WordStream,

> Black hat SEO refers to a set of practices that are used to increases a site or page's rank in search engines through means that violate the search engines' terms of service. The term "black hat" originated in Western movies to distinguish the "bad guys" from the "good guys," who wore white hats (see white hat SEO). Recently, it's used more commonly to describe computer hackers, virus creators, and those who perform unethical actions with computers.

> It's crucial to realize that implementing black hat SEO tactics and strategies can get your site banned from search engines, excluding you from the number one traffic referral source on the Internet. All SEO's need a proper understanding of black hat SEO and its consequences.

Black hat SEO tricks such as stuffing pages with keywords or creating extra menu items to try to rank well in Google for every city in which you do installations will certainly annoy your human visitors. But they also annoy Google. Even though some black hat tricks may work temporarily, over the long term they're sure to fail. And doing them may even get your website punished by Google.

Even though everyone's been told not to do them, stupid SEO tricks remain surprisingly common these days. Perhaps human impatience combined with the desire to get something for nothing create a natural market for misinformation about what will make you a star in keyword searches. So it's easy to put your website at risk with SEO tricks that won't increase your traffic over the long term but could instead earn you a penalty from Google.

How do you know you shouldn't do black hat SEO? Just listen to Google itself.

FROM THE MOUTH OF THE GOOGLEBOT TO THE EAR OF THE SOLAR MARKETER

Fortunately, defying the laws of physics and biology, the Googlebot itself—Google's own search algorithm in sentient form—has offered a handy list of SEO pet peeves in an open letter at patrickcoombe.com. I've adapted the Googlebot's list below for marketers who run solar company websites:

1. I HAVE VERY SIMPLE RULES

"Please stop trying to get around these very simple guidelines...Please do not be surprised if I decide to apply some sort of action based on your failure to adhere to these basic guidelines. Doorway pages people? Hidden text? Come on now."

So, just because you want to do more residential PV installs around Southern California doesn't mean you should create a whole bunch of duplicate pages with the same text whose only difference is the name of a city: "Home Solar Santa Monica | Home Solar Malibu | Home Solar Rancho Palos Verdes…"

2. HELP MAKE MY LIFE EASIER

"I am Googlebot. I work hard 24/7 365 days a year including Christmas and Ramadan. I don't ever take vacations and I never sleep. Many of you that call yourselves SEO's spend your days crafting elaborate plans to make me think you are better than you actually are. Please stop doing this and make my life easier by making your websites better."

This is an all-around warning against black hat SEO, which is really anything that attempts to make a website appear more authoritative and useful than it really is. So, if you want to rank well in Google searches for residential solar in your area, then don't try to do it with gimmicks intended to catapult you ahead of competitors with long-established websites. Instead, make your website better and more useful to solar buyers than those competitors by creating helpful content. Start by doing a regular blog!

3. BECAUSE ETHICS

"Just because I am owned by a big corporation does not mean your ethics do not apply. Please stop violating my boundaries…I cannot feel pain or emotion but I have sensors to detect when my physical limitations have been violated. Please do not be surprised when I react or lash out at your attempts at violating my boundaries in a negative way. Or when I wait 18 months to respond to your penalty review."

You've been warned. Trying to get away with tricky SEO now can cost you big later.

4. A NOTE TO BLACK HAT SEOS

"Chances are if you have obtained rankings as a result of black hat SEO those rankings are not going to last long…In your mind you are sliding by and getting away with it but just remember I probably just haven't gotten around to even looking at you yet."

I'll assume that marketers for solar companies, whose mission to make the world a better place is more upfront than in other industries, won't intentionally use black hat SEO. But who's to say that the SEO guy you hired has the same high standards?

Be sure to properly supervise any outside SEO jockey. And if he promises quick results (for example, "join this link-sharing network from Ukraine for $29.95 a month and you'll start to see your rank rise next week") then be worried. Any SEO that is supposed to deliver results in a few days or hours is probably garbage. Good SEO takes months or years to build.

5. I'M NOT PERFECT

"You do realize I'm trying to parse and sort through 60 trillion websites, don't you? Sometimes I make mistakes. Sometimes it takes me a few days or weeks to make an adjustment, so bear with me."

Just because you know your main competitor only has a single location in Van Nuys but they come up first in a search for "Solar Panels Bakersfield" doesn't mean it's safe for you to use the same stuffed keywords that they have. That competitor may not have been punished yet, but just be patient. Chances are, sooner or later, the Googlebot will discover that competitor's tricks and make them pay.

6. BUT I'M NOT A MORON

"I will notice when you put something like "Denver Plumbers | Denver Plumbing Company" in every HTML tag and piece of content on your website (and I don't think it's cute.)"

Ditto, of course, if you pepper your website with stuffed keywords like "Denver Solar Lease | Denver Solar PPA | Best Denver Solar Installer | Denver Solar Financing."

7. I HAVE VERY LITTLE PATIENCE

"I was programmed to give second chances. If you do clean your site up and ask nicely, I just might give you another shot. But know this: if I do give you a second chance you are still on my list. Do not think for a second that I won't permanently banish your site from my index."

If you've already been burned once by a Google penalty, then you're probably still twice shy about trying any more black hat SEO. But make sure your SEO guy feels the same way.

8. I'M MORE THAN JUST A BOT

"Don't forget I have a dedicated team of engineers constantly feeding me with information. Sometimes they make manual adjustments, tweaks, or add-ons to my base algorithm...I also accept feedback from the general public."

It can be hard to get through to Google sometimes, but with enough persistence, you can get a human for a live chat for a thornier issue, such as correcting the name of your CEO in a Knowledge Graph box.

The best way to profit from a competitor doing black hat SEO is not to copy their bad behavior, but instead to report them to Google so that they'll get punished and learn to change their evil ways. That in turn will help make the web a better place for everybody.

9. STOP TRYING TO FIGURE ME OUT

"SEO's are constantly trying to figure out a way around doing hard work. Don't forget, not only am I one of the most advanced algorithms in the world, but 1000's of the

brightest minds in the world spend every waking moment of their day to make me better, faster, and stronger. Think of the most complicated boyfriend you've ever had. Multiply that by infinity and you have a starting point of my intelligence."

Solar marketers should forget about technical SEO tricks with stuffed keywords in metatags and focus on just writing content that humans want to read. Write for the homeowner who wants solar on her roof. After that, optimize your text for one or two keywords and add those keywords to a few places where it sounds natural. But don't over-optimize.

10. STOP PINGING, POKING, AND SCRAPING ME

"You do realize most of these 'pings' and weird indexing programs I completely ignore, right? The moment I recognize any of these tools I have a built-in function to ignore them. Stop wasting your time trying to index your website. I index most pages on active sites within a few hours. If you can't wait that long then you are in the wrong business."

If your SEO guy says that he's got a neato program that is set to re-submit your page on net metering rates every 72 hours to Google, then that SEO guy is taking you for a ride.

THE REAL TRICK TO SEO

Actually, there's no real trick.

The Googlebot is just trying to give web searching humans the best experience possible when they search for solar companies.

To help, you should create the best web experience you can for those solar-interested humans. Make sure your website is mobile responsive. Pretty is nice, but easy-to-use is better. Publish content about the costs and benefits of residential solar that homeowners want to see and publish content on commercial solar that solves problems for business owners. Finally, keep putting up new content, because Google likes fresh websites better than stale ones.

Meanwhile, when you're annoyed that a more established competitor's website is coming up higher than yours in a search for "No Money Down Solar Panels" even though your PPA or lease deal is better than theirs and for the last three months your company has been putting lots of SEO love into this particular keyword phrase, have patience. Resist the temptation to take short-cuts and remember what the Googlebot says:

I favor larger websites because they are better than yours. They are far more optimized, more comprehensive, and have been around way longer than yours. They also have a ton of awesome backlinks that weren't bought or created with a tool.

SEO is one of the best ways to attract new visitors to your website, but it's risky to invest in a single strategy for web traffic. It's safer to have a balanced strategy, where you attract traffic from different sources.

The next section will help you get more traffic from one of the best sources, social media, along with email and other online marketing tactics.

LET THE SUN SHINE IN–USING SOCIAL MEDIA WITHOUT WASTING TIME

*The goal of social media is to turn customers
into a volunteer marketing army.*

– JAY BAER

Chapter 30

● ● ●

SOCIAL MEDIA GOES WITH YOUR WEBSITE

The purpose of social media for personal use is to have fun, to stay connected with friends and family, and, of course, to spread cat videos far and wide. A solar marketer should also have some fun on social media. Not only will some fun make your social media time feel less like a chore, but it will help humanize your company and make it more appealing to solar buyers, especially homeowners. But anything you do on social media for business needs to have a purpose beyond growing your fan base or getting more likes and shares. Social media for a solar company needs to help meet that company's goals, whether for more sales leads, or to build branding that will support lead generation in other media such as email or blogs.

Doing social media without a clear goal is just wasting time. So before you get started on social media, ask yourself what benefit you're seeking. And then consider how to make your social media work with your other marketing and sales activities, both online and traditional, to get the most benefit.

And never, ever do social media without first building a modern website, as I discussed in Chapter 17.

Before doing much social media, it's best to publish a few blog posts first. Once you've published a blog post and optimized it for keywords (basically, doing SEO), potential solar customers will find it through Google searches. Eventually.

Getting any decent amount of traffic to your blogs through web searches can take a few months or longer. To jump start traffic for any new blog post, push your blog content out to your audience through social media, email, and other channels online. You can even buy a few ads linking to your post. Once you've published blog posts that your customers would really want to read—not advertorials for your products and services, but articles that offer good advice in an engaging way—then you're ready to let the world see them. Follow these five steps to generate traffic to your solar blog:

1. GO SOCIAL

If you don't have them already, create a presence for your solar company on three or four of the most popular social media services. Start with Facebook and Twitter. Add LinkedIn if you sell commercial solar or if your residential solar customer is likely to be a businessperson. And consider photo-centric services like Instagram and Pinterest if you have great visuals to share that go beyond solar-panels-on-a-roof, such as unusual installations, fun events like sponsorship at a craft brew festival, or intriguing shots of customers. Each service offers easy-to-follow instructions for setting up a new account, but the next chapter will give you tips that will help make your social media profiles more effective for a solar business.

2. POST YOUR POSTS

Publish links to your blog articles when they come out on your company's social profiles. For well performing pieces, consider re-posting them after a couple days, weeks or even months, perhaps using different text to introduce them. Social media software such as HootSuite or Buffer can help you schedule posts in advance to go out on some or all of your different social media accounts.

3. SUBSCRIBE ME

Offer your website visitors the chance to subscribe to your blog by email. Ideally, you should offer options for subscribers to receive new posts daily as they're published or else together in a digest once a week. But even a simple subscription system such as Jetpack Subscriptions (for WordPress sites) that sends out posts as soon as they're published is a good start.

4. BE MY GUEST

Offer your blog articles as guest posts for other blogs or top solar news sites that accept guest articles. This is a win-win for both parties. Web publishers always need more (quality) content and in exchange, you may get more traffic from the other site's visitors. For example, I adapt posts from my own company's website into articles for web publications in the energy industry and on influential blogs that post on energy along with other topics like culture, history, and society.

5. REUSE AND RECYCLE

Once you've got a few blog posts on the same topic, consider bundling them together as an ebook that you can offer on your site for free to any visitor who fills out a form with basic contact information. Then, to promote your new ebook, write a blog post about it and then share that post using the methods discussed above. If you integrate your blog well into your website and make the blog part of an inbound marketing program, blog traffic will spill over to the rest of your website. You'll then be on your way towards converting web visitors into solar leads and customers for solar installations.

All five of these tactics can help you get relevant traffic to your website that can convert to qualified sales leads. But perhaps the king of all outreach tools these days is social media. So let's talk a bit more about how to do well on social media services.

Social media can be a good way to reach potential customers and other important audiences, especially for residential solar companies. Every day, more top residential solar installers are engaging with consumers on social media. For example:

* Sunnova, RGS Energy, and Verengo Solar are on the big three social media sites—Facebook, Twitter and LinkedIn—plus YouTube.
* SolarCity and Vivint Solar are on the usual services but also Google+.
* Baker Electric Solar might win the social media prize. Along with a presence on all five platforms mentioned above, they also engage on Pinterest, Yelp, and a company blog (which counts as social media, depending on how you define it).

Even some commercial solar developers, such as HB White Canada and Borrego Solar, display links to social media accounts on their websites. All of which shows that solar companies are responding to the new climate for solar marketing, which is characterized by two recent developments:

1. **Affordability and Competition**—The falling cost of equipment plus more financing options including PACE, equipment leases, and PPAs have made solar power, whether onsite or off, more affordable for homeowners, businesses, and government alike. This has created more demand for solar, which has in turn attracted new players to the market. To try to beat rising competition, solar companies have gotten more creative (and sometimes more aggressive) in their marketing.

2. **The Social Web**—The advent of social media, such a big deal that pundits call it Web 2.0, has made possible true two-way communication between web publishers and their audiences. That means members of the public now expect home solar installers and other solar companies to listen to them and even answer their questions online.

Both of these developments have created a Wild West environment for solar marketing, especially on the residential side. In top solar markets such as California, New York, and Massachusetts, homeowners are increasingly busy fending off telemarketers, home visits, and other forms of aggressive marketing from solar installers who apparently believe that old-school aluminum-siding-style marketing is the best way to sell advanced energy.

Though most solar companies aren't doing anything wrong, consumer complaints to federal regulators and action by state attorneys general have drawn attention to the bad apples in solar marketing, creating distrust for residential installers as a whole.

Social media can be a powerful channel for installers to develop relationships with potential customers that have value on both sides. Two-way social media communication between homeowners and a solar company can help build the trust needed for homeowners to make the big investment that is going solar.

SEVEN STEPS TO SOCIAL MEDIA SUCCESS

Unlike buying ads or hiring a telemarketing vendor, social media is free to use. But it doesn't run itself, and managing one or more social media accounts well takes up employee time. Overall, to get maximum benefit out of that investment in time, solar companies should have a solid social media plan. It doesn't have to be complicated. But you should follow each of the seven steps below for the best chance of success.

1. DETERMINE GOALS, AUDIENCE, COMPETITORS, AND CHALLENGES

Social media software company HootSuite suggests that any organization using social media develop SMART Goals: Specific, Measurable, Attainable, Relevant, and Time-bound. For example, on Pinterest you can share photos that show delighted solar customers. You can do this by posting three photos a week that will achieve five likes and a couple of comments each to start with. Once you have more followers, you can shoot for more ambitious goals.

And if you haven't yet developed buyer persona profiles for your 1-3 ideal customers, now might be a good time to start. After all, you need to understand the audiences you want to reach in order to communicate with them effectively on social media.

2. DISCOVER THE BEST PRACTICES FROM SOCIAL MEDIA PROS

While experts disagree about the exact ratio of your own content to other's content that you should share in your social media posts, the average solar company will be safe following the 80/20 rule. That is, limit your own content—company news, new products, promotions—to 20% of your total of social media posts. Fill the remaining 80% of posts with content from other organizations, news sites, companies, people, and groups.

Sharing mostly stuff from others that's helpful, informative, or entertaining to an audience interested in solar helps build trust. It also establishes your company as what *Copyblogger* calls a "likable authority." If they learn to feel comfortable with your company by seeing your posts over a period of weeks or months, social media followers are more likely to think of you when they're ready to buy solar.

3. SIMPLIFY MONITORING

Which solar marketer has time to check in on Twitter, Facebook, LinkedIn, and other services multiple times each day? All too many solar marketing pros find themselves falling behind in keeping up with social media posts from fans, followers, peers, and competitors and to reply to customer comments and questions when appropriate.

Hootsuite, Buffer, and other social media management programs make it much easier to stay on top of all your social media accounts. Buffer is a clean, straightforward tool for publishing and scheduling posts on different services. Hootsuite is a more involved program that helps you publish your own posts, monitor what people say about you or on topics you care about, and even respond when you decide to do so.

4. GROW YOUR FOLLOWING

Connecting with your social media audience is really about offering valuable content that people want to consume, like, and share. And that means going beyond sharing company news—"Hey, check out this great new racking system!"—or yet another list of tips on how homeowners can be more "green." Much better would be a short video of an unusual solar installation, an ebook busting the top myths about home solar, or a checklist of things any homeowner should look for in a trustworthy solar installer.

5. CREATE ENGAGING POSTS

People behave differently on Facebook than they do on Twitter or LinkedIn. To succeed on each service, you need to adapt both your text and pictures to what users expect. By the way, you are making custom graphics for some of your social posts, aren't you? Text content with custom graphics is more likely to get shared than text alone. And if graphics have your company's website address on them, they can build your brand and send traffic to your website, too. Fortunately, DIY design services such as Canva have made social graphics easier to create. But you can even do fine social media graphics in PowerPoint.

6. SCHEDULE YOUR SOCIAL MEDIA POSTS AND PROMOTE YOUR CONTENT

Creating a spreadsheet of planned social media posts for the next few weeks makes it easier for marketers to coordinate their campaigns, grow their social reach, and put out more content. For example, HootSuite lets you upload an Excel spreadsheet directly to their service to conveniently schedule your future posts on several social media services.

7. BE CONSISTENT

Social media profiles are just like a website. They need new content on a regular basis. A social site that you post to once a month won't grow a following or drive traffic. Consistency is the key. If possible, you should assign an employee (or hire a freelancer or agency) explicitly assigned to manage your social media accounts to keep them all fresh and make sure that your activity is effective.

The next chapter will go into how you can create a presence on major social media services that will start solid relationships with potential solar buyers in your area.

Chapter 31

SOCIAL MEDIA PROFILES THAT WORK

So, now you know you can get traffic to your blog, and the rest of your website, if you use social media services well. You also know that, for your company's online presence, it's not enough to have a Facebook page but no website. That strategy would be penny-wise and pound-foolish, as it would carry all the risks of digital sharecropping—of building your online property on somebody else's online land.

It's more important to have a website than to have a Facebook page. But once you have a good website, then it's time to start regularly using at least a couple social media services for your business. Before you can take advantage of social media, you need to set up your own accounts on the services you want to use. And I'd recommend that as a solar business, you set up two or three social media accounts. Select the services based on whether your company caters primarily to consumers or to businesses.

But don't set up more social media accounts than you will be able to adequately manage over the coming months and years.

In its need for continuous feeding and care, a social media account is just like a website. It's not an online brochure that you write up, lay out, print, and then forget until you reprint it again in five years. Instead, a social media account is more like a conversation. If you don't say something every so often, the people you're talking with will think that the conversation is over and will move on. An abandoned Facebook page isn't much value to your company. it may even hurt your credibility, by making solar buyers wonder if you're still in business.

WHICH SERVICES TO CHOOSE

Every solar company, whether one that installs solar arrays on home rooftops or one that manufactures inverters, should be on Facebook. Facebook is the largest and best known social media service, with more than 1.65 billion people actively using it every month as of mid-2016. That's more than the population of any country on earth. Both residential and commercial solar contractors should set up Facebook pages. But makers of components such as storage equipment, racking systems, or inverters that sell only to other businesses have also made very good use of Facebook, for example, to create demand among end-users for their products.

After Facebook, Twitter and/or LinkedIn may make sense, depending on your offerings and your audience.

Let's start with Facebook. You'll be more likely to find value in using Facebook for your solar business if you have the right expectations from the beginning. First, you'll get less free traffic than you may have expected. We've already talked about the change to Facebook's algorithm that downgraded business posts. As a business rather than a person or a non-profit organization, you'll get less free traffic from your page than you would have gotten a few years ago. In an effort to provide more relevant content to its members, by downgrading business posts Facebook also created more demand for ads. How convenient—for Facebook's profits, that is. Of course, it's not so convenient for businesses accustomed to getting a good flow of free traffic to and *from* their Facebook pages.

Nonetheless, a solar company can use this to its advantage. I'll talk a little below on how to buy ads effectively on Facebook. In the meantime, even if you don't plan to buy ads now, you should still start a Facebook page just because these days your audiences will expect your company to have one. If nothing else, buyers will use your Facebook page—along with your website—to do basic research on your company and check you out before they make their decision on where to get solar.

So you need to be on Facebook. But selecting another social media service or two will depend on who your solar business serves and what audiences you most want to reach in your marketing. A residential solar installer may want to be on Twitter. An installer with lots of great photos to show off will want to share them on Pinterest or Instagram. The additional benefit of those services is that they have a high proportion of members who are women, an audience traditionally ignored by solar installers but with great influence over household purchasing decisions. For all of these services, be sure to follow and/or "like" popular local companies, events, attractions, and groups, a tactic that helps your company establish itself as engaged with your local and regional scene.

A commercial solar contractor or developer should certainly be on LinkedIn, which is not just for job-seekers but also for companies looking to connect with potential customers and partners.

Other social media services can be useful to your business as well, once you're a bit further along in your social media outreach. If you have videos, post them on YouTube. The social media landscape is constantly changing and individual services will rise in popularity. In the early days of social media, it was all about MySpace and Digg. Today Facebook and Twitter are the ones to beat with Instagram rising fast. In a few years, a service you haven't even heard of may be on top.

But for now, it's safe to get started with the three established services used by solar businesses, Facebook, Twitter, and LinkedIn. The next three chapters will cover each one.

Chapter 32

USING FACEBOOK FOR BUSINESS

To use Facebook for business, you must first have set up a Facebook account for yourself under your own name. That means you'll have to have a Facebook personal profile. If you're worried about privacy and want to keep your business and personal lives separate online, your personal page can remain accessible only to your friends and family if you choose. But since you want the maximum exposure for your business on Facebook, you'll want your business page to be open to the public. Fortunately, they're two separate things on Facebook and if someone likes your business page it doesn't mean they can see your personal profile.

Once you have an account with Facebook and a personal profile, then you can create a page for your business. First, go to this URL to get started:

https://www.facebook.com/pages/create.php

Then, you'll have to select from one of six categories for your page. Depending on the size of your company and how big your service area, you should either choose "Local business or place" or "Company, organization, or institution." You can change the category and even the name of the page later if you need to.

For a local business, a physical address will show up prominently on your page. This can be handy to highlight your office and make it easy for people interested in solar to find you. But if you have multiple locations, then you should probably create your business page as a company rather than a local business. Don't create separate Facebook local business pages for each of your locations. Having more than one business page will be difficult to manage and won't add much value for your potential customers. Instead, just start one single Facebook business page where you can mention the areas that you serve. Then link to your website there with your full list of locations and contact information for each.

Facebook will then walk you through the rest of the process to put in a short description, select a URL and put in a profile picture, which should be at least 180 pixels wide by 180 pixels tall in size. Square images work best.

Next, you should put in a cover image, which will go in the rectangular area that goes all the way across your Facebook page at the top. In the longer term, you'll want to have an attractive header shot formatted just for Facebook and cropped to the correct size. If you don't want to hire a designer, one of the DIY design programs online such as Canva offers attractive templates for a Facebook cover image.

However, if you want to get started quickly and get your business page out to the world, you can certainly put up an existing photo. Some ideas for a solar installer:

* A shot of your installation staff in front of your office
* A photo of you or one of your people with a happy customer
* A view of an attractive rooftop array from one of your customers

Since Facebook cuts off about 15% of your picture on both the left and the right when your page is displayed on a phone, select a shot with the interesting stuff somewhere in the middle rather than on one side or the other where it might get cut off.

When you've got your image ready, just upload it following Facebook's instructions. If it's not cropped exactly right for the available area, you can move the image around to get the positioning you want. Since the photo will appear as an update in your timeline once you post it, you may also want to put in some information about it. Facebook lets you add a description along with tags, location, and a date.

There are a few more things you should do before you let people know that your new Facebook business page is online. First, fill out the profile as completely as you can. This will include when your company started, a longer description with your mission, a phone number, and an email address. Don't skip this step and plan to come back later. You'll lose credibility with your visitors if this basic information isn't filled out when you launch your business page.

If your solar firm has walk-in business hours, it's important to list these on your Facebook page in the hours section. Customers are very turned off by businesses that don't list basic things like addresses, hours, and availability.

Then, if you have anyone else in your company who you want to let make changes to your new business page, add collaborators using the **Page Roles** tab in the page settings section. You can give people different levels of access. For example, Facebook automatically makes you the Admin of any page that you start. You could add another Admin if you want your partner, co-owner, or marketing director to be able to change anything on your business page. Or, you could leave yourself as the sole Admin and add other employees at lower levels of access, so they can add posts but can't change your company information or delete your page.

Finally, before letting people know about your page, publish your first status update. Here are some ideas for your first post:

* A link to an article from a newspaper on the spread of solar to businesses in the area
* A photo showing customers standing in front of their home with PV panels on the roof

* A video covering something like installing or turning on a new solar array
* An event such as a seminar you've scheduled for homeowners at a community center
* A milestone such as your 1,000[th] rooftop PV installation

But whatever your first update, make sure it has a picture, as updates with images get much more attention than those without. As of this writing, videos that play right in your Facebook window rather than making you click through to your website, YouTube, or somewhere else, seem to do better than anything else on Facebook right now. But in the future there will no doubt be a new hot way to get more attention with multimedia on Facebook. The point is, you should give the people what they want, and what the Facebook people want is images and short videos.

Just a reminder that the culture of social media is non-promotional. That means you should not use your business Facebook page to run free commercials for your new products or special discounts. You can mention these things once in a while, but 80% of your posts should be just information or entertainment. You might think it's silly, but your fans probably wouldn't mind if you posted a video of kittens once in a while (or, say, kids splashing in the wading pool at the company barbecue). It might soften your image and make your company look more approachable, which can only help sales.

And if you could find a video with kittens, kids, and PV panels, well then, you might just have struck Facebook solar marketing gold.

Once you've published three to five posts, then you're ready to work on getting the first 100 friends for your business page. Start by asking your personal friends to like it. Then, if you have employees or colleagues, invite them. Ask your colleagues to invite their family and friends also. Once you have a couple dozen people on the page, then add it to your website with one of the common website widgets out there, such as Page Plugin. You should even list your business Facebook page with a link to its address in your email signature. Doing all these things will help you get early fans, which will make your page look more appealing to people who come along later. Success, after all, breeds success and people are more willing to join a club that already has members.

WHAT FACEBOOK ADS CAN TEACH YOU

As we discussed earlier, sometimes the only online marketing activity that a solar contractor will undertake is to buy ads on Google or Facebook. We've seen the challenges with this tactic. For example, an advertiser can blow through their budget pretty quickly without giving their company much to show for it in terms of website visitors, leads, or customers.

But, as I also mentioned, sometimes ads can be helpful to drive traffic to a new website or a new offer until you are able to attract visitors from longer-lasting sources such as organic Google searches or your email list. And for now, Facebook ads are a better value than those on Google.

I won't spend much time with Facebook ads here, since you can find plenty of guides online about how to buy them effectively, and this book is really about earning attention organically online rather than paying for traffic. But for those who'd like to check into Facebook ads, I'll just give you the link to start buying ads (https://www.facebook.com/business) and let you know that you can buy different kinds of ads that will get you different things on Facebook:

* More likes for your business Facebook page
* Clicks through to your homepage or a landing page on your website
* More views for a particular Facebook update ("boosted post")

Targeting your ads on Facebook has become a fine art—or a science, if you use a lot of data—and Facebook marketer Ed Leake recommends that you set your ads to go to four kinds of audiences to get the most benefit:

1. Your Current Page Fans
2. Current Customer 1% Lookalike
3. Your Website Visitors (aka remarketing/retargeting)
4. Your Website Visitors 1% Lookalike

His video "4 Winning Facebook Audiences for Better Results" will give you all the details.

USE FACEBOOK FOR RESEARCH

Even if you don't plan to buy ads on Facebook, you can use their ad buying tool to do quick market research free of charge. Facebook lets you target your ads by geographical location, age, gender, languages and, most importantly, interests.

To select interests you can browse Facebook's categories or put in your own term, to see what it brings up. For example, I told Facebook I wanted to reach men and women across ages in the San Francisco Bay Area who are interested in solar power. Facebook then showed me how many people I could expect my ads to reach as well as the potential reach, which is the total audience of Facebook users who have indicated an interest in solar power in the Bay Area, which was 42,000.

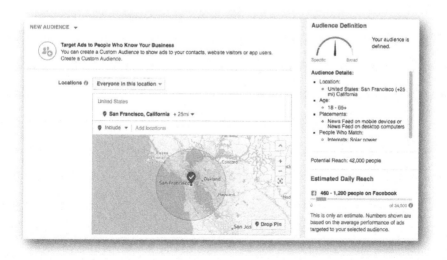

Now, since most Americans are on Facebook these days, is it fair to say that this number might give you a sense of the total market for solar in the San Francisco area, both residential and commercial?

Not necessarily. There will be people on Facebook who haven't expressed an interest in solar explicitly but who still might want it on their home or business. Likewise, just telling Facebook that you like solar energy doesn't mean you're ready to get a new array installed next week. But, knowing that more than 40,000 Facebook members have indicated an interest in solar power means that there is a substantial market in the area.

Of course, given that it's the Bay Area, where people are famous for being into both the environment and into new technology, it's no surprise that lots of people there care about solar power. But if you're somewhere else, you may be surprised to see the figure in your local area. For example, in Kansas City, Missouri, as of this writing you can find 25,000 Facebook members interested in solar, while in Atlanta, even more people on Facebook have an interest in solar than in the Bay Area—61,000. Since there are many fewer solar contractors serving Georgia than northern California, Atlantans who care about solar may be underserved by solar companies currently doing business in their area. For a local installer looking to expand to a new market, this could be good market intelligence.

Chapter 33

TWITTER AS A BUSINESS TOOL

As of June 2016, Twitter boasted 310 million active monthly users, with 21% of its accounts in the United States. That would mean more than 50 million Americans use Twitter on a regular basis. The question for a solar contractor is, are those people likely to be your customers? And is Twitter a good place to reach them?

According to a study done in 2015 by the Pew Internet and American Life Project, the biggest group of Twitter users by age is people in their twenties and thirties. Not surprisingly, people over 65 hardly use the service at all.

On the one hand, people at the beginning of their careers own homes at a low rate. On the other hand, as young people start to get into their thirties and forties, more of them are buying their first place. That alone makes them good emerging buyers for solar. If they're not in the market this year, they may be next year, so it's good to form a relationship with them now. Also, younger adults are more aware of and friendly to solar than older generations, so even if they're not ready to be your buyers yet, they may be willing to become your ambassadors, spreading good news about solar to their friends and family who may be ready to buy.

The other demographic quality of Twitter users in particular that makes them attractive for solar companies is that they tend to live overwhelmingly in cities and suburbs where demand for solar is highest rather than rural areas where solar adoption is slower.

So, while Twitter is not yet—and may never become—as crucial as Facebook for any kind of company that installs solar panels, whether at residential, commercial, or even utility-scale, Twitter is definitely a good bet for residential solar installers. It's probably worthwhile for commercial solar contractors as well.

How to get started? Even if you know nothing about Twitter, you probably know that unlike status updates on Facebook or LinkedIn that can be as long as you like, on Twitter you post "tweets" that are limited to 140 characters long. You can like tweets, share them by retweeting, receive comments on your tweets, and comment back to your commenters.

What you may not know is that just like Facebook or LinkedIn, on Twitter you can also attach links, photos, and videos to your tweets. Adding multimedia makes your updates more appealing and gets you more likes and retweets. As of this writing, Twitter is planning to exempt links and multimedia from the 140-character limit, giving you more text to use for your tweet.

So, if you don't have one yet, to get started, you need to open a Twitter account. Unlike Facebook, you need not first have a personal account. All you need is a valid email address to go with the account. Choose a username that reflects your company branding. You can either use your personal name or your company name (or a variation on either one, depending on what's still available on Twitter). If you are already known in the industry as a leader in some way—for example, you speak at events a couple times a year or more or you've written a book—then you should stick with your own name. Otherwise, to get maximum benefit for your company, you should choose a Twitter username that represents the company brand.

As on Facebook, you can post two profile images. The small one can be your face if you've started a personal account, or your logo for a company account. If your logo isn't the right shape for the little image, then use some other image there, such as a photo of a PV panel, and put your logo in the bigger image. Just as with Facebook, it helps to have attractive, professional-looking images, especially in the bigger spot. If you don't want to hire a designer, use a DIY design tool such as Canva. Just as such services offer templates for Facebook images, so they offer Twitter image templates too.

On Twitter you can add also a third image to customize your background. I'd recommend restraint here. Too many Twitter accounts are cluttered up by bright colored backgrounds that wind up looking garish and distract from the Twitter feed.

Then, as on Facebook, fill out your profile information completely. Be sure to include a link to your website. For a solar contractor, all your social media accounts should support what you do on your website. It doesn't mean that every tweet has to have a link to your site. In fact, to avoid looking too promotional, only the occasional tweet should point to your site. But if your Twitter followers are inspired to learn more about you, make it as easy as possible for them to get to your website.

Once you have pictures up and your profile filled out, then you should start seeking followers for your new Twitter feed. And ironically, the way to get your own followers on Twitter is to start by following other companies and people. That's because, unless you're already super famous, Twitter has its own etiquette that's different from, and more egalitarian than, Facebook. On Facebook your page will get fans but on Twitter your account will get followers. And the custom on Twitter is that if someone follows you, then you should follow them back in return. That's actually how most new Twitter accounts get their first few hundred followers.

Ultimately, for Twitter to be really useful to your company, it's better to follow a few hundred good feeds than thousands of accounts that don't interest you and add little value for your followers. So, focus on accounts that tweet about solar power. I recommend that you seek out accounts in a few related industries and areas:

* Your customers
* Other local solar installers in your area (if they're your competition, it's good to see what they're doing and perhaps even give them a like or retweet once in a while just to keep things friendly)

* Big national solar contractors (ditto)
* Your business partners, suppliers, contractors, and vendors
* Realtors in your area, especially green-friendly ones
* Solar industry groups and publications
* Environmental groups that post about clean energy
* Personal Twitter accounts that post about clean energy

Twitter can help you find people you know by scanning your email address book.

Don't worry if your feed starts to get followed by people or companies you don't know. At the beginning, stay focused on whom you follow. After setting up a Twitter feed for your solar energy company, I recommend that you follow nearly everyone who follows you, unless they're spammers, such as people who sell Twitter followers. (By the way, you should never buy followers or fans on Twitter or any other social media service). Also, don't follow back accounts that post tweets that are inappropriate to appear in a company feed, such as accounts offering pictures of women in bikinis from some Eastern European country.

Once you do have your first couple hundred Twitter followers, you can get pickier about who you follow back.

Finally, once you've got a few followers, start to participate. First, read other people's messages. Then, once you feel comfortable with Twitter's format, start putting out your own messages. You'll notice that there are five types of message on Twitter:

1. **Tweet:** a short message you send out to everyone who follows you, which shows up in their own Twitter feeds. This is the heart of Twitter communication.
2. **@Reply:** a message you send out as a reply to a message you received. The @reply is a public message that mentions the Twitter username of the person. It shows up in the tweet stream of the Twitter feed that you mention.

3. **Mention:** a message you send out that mentions another Twitter username. A mention tweet includes the name of a Twitter user but is not a reply to a previous tweet from that person. To be successful in mentioning another user but landing this tweet in your own feed too, the @name of the mention cannot be the first entry in the tweet field. Instead, it should be located somewhere in the body of the tweet after the first character, eg., "Great @hubspot review of @adobe's new design platform @adobespark; very thorough, instructive. #design #socialmedia"

4. **Direct message (DM):** a message you send privately to another Twitter user. You can only send a DM to someone who follows you.

5. **Retweet (RT):** a message created and sent by someone else that you share with the people who follow you. It's very easy to share tweets—just click the retweet icon under any tweet.

A few tips will make your tweets work well for your solar contracting company.

First, unlike Facebook, where posting two or three times a week is sufficient but once a day is a good maximum, on Twitter you can post every day, multiple times per day. Since Twitter is more of a news feed, it's easy for your followers to miss a particular tweet if they don't happen to be online when it goes up. So you can even re-publish tweets over a period of several days. But if you do this, it's best to modify the phrasing of your tweet a bit each time, so those followers who do see it more than once won't find your tweet repetitive.

Second, listen to what your audiences on Twitter are talking about, especially when it comes to solar. Then, jump in to help. If they have questions, offer answers, perhaps including a link to more information. If they bring up a controversy, weigh in with your perspective. If they've posted a photo that you like, like and retweet it with your own comment.

Third, drive traffic to your website, and especially your blog, by posting stuff that will be helpful and interesting to your audiences, whether it's a your latest blog post on the current solar incentives in your area, an infographic you did on how double-sided PV panels work (with a link to your product page on those panels), or a checklist of the top ten things that will qualify your house for rooftop solar.

However, don't just post boring, routine pages from your website, such as your products or services listings. A video of an unusual solar installation—no matter who installed it—would be more interesting. And too many posts on what you're doing will turn off your Twitter followers. On average, for every one tweet about your company or from your site, share four or five tweets that are about solar in general and come from other websites.

You can even share selected tweets from your competitors once in a while. You may not want to share a customer case-study or their pricing page. But if they tweet news about solar incentives in your state, for example, your followers would probably want to know about that too. We call this the Macy's and Gimbels approach from *Miracle on 34th Street*. You'll remember in that classic Christmas film, the new Santa Claus at Macy's started sending customers to Gimbels if Macy's didn't have the toy the customer wanted. At first, Macy's management was furious. But then, the policy started creating so much goodwill among customers that it actually increased business for Macy's.

It may seem counterintuitive to post content from competitors. But this low-key (and confident) approach actually makes you appear more likable, more helpful, and more of an authority. And that will make you more trustworthy to followers and customers alike, which will lead to more business from solar buyers.

Fourth, back on your website, make it easy for visitors to connect with you on Twitter. Display at least two kinds of Twitter buttons on your website. First, in the header and/or the footer of your site, post a button for visitors to follow you on Twitter. Second, at the top and/or bottom of pages and posts, display a button for visitors to share that page or post on their Twitter feeds (your site should also display buttons to let visitors post on other major social media services too, from Facebook to LinkedIn).

Fifth, if you're active on Twitter, you should consider posting your Twitter feed on your website, perhaps in the sidebar on in the footer. Twitter offers a widget that will let you do this easily. Only add it to your website if you're committed to regularly posting on Twitter. A live website feed from Twitter displaying your last post dated four months ago makes you look unengaged with the web, and so behind-the-times, which is bad for business in today's connected world.

Using Twitter well is a big topic in itself that will change over time as Twitter adds new features. You can get the latest advice on using Twitter from blogs such as those run by HootSuite or Social Media Examiner.

A key feature of Twitter is hashtags. Since first appearing on the service in 2007, hashtags have spread to other social media services, including Facebook and Instagram. As Rebecca Hiscott explains on Mashable:

> On Twitter, the pound sign (or hash) turns any word or group of words that directly follow it into a searchable link. This allows you to organize content and track discussion topics based on those keywords. So, if you wanted to post about the Breaking Bad finale, you would include #BreakingBad in your tweet to join the conversation. Click on a hashtag to see all the posts that mention the subject in real time.

People use hashtags to follow and to share share celebrity news (#MerylStreep), promote causes (#WorldMeatFreeDay), get psyched for the workweek (#MotivationMonday) or even connect with other people on Twitter (#FollowFriday, now shortened to #FF).

Businesses can use general business hashtags (#SMB, #startups, #marketing, #sales, #networking) to get or share business advice. Bigger businesses, especially brands that are well known by consumers, may create their own hashtags about their company (#Coke, #DietCoke, #MyCokeRewards) or around a marketing campaign. For example, Domino's Pizza encouraged followers to tweet with #letsdolunch. Then, once the number of tweets reached 85,000, Domino's dropped prices by more than half during the hours of 11 a.m. and 3 p.m. that day.

In the solar industry, big national installers do the same thing, with the most popular example being #solarcitychat. But even a smaller company can invent its own hashtag and try to get people to use it.

All solar companies should try tweeting with the hashtags #solar, #solarenergy or #solarpower and see if it gets them more retweets and responses. More specific industry hashtags such as #PV or #solarpanels can reach a more targeted insider audience, while more general hashtags such as #RenewableEnergy or #ActOnClimate will reach a broader audience that is likely to include homeowners and businesspeople who may be interested in getting solar for themselves.

A variation on the hashtag is to use the @ symbol. As Hiscott explains,

> Keep in mind that the @ symbol does something completely different. Using @ before a person's Twitter handle will tweet at him directly, letting him know you have written to him via the @ Connect tab. A hashtag will not. Sometimes users will hashtag a celebrity's name instead of using her Twitter handle—it is acceptable to tweet #Lorde or @lordemusic. But if you are trying to reach someone directly, don't use a hashtag.

The @ symbol can be very useful to reach a particular person with a tweet that you think will interest them. For example, when I quote someone in a blog post or article I've just published online, I will mention the author or her organization with the @ symbol, for example, @RockyMtnInst. A residential solar installer could use the @ symbol to reach an existing customer whose story of home solar you just posted on your website. That way, the customer can like your tweet and hopefully, retweet it to their followers, which will get you more attention on Twitter.

As with anything online, less is often more. Don't use more than two or three hashtags or @ mentions in a single tweet. If you're going to invent your own hashtags, don't make them too long (#KickCoalToTheCurbWithSolar) or people will be unlikely to use it. Also, if your hashtag is too promotional (#LongIslandSolarBigSavings) it will make you appear spammy.

A Twitter feed can quickly get so crowded that it's hard to follow. Hashtags can help cut through the clutter. If you're using a service such as HootSuite or TweetDeck to monitor Twitter, you can set that service up to give you a feed of all the posts in a particular hashtag such as #PV or #solarpanels.

Finally, if you're new to hashtags, it might seem like an extra step that you can safely skip. However, hashtags can get you much more attention on Twitter or other services, so try to start getting in the habit of putting at least a single hashtag in your tweets. And though hashtags often come at the end of a tweet, you can also put them in the middle, which will make it easier for you to use them (eg, "It's time to remove barriers to #solar power in every state").

Chapter 34

USING LINKEDIN TO MARKET SOLAR

Unlike Facebook and Twitter, LinkedIn is all about business. "If I were forced to choose between using only one social networking site for my business, from Twitter, Facebook, YouTube, and other social networking sites, I would choose LinkedIn, hands down," writes LinkedIn marketer Lewis Howes. "I still love these other social networking sites, but LinkedIn is by far the most powerful for your business and career."

As Howes puts it,

Being that it is the largest business networking site in the world, there is a mindset shift when users log on to LinkedIn compared to logging on their cousin sites, Twitter or Facebook. The mood changes, the messages are more professional. Conversations are geared toward partnerships and transactions, as opposed to how funny you looked in your birthday pictures, and everything is centered around advancing careers or building businesses.

With 433 million total members (and 128 million in the United States) as I write this, LinkedIn is the largest social media service on earth for business networking. And it's growing—two new members join every second. Its focus on business is partially why LinkedIn has more CEOs as members than any other social media service and also why 59% of LinkedIn members have a household income higher than $50,000 per year, with 28% passing $100,000 annual household income.

If you do commercial solar or you sell solar services to businesses, then you should have an account on LinkedIn. But even if you only install roof-top arrays on homes, you may still want to consider establishing a presence for yourself on LinkedIn, as it's a good way to reach affluent consumers.

As on Facebook, LinkedIn requires you to have a personal profile but will also let you create a page for your business. Most LinkedIn gurus will tout the advantages of a business page but I'm not convinced that it's worth the time to maintain both a personal profile and a business page on LinkedIn unless your customers are mostly other businesses. However, it can't hurt to create a LinkedIn business page even if you only update it a couple times a year, because it's free and it's another way for people to find you. As with your own website, on a LinkedIn company page you can post information about your products and services, including video.

Unlike Facebook and Twitter, in theory, you can't just connect with any other member you want on LinkedIn. To make the service more valuable to its preferred audience of busy corporate executives, LinkedIn encourages you to connect only with people you already know or to seek out new people by asking for introductions from contacts you already have.

But as of this writing, you can now connect directly with people who are second-degree contacts, which means that you have one connection in common. And for people who are separated from you by three degrees, there's nothing to stop you from trying to connect with them also. After you hit the Connect button, another screen will appear, asking how you know the person. You can simply say that you work with them through your current company, which is technically true since you're with that company now when you're trying to contact them. Since the person probably won't recognize your name, if you customize the message to explain why you want to connect you'll have a better chance that they'll accept the connection.

And speaking of free, LinkedIn is the only one of the three established social media services that offers a paid membership—and even if you buy it, they still show you ads. The primary benefit for members of LinkedIn Premium is the ability to get more data on other members and to send them InMail messages. Depending on how many messages you want to send per month, premium membership starts at about $30 a month for three messages and goes up to more than $100 for dozens of messages. Near the top of this range, LinkedIn's Sales Navigator Professional version provides a lead-builder tool, lead recommendations, and real-time insights on existing accounts and leads, making LinkedIn Premium a good investment for well-capitalized salespeople. But for most solar installers, the free membership will be sufficient to get started. Once you've gotten a feel for their free tools, you may want to consider a paid subscription to LinkedIn.

Brian Halligan and Dharmesh Shah of HubSpot suggest that, once you've filled out your own profile fully and added a page for your company, that one of the best ways to market your business on LinkedIn is to start your own group.

"Groups are a very powerful feature of the LinkedIn system," they write in their book *Inbound Marketing: Attract, Engage, and Delight Customers Online.* "A LinkedIn Group is essentially an online community of people interested in a particular topic (whatever the focus of the group is)."

As of May 2016, there were more than two million groups on LinkedIn. Many of them are dormant but many others are also active, with new posts every week or even daily. Starting your own group is fast, easy, and free, and helps you establish authority on LinkedIn while connecting you to people who might become new solar vendors, partners, employees, or even customers. Depending on what your company does in solar, especially if it's residential or commercial, you should look for an existing LinkedIn group that seems likely to have the audience you want and appears to be active. Then, based on what's already out there, you can decide if starting a new group might meet a need that existing groups are not serving.

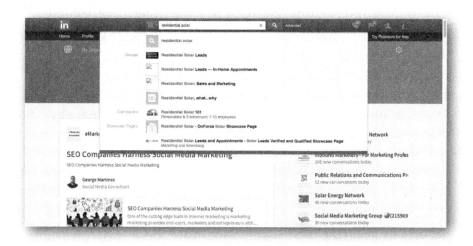

You can search for groups by keyword in the search box above the main navigation bar. The screenshot shows a search for "residential solar." Unfortunately, it's not promising. Though there are four groups listed, the thumbnail image for two of them are broken, a sign that the groups have gone dormant. And the icon on the fourth group indicates that it was auto-generated by LinkedIn. Only the first group listed, Residential Solar Leads, has a custom thumbnail image that shows up properly.

The next screen shows that when you check out the group, it does appear to be big, with 766 members, but there's no way to tell how active the group is until you become a member. You can request membership in the group by clicking the "Ask to join" button circled in the image. Before that, you can decide if the group interests you by reading the description:

ABOUT THIS GROUP

Residential Solar Leads - Was created for to [sic] introduce Marketing directors of Solar Energy Companies and lead generation companies that specialize in generating solar leads.

As someone who advises solar installers to make their own leads instead of buying them, this group doesn't sound very interesting to me. However, if you're in the market for residential solar leads, then there's probably little harm in checking out the group to see if anything interests you or if you can make some good connections for your business. Once you join, you'll get updates from the group via LinkedIn and also, if you want, by email. And if it turns out that you don't like the group, you can always leave it later.

Another search for solar industry groups may bring up more results and lead you to a group that is both active and interesting to you. I'm a member of a couple solar industry groups that host multiple posts daily, the Solar Energy Network and Solar Energy Professionals - PV & Thermal. There are also solar industry groups for major solar markets by state, such as Solar California with nearly 2,500 members or Massachusetts Solar and Energy with more than 500 members.

Since marketing is my field, I've been active in a couple groups dedicated to solar marketing. Whenever I've looked, members in those groups mostly discuss marketing tactics that are traditional in the solar industry, from trade shows to direct mail and ads, but don't bring up much about solar marketing online aside from some general posts about the growth of social media or mobile usage. This experience has shown me that there might be a need for another group that's more specifically devoted to online marketing for the solar industry. After spending time in existing solar industry groups, you might find a similar opportunity to start your own new group on LinkedIn.

Similar to Facebook, you can also buy ads on LinkedIn. You can target ads to reach LinkedIn members by size of the company they work for, industry, sex, and location. You can buy ads either by impressions (cost per impression or CPI) or by clicks (cost per click or CPC). If you have budget, ads might be a good way to recruit early members to your new group.

After you've started your group and have recruited some members, then you'll want to offer enough value frequently enough to make those members glad that they joined your group. A nice advantage of groups is that LinkedIn allows you to privately message all your members. This is a handy feature that you should use sparingly, as you would with blast email or any other mass communication tool. Don't contact group members too often and don't push your own products and services, or else you'll seem spammy and people will start to leave your group. Instead, email members once a week or a couple times a month with information that you think will interest them and help them in their business, whether it's advice on managing a solar contractor, hiring new installers, or news about trends in the industry.

Post the same kinds of messages in the group and then ask a question to stimulate discussion. Be sure to reply to comments that other people make, especially at the beginning of your group when membership is still low. Doing that will make people feel that their comments have value, which will encourage them to stick with the group and help recruit their own contacts as members. And while any member can post a message to the group, only you as the administrator can "pin" a message to the top of the discussion forum so it doesn't get pushed down and can always be easily seen.

So that's it for LinkedIn, and for social media. While social media can be helpful to connect with potential solar buyers and other audiences, don't let it eat up your life. If you're spending more than an hour each day on social media, then you need to cut back. In the end, social media may or may not bring much traffic to your website, which is where all your online marketing magic will take place. Building a great website and publishing a blog are more important than making posts on social media. So, if you have to choose, then choose to invest your valuable time and effort in your own online property—your website and its organic SEO efforts—rather than digital sharecropping on somebody else's property.

The next section is about one of the primary benefits of marketing online, being able to generate your own solar sales leads.

NEW UNDER THE SUN—GENERATING LEADS YOURSELF

*Many of life's failures are people who did not realize
how close they were to success before they gave up.*

— THOMAS EDISON

You are out of business if you don't have a prospect!

– ZIG ZIGLAR

Chapter 35

● ● ●

CREATE CLICKABLE CALLS-TO-ACTION

Generating leads online begins with an excellent website. It continues with content that potential solar buyers want to see. And it winds up in SEO and social media that bring visitors to your website.

But in the end, if your goal is to generate your own sales leads online, then things don't really get interesting until you get a good number of visitors to your website. That's when you can present those visitors with a lead-generation sequence that's more likely to pull them in than the usual "Free Quote" button. And any lead-generation path begins with a call-to-action.

In marketing, a call-to-action (CTA) is an instruction to the audience to provoke an immediate response, usually using an imperative verb such as "Call Now," "Find out More," or "Visit One of Our Locations."

The most common CTA on a business website is "Contact Us." Unfortunately, this offer is as ineffective as it is pervasive. I'm not saying you shouldn't have a way for people to contact you via your website. But such a passive and unspecific offer—basically, you're inviting the whole world to ask about or tell you anything that's on their mind—will generate very few sales leads. Instead, many contact forms on websites just become an easy way for salesmen from other companies to try to reach you with their pitches for eco-friendly office supplies, shady SEO tactics, or discount customer service from call centers overseas.

Aside from "Contact Us," most solar company websites offer a single call-to-action that is not much more effective: "Free Quote" or "Free Solar Assessment." If you've made your button or link for this offer stand out from your competitors somehow, it may appeal to the 4% of your website visitors who are ready to buy. But what about the other 96% of your website visitors who aren't ready to buy yet but with whom you want to begin a business relationship? If all you offer is a solar assessment, which is just a chance to have a salesman come to their home, then you're giving them nothing—and doing nothing to convert those visitors into early-stage sales leads.

To generate leads at all stages of the Solar Buyer's Journey, you need to offer your most desirable web visitors things that they'd find valuable at their stage of decision-making about solar, such as an ebook or checklist. In this age of spam and robocalls to cellphones, web surfers today are more protective than ever of their email addresses and other contact information. That's why it's not enough to expect them to use your contact form out of thin air. Instead, you must give web visitors a good reason to surrender their digits to you. This is what some web marketers call an "ethical bribe." Give the visitor something valuable in exchange for their contact information, and you'll start generating solar leads right on your own website.

While calls-to-action are a proven tactic to generate leads in many industries, few solar companies, including the big national installers, do calls-to-action well. That's a shame, because it means they're leaving money on the table.

Think about it. The top solar installers have clearly spent tens of thousands of dollars on building attractive websites. In some cases, as we saw earlier, their home pages are good at building excitement in website visitors with stories of happy homeowners bragging about their rooftop solar. The bigger solar companies also do good work using content to generate web traffic, whether by publishing a blog or being active on social media.

But after all that investment in generating traffic and then making their sites attractive for the visitor, without effective calls-to-action for their different kinds of visitors, these solar companies are then just leaving the visitor to figure things out on their own once they arrive on the solar company's website. And that may or may not ever turn into new solar leads.

It's like sending out lots of invitations to a party and then making your house ready by hanging festive decorations, hiring a guy on acoustic guitar, and filling a couple of coolers full of craft brewed IPAs—but then failing to answer the door when visitors arrive.

Building a sleek solar website and attracting visitors to it is a good start. But once you've got a website visitor, it's not enough to just hope that she will figure out whether she wants to take the next step and if she does, how to do it.

And an online form to get a free home solar assessment and then receive a call from a salesperson doesn't count—it's too premature for most folks. Remember, each potential solar customer goes through their own version of the buyer's journey. Eventually, that buyer may decide she's ready to make a purchase. But it could take her months or years of research and thinking to arrive at that final point. In the meantime, she's not going to want to fill out any form that will trigger a call from a salesperson. She's just not ready for that level of commitment—yet. So offer her something less intimidating to do while she's still thinking about whether to get solar in the first place and, if so, whether to get it from your company or somebody else.

Your website needs to help your visitor, at each stage of her buyer's journey, to find the content on your site appropriate to the current stage of her decision-making process. Menu bars and other navigation links help visitors get around a website, but they're not strong enough to convert visitors to leads unless they offer something of real value in exchange.

Using a call-to-action for a premium content offer such as an ebook or checklist is the best way to guide a potential solar customer to the next step of the solar buyer's journey. And that next step is getting that visitor to fill out a form to become a sales lead. Of course your ebook or other content offer needs to be appealing enough to get a visitor to surrender their contact information to your sales team. And making your offer attractive starts with a clickable call-to-action graphic.

Usually a banner ad placed at the bottom of a page or blog post, a clickable call-to-action graphic can also appear in the middle of the text or in a website's sidebar or footer. Wherever you place it, a call-to-action must be enticing—visually attractive and/or verbally compelling, like the example we saw earlier from Sunpower by Infinity Solar in New York State, displayed again here.

As you can see, this is an offer for the middle stages of the Solar Buyer's Journey, when your potential customer already knows the benefits of solar power but needs to deal with some key questions before he decides he's ready to get it. These questions include whether his house qualifies for solar, how much money is he likely to save with solar, and how the installation process works.

The call-to-action makes it clear that this ebook is not just an extended advertisement for the company, but instead, a guide with helpful advice for a home solar buyer who might never buy from the company at all. He may decide that solar is not for him, or he may want to wait a few years, or he may decide that he wants solar now but likes another company better.

Now of course, the text will be written to make the company's offerings for home solar look attractive, but the ebook is not a product spec sheet. Its immediate goal is not to lead to a phone call to inside sales but simply to generate an inquiry online. The longer-term goal of the ebook is to help nurture the new early-stage lead along his Solar Buyer's Journey so that, if he does decide to get a solar system for his house, that he'll think of Sunpower by Infinity Solar first, before he'll think of other residential solar installers.

To create an effective CTA graphic, HubSpot offers critical do's and don'ts for calls-to-action, including:

* Don't use the word "Submit" on a button but do offer action-oriented language like "Download White Paper"
* Don't hide your calls-to-action where nobody can find them but do put them above the fold where they stand out
* Don't be too wordy but do make your offer easy to understand

Visual calls-to-action often perform best, and you can create little banner ads easily with Canva or any other graphics program. HubSpot includes a call-to-action generator in its suite of Marketing Automation tools that doesn't require either any design skills or any knowledge of code. But testing has shown that CTAs in text form located near the top of a page or post may outperform a graphic CTA placed at the end of the text. The reason for this is that, if you've done your SEO right for your ebook or other offer, then visitors have arrived at your website looking for that offer. The easier the offer is to find, then the more downloads you'll get.

Ultimately, if you want to generate solar leads yourself online, you should have calls-to-action in both text and graphic form located throughout your website, especially on the most popular pages and posts.

Any call-to-action must take the visitor to an effective landing page where he can learn more about the offer, which is the subject of the next chapter.

Chapter 36

●　　●　　●

USE TEMPTING LANDING PAGES

At what point does a website visitor who's maybe interested in residential solar become a lead? It's simpler than you might think: When a web visitor gives you his contact information by filling out an online form, he becomes a solar lead, at least from the marketing standpoint. Does that mean the lead represents a person who's ready to buy solar right now from your company? Unfortunately not. Indeed, someone who filled out a form on your website to get an ebook or checklist may never become a lead for your company at all. He could be:

* A competitor or potential vendor checking you out
* A solar buyer outside your service area
* Somebody with a lot of time on his hands who trolls the web for free offers

So, someone who's filled out a form on your site to get an offer should be considered an inquiry. It will take some research by a solar marketer into that person and his activity on your website to qualify him as a lead for marketing purposes. And it will take even more scrutiny to qualify the same person as a lead ready to hand off to Sales.

But given how inexpensive and easy it is to generate online inquiries once you've got your lead-generation path set up, it doesn't matter if some inquiries fail to qualify as leads. If you do it right, you'll get enough traffic and enough inquiries that there will be plenty who do qualify as sales leads. And those leads will likely be higher quality than leads you buy from a vendor.

The first step towards getting those leads is to generate inquiries, or conversions, on your website. Here's how to do it.

"Real and actionable conversions come if you fulfill two conditions: overcoming psychological obstacles + screening out the tire kickers," according to Laura Moisei at Unbounce. Moisei continues:

> In other words, a pro conversion is all about getting a lead that has a genuine interest in your business and your product offering. As Mona Elesseily said, "collecting information from prospects with your form is a negotiation, a process of easing into a relationship—and not a sudden event."

If someone's just kicking the tires, they probably won't fill out an online form because they're not ready to talk to a sales rep yet. So if your website is clear about what you offer and to what kind of solar customers, then you don't really have to worry about your contact form generating a lot of irrelevant inquiries. If your form is generating too many unqualified conversions, then maybe you need to go back and re-orient your website content towards your ideal solar buyer persona.

It's the opposite problem that most solar companies have to worry about—namely, not enough people filling out their online contact forms. And that's because those companies are asking web visitors for too much, too fast. Here are the top six mistakes in forms that lead to low conversions on solar websites.

1. WRONG OFFER

A form to "Get a Free Quote" or even receive a "Free Home Solar Assessment" will scare off website visitors who are at the early stages of the solar buyer's journey. You wouldn't ask someone to go steady on a first date, right? Likewise, when someone just finds your site, they're usually not ready to get a visit or phone call from a salesperson. As we've already discussed, 96% of your website visitors are not yet ready to buy.

So, if all you're offering is the chance to get a call from a salesperson to start a solar assessment, then very few visitors will fill out your form. You'll get more form submissions if you offer your web visitor something that will help them move forward with their buying decision at the stage of decision-making they're at now and at their own pace, such as an ebook or checklist.

2. TOO MANY FORM FIELDS

The sweet spot for forms is 3-5 fields, according to the experts at Unbounce. Any more than that, and fewer visitors will fill out your form. This means that you have space to ask for a visitor's name, email address, and city and state. But you probably don't have space to ask the average amount of their monthly electric bill, the name of their electricity provider, or how recently their roof was replaced.

3. TOO MUCH CLUTTER ON THE LANDING PAGE

As I discussed earlier, your form should be placed on a landing page. And that page should have a bit different format than the rest of your website. It should be much simpler. Once your visitor gets there, through an appealing call-to-action, then your landing page should be laser-focused on one thing and one thing only: getting the visitor to fill out the form. So remove anything else that's usually on your site pages, including sidebars with blog posts and ads and even your top navigation menu. Don't give the visitor anything to do on that page but fill out and click on the form.

4. NOT ENOUGH TO PROMOTE THE OFFER ON THE LANDING PAGE

The landing page should be simpler than the other pages on your website, but that doesn't mean the landing page should be bare. In order to entice a visitor to fill out the form in exchange to receive the ebook or whatever you're offering, you need to describe your offer well enough to make it sound attractive. If it's not clear that the solar web visitor will get something valuable in exchange for his contact info, then he won't bother to fill out your form.

So, as you remove distractions from the landing page, remember to add in enough text and pictures to show what your visitor will get if he sends in the form. If you're offering an ebook, for example, have a few bullet points about the content along with an image of the book's cover. Or, you could display a photo of someone who looks like the ideal reader for this offer, such as a homeowner like Ranch House Ralph who we met earlier. But don't put too many images on the landing page. One is ideal and two may be the maximum.

5. BORING BUTTON

A grey button that says "Submit" will get very few clicks. Get more clicks by making your buttons as attractive as possible. Make your button an action color such as orange or blue. Then, depending on your offer, the text should say "Download ebook," "Reserve Yours Now," or even "Get It!"

6. FEAR OF SPAM

If you ask for an email address or phone number (and I don't recommend requesting a phone number from early-stage solar buyers, as I wrote earlier) visitors won't give it to you if they worry that they'll start getting cold calls and spam emails as a result. So right in your form, include a link (eg, "We respect your privacy" or "We'll never sell or give away your info" or even "Privacy Policy") to your site's privacy policy, written in regular non-legalese English, to reassure visitors that you can be trusted with their digits.

Of course, to be really useful to your sales effort, your form should be connected to your Customer Relationship Management (CRM) system, automatically feeding contact info straight into your company's lead-tracking database. And for your solar marketing team to be able to track the results and optimize the form based on usage, the form should also be integrated with analytics. The leading marketing automation software suites offer this kind of analytics to help track the performance of landing pages. Or, if your website is built in WordPress, you can get simpler lead conversion tracking by installing the LeadIn plugin.

After your web visitor submits the contact form on your landing page, that visitor goes to a page where the offer will be delivered. Called a thank you page, this next destination is similar to the landing page in that it's focused on a particular goal. In this case, that goal is making it easy for the visitor to download or otherwise take delivery on whatever you offered them on the landing page, whether an ebook or a private webinar. So a big button saying "Download Ebook" would also be appropriate on the thank you page.

But a thank you page doesn't need to be as simple or as focused as a landing page. Your visitor has already taken the one action that you wanted her to take. So now, you can relax a bit. Sure, make it easy for your new lead to find her offer. But also make some other offers too:

* Bring back your site's navigation menu. You now want to make it easy for the visitor to click around your site, if she wants to.

* List a blog post or two on the same topic as the offer she just requested. So, for example, if the initial offer was a checklist on "10 Questions to Ask Any Solar Installer" then you could display blog posts on how to choose the best solar installer for you or easy ways to check out a solar installer and make sure they're trustworthy.

* You could even show another call-to-action graphic for another premium content offer that you think would interest your new lead. The offer should help move her a little further through her buyer's journey for solar. So, if your first offer was very entry level, for example, an ebook on the main benefits of home solar, then your second offer could be a little more advanced, say, case studies

of home solar buyers. But if your first offer was more advanced, such as a cheat sheet comparing pricing and payback time of three different financing options, then your second offer should also be more advanced. For example, since your buyer is at the decision stage and has reached the point where she's ready to talk to a salesperson, this might finally be the time to offer that free on-site home solar assessment through a link to its own contact form.

So that covers landing pages and thank you pages, key components of any online lead-generation sequence. If its website attracts enough traffic, then this sequence will start to bring in more and more inquiries. A solar marketer can sort through those inquiries and qualify those that appear to be potential solar buyers as leads that can be passed along to the sales team. And that's where doing sales the inbound way comes in, the subject of the next chapter.

Section 8

●　●　●

MAKE HAY WHILE THE SUN SHINES— DOING INBOUND SALES

Selling to people who actually want to hear from you is more successful than interrupting strangers who don't.

— *SETH GODIN*

Best way to sell something: Don't sell anything. Earn the awareness, respect, and trust of those who might buy.

— *JEFFERY GITOMER*

Chapter 37

HOW NOT TO DEAL WITH SALES LEADS

Congratulations! Now that your visitor has filled out the form on your landing page, you've started generating your own solar inquiries online. Some of those will turn out to be qualified sales leads. If the form didn't ask for a phone number but only an email address as I've recommended for early stage solar buyers, then you can start to cultivate that lead online as the next chapter will explain. But if you did get a phone number, then you've got the chance to make a more impactful sales contact by calling.

And if the lead came in the old fashioned way, by phone, then you should get back to them the way they taught you in Sales 101: as quickly as possible.

Unfortunately, it appears that many sales reps in the solar industry didn't take Sales 101. Nor did they learn from the guys before them, or anywhere else, the most obvious point in any kind of sales of any product or service: If somebody wants to buy something from you that you're selling right now, then you should sell it to them.

But according to a new study done in 2015 by Velocify, a maker of software to help salespeople, lots of solar companies seem to be taking a pretty chill attitude towards customer inquiries, letting hot leads go cold.

Whether the sales department totally blows off a homeowner who's requested a quote on the company's website or the company can only be bothered to send out a couple of follow-up emails to prospects before salespeople get discouraged, it looks like too many American solar installers are acting like the grumpy guy who puts in hardwood floors and won't return your call because he has an eight-month waiting list and doesn't plan on hiring any help anytime soon.

TWO WAYS TO SCREW UP A PERFECTLY GOOD SOLAR LEAD

Velocify's secret shoppers found that, across the industry, solar sales is not as aggressive as you'd expect from all the cold walking and cold calling that goes on, as shown by the two big mistakes that solar installers are making in the way they treat new customer inquiries:

1. **Solar companies aren't responding to qualified leads.** "Nearly 40 percent of prospective solar customers waited weeks for a quote response, and many never received a response at all," writes Julia Pyper at Greentech Solar. "When companies wait an extended duration before responding to requests from prospective buyers, it has been shown to put them at a significant disadvantage compared to companies that respond within minutes."

2. **When solar installers do respond to leads, they're not following up enough.** Nobody likes salespeople who pester them endlessly about something they don't want. But when a homeowner contacts a solar company, just making that contact shows that the person is very interested in solar and may even be ready to buy. It may be just a question of whether they'll buy from you or from your competitor. But 77% of solar installers contacted prospective customers by phone four times or fewer, which just isn't enough. Velocify says that six calls is what's really needed to close sales across a variety of industries.

DON'T BECOME THE "NO-CALL-BACK" SOLAR COMPANY

Even if you have all the new customers you can handle now, it will hurt your brand if you just let qualified leads go cold by ignoring inbound inquiries. You'll get a reputation as unresponsive and inefficient. Meanwhile, competitors who know how to handle leads better than you do will eat your lunch. Then, sometime in the future when you're not so busy, you may wonder where all the new customers have gone. But once you're known as the "no-call-back" solar company, it'll be too late to fix your damaged reputation.

If your installation crews are really so maxed out, I'll leave it to your management to get out and do some hiring quick. Last time I heard, Americans still need jobs. And "green jobs" are hot.

But as a solar marketer, you should take responsibility for working with your sales department to respond to qualified leads in a timely way and to follow up enough to give you a chance to make the sale. Your company can get help streamlining your sales process from companies like Velocify mentioned above or other companies that help you automate key sales response tasks like tracking leads and sending out a chain of automatic email responses spaced out over a couple weeks.

Software company HubSpot uses the goofy term "SMarketing," which sounds like a new snack food but is actually an okay way to talk about how sales and marketing need to be better coordinated in order to close more customers. I'll talk about it more later, but in the meantime let me just leave you with a little quote that might possibly apply to your solar company:

> SMarketing is the alignment and connection between sales and marketing. Since Sales and Marketing work closely together in most organizations, it's often typical for these two revenue generating groups to be in conflict with one another. The typical battle looks like this: Sales complains that Marketing isn't generating enough quality leads, and Marketing criticizes Sales for not

working their leads hard enough. But if you improve SMarketing at your company, you'll spend less time bickering and more time closing business.

Whether you're a solar marketer or you work in sales, you'll find ways to help these two crucial parts of any solar company to work more effectively together to help everybody later in this book. In the meantime, let's talk about how to best handle new sales leads that come in without a phone number but only an email address.

Chapter 38

●　　●　　●

WELCOME NEW LEADS BY EMAIL

Once you've got a lead with an email address, you can start cultivating your new lead, nurturing her over several weeks or months into a prospect for your solar products and services.

But with all the spam out there filling up the inboxes of nearly every email user on earth, is email marketing even effective anymore, you may ask?

In contrast to social media, which is new enough that people are still getting used to using it as a business tool, email is a technology that even the most tech-averse company executives can't do without. More than 200 million emails are sent out every day, according to data service Domo. This volume proves that email is still a serious business tool, according to Daniel Newman, president of online marketing agency BroadSuite. As he writes in Entrepreneur magazine:

> This isn't the only piece of evidence that proves it's too soon to contemplate the demise of email marketing. Consider the following stats: Seventy-two percent of US adults say they prefer companies to communicate with them via email, and 91 percent say they'd like to receive promotional emails from companies they do business with. Meanwhile, 73 percent of companies agree email

marketing is a core part of their business efforts, and 25 percent rate email as their top channel in terms of return on investment.

You probably already know that most potential solar customers, at least until they reach the end of the buyer's journey, would rather hear from you by email than by phone. That's reason enough to use email as the initial follow-up method for a new lead from your website.

Newman gives three other reasons why email is here to stay as a marketing tool. First, email is more effective than social media to reach potential customers with marketing messages. Subscribers to your email list have asked to hear from your company directly, unlike casual followers on social media who might tolerate the occasional post from you on their feed but will un-like or un-follow you if you come off as too spammy. Second, new technology like wearable devices and location-sensing will allow email to reach people in more places and to do so more effectively. Finally, email is still very effective for both marketing and sales if you use it correctly.

As Newman explains, "People who think email is passé are probably not using it properly. For instance, one of the biggest challenges of email marketing is that a very small percentage of subscribers actually read newsletters. Now, if the read rate of your newsletters is pathetically low, it doesn't necessarily mean that email is dead or dying. Instead, it means your newsletters fail to pique audience interest, or your calls to action aren't up to scratch." If you're not doing well with email, Newman suggests that you ask yourself three questions about it:

1. Is the tone of your content impersonal and promotional, or is it friendly and helpful?
2. Are you having a conversation with the reader, or are you talking "at" them?
3. Are you driving meaningful one-on-one engagement?

These are the kinds of questions that beg an obvious answer. Yes, your email messages should be friendly and helpful rather than overly promotional. You should talk with the reader rather than pushing him canned advertising copy. And your email messages should encourage your readers to interact with you—not just by filling out the dreaded "Contact Us" form on your website but by downloading additional ebooks, watching your videos, or asking your expert staff members a question on Facebook.

Once you understand that email only works these days when you treat solar buyers not like eyeballs for advertising but like your own business contacts, then you'll be ready to start using email to convert leads into prospects and sales. And it all starts with the email you send out after a visitor downloads an ebook or another premium content offer on your website for which that visitor has to give you an email address by filling out a contact form.

At a minimum, you should connect your contact form to send out one automated email message to your new lead. The email message should do three things:

First, thank the person for his interest in the content offer and give him another link to download it. This is the same link you already provided on the thank you page, but you should offer it again for the visitor's convenience.

Don't worry that your new lead may forward the email to a friend so that friend can download your content offer without filling out your form. Yes, you may not capture that second person as a lead through this particular offer. But if that second person gets your offer and likes it, he may come back to your site on his own and download some other offer directly, making him a lead then. And frankly, the more your content spreads around the web, the more people will know about your company and have the chance to see you as an authority.

So, think of people sharing your ebooks as a form of free marketing. Extra downloads of your content offers don't cost you anything, after all. But if your stuff is so good that the general public wants to spread it around on its own, then that's a sign that your inbound marketing is a success.

The second thing you should do in your thank you email is to say a couple things about the offer that will entice your new lead to read the offer right away and take some action. For example, if the offer was an ebook on questions to ask a solar installer, then repeat a couple of the questions in your email message and then give a summary of your advice on checking out solar installers. That advice could go something like this: "A reputable solar installer will be happy to answer your questions or to get back to you with the answers if necessary. But if an installer can't give you a straight answer to any of these questions, then that may be a signal that this installer is not a good fit for you and that you should look for someone else."

Third, in the followup email just as on the thank you page, offer additional related content. This can be open content such as blog posts or another premium content offer available on its own landing page and through its own contact form. Either way, any content you list here should be related to the topic of the offer that the person just requested to receive.

It's easy to program Gravity Forms or other common online form software to send out a single message to a web visitor who submits a form on your site. However, for nurturing leads into sales, it's more effective to send out more than one follow up email, even a series of a half dozen or more email messages. And better than sending out all those messages manually is to program them into a email system that will send them out for you at intervals that you specify in advance. The next chapter will show you how to put together an automated email sequence for a solar buyer.

Chapter 39

NURTURE LEADS WITH DRIP EMAIL

There are various names for an email system that works for you, auto-matically, over a period of weeks or months to keep in contact with solar leads and help move them along the Solar Buyer's Journey: drip email, email workflow, or even marketing automation. Each name is use-ful because it tells you something about how an automated series of email messages would work:

Drip Email—Related email messages in a series are dripped out one at a time to recipients over a period of several weeks or months. For exam-ple, after a visitor has downloaded an ebook on your website, you could send them one email on the same subject but with different content every ten days for twelve weeks.

Email Workflow—A more sophisticated version of drip email, in a workflow sequence you can actually specify alternative email messages depending on what action your recipient takes to a message in your series. For example, let's say someone downloads an ebook on your site. This gets him subscribed to a series of eight follow-up emails over a few weeks. The first email offers a second ebook. If the recipient clicks the link to down-load the ebook, then he receives an email message offering him a free

15-minute consultation by webinar. But if he doesn't click the link for the ebook, then the visitor will receive a different email message, one containing a link to a blog post. An email workflow can be simple, offering the reader only one or two messages on which a choice will trigger different responses. Or, a workflow can be more complex, offering several messages each with a choice that leads to a different response.

Marketing Automation—technically, automation includes a larger suite of software products and services, such as a customer relationship management database, a keyword tool, and a system to schedule social media posts and monitor activity on your social media accounts. Companies including HubSpot, InfusionSoft, and Pardot offer such marketing automation software suites. However, the heart of marketing automation seems to be drip email workflows. For some marketers that's all the automation they're interested in. There's even a service called Drip that only offers automated email marketing and advertises itself as "lightweight marketing automation." The most popular choice for setting up an automated email sending series is probably MailChimp. It's attractive, affordable, and easy to use.

Email followup is the last step in the inbound marketing process before you start calling leads over the phone or setting up an on-site solar assessment. But email followup is crucial towards nurturing early-stage buyers to the point where they're ready for a phone or in-person contact. Most marketing and salespeople don't have time to follow up with website inquiries or leads manually. That's why the best way to make sure you do that follow up is to automate it.

These days, software can make automating emails easy. Stand-alone email marketing programs such as MailChimp or full marketing suites such as those offered by HubSpot or InfusionSoft allow you to create workflows or drip sequences of email messages timed to start going out in response to an action by a website visitor and then to keep going out automatically at intervals that you determine. And of course, these programs all follow the principles of permission marketing—not to mention the federal CAN-SPAM Act which regulates commercial email, which we'll discuss below. But for now, you should know that unlike sending out your own emails to a list through Gmail or Microsoft Outlook, email marketing providers offer an easy way for the recipient to unsubscribe to your emails at the bottom of each message. Not only does this keep you in compliance with the law but it also keeps you from annoying your prospects with unwanted email messages.

SAMPLE DRIP EMAIL CAMPAIGN

By now, you may be wondering, how would a drip email campaign for a solar company work?

For example, let's say you offer an ebook on the "Top 10 Myths of Home Solar." The ebook is free, but in exchange, you ask for the visitor's name and email address through a web form. On the back end of your website, the form is connected to your email automation system. So, once the visitor submits her information in the form, that form sends her email address to the email system. In turn, the email system sends her the first email in a series of eight or ten in a workflow.

Then, for the next few months, the email system will automatically send the visitor additional email messages every ten days. Those email messages will help to nurture this new sales lead into a hotter lead and will contain content such as links to blog posts, offers of additional ebooks or, towards the end of the series, product and service information that compares you to other solar companies (favorably, of course). The messages can contain any content that would interest a potential customer who downloaded the original ebook on myths of home solar and would help to move her along the buyer's journey from initial awareness to decision-ready.

If you want to get fancy, you can even set up your workflow to respond to an action that the recipient might take when she gets any of your automated email messages. For example, email #3 contains an offer for a second ebook, this time on the subject of how to avoid solar scams. If she doesn't click the link and download the offer, she will continue to receive the remaining emails in the original series based on the solar myths ebook. But if she does click on the link and download the second ebook, then you can take her off the first list and put her on a second list, to start receiving emails from a series based on that second ebook. Or, if she gets so far along in her decision-making process that she takes the step to request a free solar home assessment, then you can remove her from any email workflow she may be in, and let your salespeople start making live contact with her by email, phone, or in person.

Here's what a typical automated email series might look like for a website visitor who downloads an ebook on "Top 10 Myths of Home Solar":

Message	Timing	Content
1	0 days	Thank you for downloading our ebook, here's a link to it just in case you need it again, along with three links to learn more about the reality of home solar
2	7 days	Teaser and link to a blog post about how affordable home solar has become
3	10 days	Video from a customer who was skeptical but now loves her home solar system
4	10 days	Offer of another ebook on avoiding solar scams and finding a reputable solar installer
5	10 days	Teaser and link to a blog post about the newest trends in solar financing
6	10 days	Teaser and link to a case study of a customer who got solar because he cares about the environment
7	10 days	Offer of a checklist on what to look for in a good solar installer
8	7 days	Teaser and link to a chart comparing your solar offering with likely competitors
9	7 days	Link to solar savings calculator on your website, which triggers a separate email sequence to follow up on leads who are further along in the buyer's journey

Remember, for one reason or another, the potential buyer might not complete the whole series. She may unsubscribe. Or she may take an action that moves her out of this series and into another drip campaign, or even into personal contact with your salesforce. But a good email automation system will help you guide your email audiences into another email series, some other content or contact with a salesperson—whichever is most likely to meet her needs at that point.

Automated email works with everything else in inbound marketing. So, first, you need to get the right traffic to your website—people most likely to become your most desired solar customers. Then, make it easy for the solar-curious web visitor not only to learn about your company and its offerings but also to learn about solar in general. Help the buyer to educate himself on his solar options. Then, guide that visitor towards starting a low-pressure relationship with you by offering him something he'd want, such as an ebook with helpful advice, in exchange for filling out your lead generation form.

Finally, build your authority and trust with the potential buyer by communicating for a few weeks or months by email with helpful, non-salesy advice that makes him feel empowered to make a decision on solar when he's ready. That's how you'll get more web visitors converting into more qualified solar leads that your salespeople can really use.

Chapter 40

AVOIDING COMMON EMAIL PROBLEMS

The biggest mistake most solar companies make with email is to pay lead-generation vendors to send out cold emails to potential solar buyers. Blast emails from such dubious senders as Solar America, the National Solar Network, and the US Solar Department have become all too common and have eroded trust for the solar industry. Company salespeople also sometimes send out cold emails to lists that they buy themselves. Either way, cold emailing isn't much better than cold calling. And unless cold emailing is accompanied with other Internet marketing, the conversion rate is very low.

On the positive side, at least cold email is less annoying than a cold phone call. But is it legal? You've certainly heard that there are laws against sending out spam, or unsolicited commercial email. But it turns out that the law has some surprising twists. We'll look at those below.

But first, I want to share a story about email marketing gone totally wrong.

Once, I heard a speaker at a marketing industry event tell the audience that harvesting the emails of your visitors without their knowledge was good marketing practice.

I kid you not.

The speaker certainly should have known better. She was a high-paid branding consultant for large consumer marketing companies from the Washington, DC area. She told a story of how, after she visited a website, she received an email from that very same site. She was surprised that they even had her email address, since she hadn't signed up to get any email newsletter or even filled out a form on the site. Yet, though the email was completely unsolicited, she said it was still an example of effective outreach in today's marketing environment where brands have to put their name before consumers five or ten times before that consumer might be ready to buy.

I was appalled by her response. And pretty confused.

We've already discussed what Seth Godin says about "permission marketing," that these days, consumers have nearly zero tolerance for unsolicited interruptions. But perhaps this marketer was stuck in some kind of time-warp, still back in her office cubicle during the 1990s, back in a simpler time when people actually wanted to get more email?

I also wondered: Wouldn't sending unsolicited email in the first place be illegal under federal anti-spam regulations? Finally, I was doubtful about the technology. Since the branding consultant didn't fill out any kind of form, how did the website even get her email address in the first place? It didn't seem possible.

So, I went home and Googled the laws about spam as well as the technology for a website to collect email addresses from visitors without their knowledge or participation. I'm still convinced that sending somebody an unsolicited email after a single visit to your website is bad marketing. And secretly getting an email address from a first-time visitor to your website is super creepy. But it turns out that I had a lot to learn about both the technology and the law.

HARVESTING EMAIL ADDRESSES

First, the technology. Believe it or not, a shady website can in fact harvest your email from your web browser from a single visit.

And it can all be done automatically through various technical tricks, without needing you to fill out a single form on the site. In fact, you won't even know it happened until you get a spam email from the site after your visit. According to Uri Raz at Private.org, a website can get a web visitor's email in a few different ways. For example, the site can make the visitor's web browser fetch one of the page's images through an anonymous FTP connection to the site. Or, the site can use JavaScript to make the browser send an email to a chosen email address with the email address configured into the browser.

This is probably pretty rare technology-wise and of course no reputable website would pull this kind of stunt. Because even if you have the technology to harvest email addresses, it turns out that sending email to a harvested address is illegal in the United States. So I was right that what this website did to the marketing speaker could get the site in trouble. But I was wrong about the reason. It was the harvesting and not the spamming that was the problem. In fact, it's perfectly legal to send a certain amount of spam as long as you don't send it to an illegally harvested address.

ONE STRIKE AND YOU'RE NOT OUT—YET

The federal law that regulates commercial email in the United States is called the CAN-SPAM Act. "The Act does not require opt-in by recipients, however, and so unsolicited messages are still lawful," explains cybercrime expert Alex Kigerl. The bill does not prohibit spam, but rather regulates the way it is sent and the content that is delivered. Any commercial messages sent, even unsolicited, must be truthful and not fraudulent. The sender must also comply with a recipient's express request to opt-out of all future emails and provide a link in the email to do so easily.

So, though the site that the branding consultant visited did indeed break the law by harvesting her email address from her visit, the site was allowed to send her unsolicited email. However, if she asked to get off their list and they didn't remove her within ten days, then they'd be breaking the law on that point also.

But whether it's illegal or not, sending unsolicited email still wouldn't be good marketing practice.

"If I meet you and you add me to your mailing list without asking me first, I'll be annoyed but I'll give you a few emails to show how you add value to my life," as lawyer Ruth Carter writes. "But if we've never met and you're sending me unsolicited email, I don't like you. It's because of people in the latter category that I'm glad we have the CAN-SPAM Act."

CRACK THAT WHIP, CAN THAT SPAM

Let's do a little history here. In 2003, Congress passed and President George W. Bush signed the Controlling the Assault of Non-Solicited Pornography and Marketing Act. As attorney Zachariah Parry explains,

> The cleverly titled acronym, CAN-SPAM Act, sought to provide refuge to consumers weary of unsolicited emails. (It did not, however, make any attempt to shield the feelings of legitimate marketers who resent being lumped in the same category as pornographers.)
>
> The Act, which itself does not use the word "spam," defines "commercial electronic mail messages," i.e. commercial email, as "any electronic mail message the primary purpose of which is the commercial advertisement or promotion of a commercial product or service (including content on an Internet website operated for a commercial purpose)." 15 U.S.C. § 7702(2)(A).

Commercial email for the purposes of the law is not just bulk email but all email sent out by companies or employees to try to sell you something. An online purchase receipt or some other service message not subject to the restrictions on spam doesn't have to meet the requirements of the CAN-SPAM Act.

SEVEN DEADLY EMAIL SINS

Common small business email marketing systems such as MailChimp or Constant Contact are set up to help you avoid the biggest legal mistakes on your next email blast. But, keep in mind, the CAN-SPAM Act doesn't just apply to big spammers but it covers even the little guys too. And the Federal Trade Commission, which enforces anti-spam laws, doesn't care if you send 1,000 emails or just one. As long as the email tries to sell something or comes from a commercial website, then it has to follow the law.

So especially if you're sending unsolicited emails to customers one at a time from your Outlook or Gmail account, avoid the temptation to play clever with the law. The FTC lays it out for you:

1. **Don't use false or misleading header information.** Instead, use your real name and company name in your "From," "To," "Reply-To," and routing information. Commercial email is not the place to be anonymous.

2. **Don't use deceptive subject lines.** My favorite, "Re: Information You Requested," is totally illegal coming from a company I've never had any contact with.

3. **Don't be too cute pretending the message is not selling something.** You probably don't want to label your message "advertisement" but you can come up with more subtle ways to show that the message is selling something.

4. **Don't try to hide behind the Internet.** Even if your business is 100% online, to send commercial email, you also must demonstrate a presence in the physical world. Any commercial email message you send needs to list a current street address, a post office box, or a private mailbox.

5. **Don't make it so damn hard for recipients to opt out of your email.** Forget the tiny type or the need to email you back to unsubscribe. Instead, follow the example of one popular email service that inserts at the bottom of each of its customers' emails an

easy-to-find "SafeUnsubscribe" link. Make sure your spam filter doesn't block these opt-out requests.

6. **Don't ignore opt-out requests.** You need to give recipients 30 days to opt out after getting your email and you need to stop sending to them within 10 days. And once someone has opted out, you can't send emails to them anymore in the future unless they opt back in. This means you need to keep a record of an email address even after it's opted out. Again, the commercial services do this for you automatically. That's yet another reason to scrap your manual email list in Outlook or Gmail and sign up for Constant Contact already!

7. **Don't let your email guy go rogue.** Hiring an outside contractor to send your emails is no excuse for breaking the law. And when the FTC comes calling, your email guy will get in less trouble than you will, since it's your email that started the fuss. Only hire reputable email marketers who can demonstrate a history of knowing the law and complying with it.

I DON'T NEED NO STINKIN' ANTI-SPAM POLICY

If you think that your residential solar installation company is too small to get dinged by the FTC for sending out spam, then you should think again. Anybody who gets really annoyed that your unsolicited emails won't stop even after they opted out can report you to spam@uce.gov. "Their site On Guard Online has some other useful tips for managing and reducing the amount of spam email you receive," writes Ruth Carter.

And the penalties for breaking the law on spam are no joke. The fine for one single incident of violating the CAN-SPAM Act is $16,000. And since that doesn't seem to deter the big nasty spammers, the FTC can also throw in jail time to boot. That's what happened to 34-year-old Milos Vujanic. In April of 2015, a Texas court sentenced the uber-spammer to spend 48 months in federal prison and pay $17.3 million in restitution. A couple of accomplices got smaller fines but much longer prison sentences—a mind-blowing 30 and 40 years respectively.

Vujanic and his gang don't appear to have been in the solar industry, but there are plenty of instances of solar marketers sending out spam. For example, here's an email offer from 2015 reported to the anti-spam site Discard.email, with the subject line "Home Solar Panel Savings & Rebates Available":

Eliminate Your Energy Bills Today - Click Here to Get Started: [link]

YOUR AREA HAS BEEN APPROVED FOR SOLAR!

Federal, state, and local governments are offering limited time incentives in 2015. Learn more about Rebates and incentives. Available by clicking the link below: [link]

Savings-on-Solar-Panels—Rebates

How Does it Work?
* Save up to 80% off your monthly electric bill by going solar
* You can quality for $0 upfront costs
* Protect Against Rising Energy Costs
* Learn how much you can save with solar today

Click Here For Quotes: [link]

To stop receiving messages, please visit here [link] or mail your request to:
Home-Solar-Rebates II 804 Congress Ave, Suite 400 II Austin, TX 78701

Fortunately for these folks in Texas, they did include both the un-subscribe link and a physical address. If they honored unsubscribe requests, then they may have been in compliance with the law. But even if this email is entirely or even mostly legal, there's so much that's just bad practice about this approach, primarily a tone of hype (all caps, exclamation points, and repetition) that leads to distrust. Email copy like this would never pass the solar inbound-marketing test and a campaign with messages like this would not set up a solar installer for long-term success.

I'm no lawyer, but if you forget to take somebody off the "Residential Solar Prospects" email list you have in Outlook even after they've sent you two angry emails about it, my bet is that even if the person complains to the FTC, your chances of doing time at Club Fed are probably small. But everybody hates spam, and following the law on your commercial email is just doing the right thing. Whatever the law says, that's the best kind of marketing these days.

Solar installers in a hot market may be tempted to try to shout louder to be heard above all the noise of competitors. And they might be tempted to use email to try to push their way in even after a customer has already said they're not interested. But even if that weren't illegal, since every-body's email inbox is stuffed with spam these days, emailing people who don't want to hear from you wouldn't be effective.

As Seth Godin puts it, marketing today needs to be so good that con-sumers won't want to opt out of your email list. And you need to start by getting permission to send your customers an email or any other market-ing content.

Real permission is different from presumed or legalistic permis-sion. Just because you somehow get my email address doesn't mean you have permission. Just because I don't complain doesn't mean you have permission. Just because it's in the fine print of your privacy policy doesn't mean it's permission either.

Real permission works like this: if you stop showing up, people complain, they ask where you went.

Email is a key tool of both marketing and sales today. The next chapter talks about how to make those two crucial functions for a solar company work together more effectively in the context of online marketing.

Chapter 41

●　　●　　●

INTEGRATING MARKETING AND SALES

The solar industry handles marketing in an unusual way. Larger residential solar installers do a small amount of marketing, led by an in-house staff that employs outside consultants for tasks from writing to developing multimedia. As in other industries, the smallest startup solar installers lack a marketing staff and simply do a little bit of marketing, such as taking out ads, to drum up leads. So far, this is fairly typical of other industries. Big companies almost always do more marketing than little companies.

But what makes solar different is that even mid-sized companies do very little marketing, focusing nearly entirely on sales. This includes both residential solar installers and commercial solar developers, both of whom have largely outsourced their marketing to third parties. And in this case, as we saw at the beginning of this book, those vendors are not marketing agencies, but lead-generation vendors. In fact, lead-generation vendors do most of the marketing that happens in the solar industry today, as they have for years.

I don't know exactly how this happened in the solar industry in such a big way, but I'm always surprised how the management of solar installers with millions of dollars in revenue each year don't see the need to do any of their own marketing. They seem content with buying leads from telemarketers and the newer online lead-generators. The only problem is that their salespeople are not content with purchased leads.

I've talked to dozens of solar sales reps from across the country in phone consultations and these men and women are frustrated. The leads are poor quality, they tell me, and those leads close at a very low rate. Now of course, I haven't talked to their sales managers or directors or to the guys at the vendors who are providing leads to those disgruntled salespeople, though I have researched the methods of lead-generation that they largely rely on. And perhaps from them I'd hear a different story—that the salesforce is lazy and doesn't hustle enough to close sales.

But if the methods those sales reps have available to them are the same ones we discussed earlier—the very same sales tactics that make the solar industry look sleazy like door-to-door canvassing and telemarketing calls that offer a weekend in Los Vegas for a homeowner to book a solar home assessment—then I don't blame the salespeople for lack of hustle. In this case, too much hustle might be exactly what's hurting the company's sales.

Solar customers today don't want to be the target of "hustle." They don't want to be "sold" or "pitched" or "gamed" or manipulated in any way to "sign on the line that is dotted," to quote the high-pressure sales trainer played by Alec Baldwin in the movie *Glengarry Glen Ross*, perhaps the best film ever about the pressures of working as a commission salesman.

Writing in *Entrepreneur* magazine, Jason Wesbecher, a B2B sales analyst, explains how sales has changed in the last few years, with the rise of the Internet. His insights on B2B buyers also apply well to consumers in general and solar buyers specifically:

> There is something unique about today's selling environment that represents an opportunity to forever change the dynamics of this relationship. Today's B2B buyers simply don't need the assistance of a salesperson in the same way they did a decade ago. Instead, they rely on thought-leadership content, product reviews, case

studies, and peer recommendations that marketing teams develop to nurture prospects.

I'll get to the way that marketing and sales work together at the bigger solar companies in a minute. But let's deal with the smaller solar companies first, those companies that do little or no marketing for themselves but simply buy most or all of their sales leads.

Those companies need to know that most of their lead-generation vendors are not producing the kind of content that Wesbecher describes. With the exception of a few very good vendors such as the solar marketplace EnergySage which I discussed earlier in this book, most solar lead vendors are not putting out case studies, highlighting thoughtful product reviews, offering high-quality ebooks to empower customers to make the best decision on solar, or blogging with helpful advice for solar buyers at all three stages of the Solar Buyer's Journey.

Instead, most lead generation vendors aren't doing much online at all. They're just cold calling people from lists that they buy and, in many cases, pressuring a reluctant homeowner to agree to a home visit that the homeowner then doesn't show up for.

But if a lead-generation vendor is getting leads online, it's usually through the most primitive approach: that's right, the good ol' "free solar assessment" form. Since the form is usually generic and not especially appealing, the vendor is lucky that anybody fills it out at all. Yet, somehow the vendor does manage to generate a few leads online, which they sell to solar installers. Not surprisingly, those leads convert at a low rate because the solar buyers don't appreciate being passed from one company to another like a hot potato.

So, if you're at one of those many solar companies that does little or no marketing yourself and then wonders why your sales leads get worse and worse every year, I hope you'll rethink your approach. Stop relying on lead-generation vendors to do all your marketing for you, and bring some of your marketing in house. In the next chapter, I'll talk about how you can get help by hiring your first marketing employee.

Once you do hire that first marketing staffer, or if you're with one of the larger solar companies that already has one or more marketers in-house, then you'll want to make sure that your marketers are working well with sales. And for that, your company needs to bring both sales and marketing together to focus less on the company and more on the customer, according to sales researcher Christine Moorman writing in Forbes magazine. Below, I adapt what she says to the particular needs of solar companies:

1. DESIGN MARKETING AND SALES RESPONSIBILITIES AROUND THE CUSTOMER BUYING PROCESS

You want to sell solar to humans, not leads. So, organize your sales and marketing work around the customers you are trying to reach. The Buyer Persona Profiles that I talked a

out earlier are key here. And then, think through how each type of customer likes to learn about solar and what will help them move along the Solar Buyer's Journey. As Moorman says: "Outline these steps and then assign marketing and sales responsibilities at each stage. This way both functions work together to meet the customer needs during each stage and support the customer's progress to the next."

2. CREATE A UNIFIED FOCUS ON THE MOST VALUABLE CUSTOMERS

Don't make salespeople waste time on customers you don't really want, whether it's because they buy small PV installations, make lots of complaints because they don't understand how solar works, or don't pay on time—even if this type of customer is your main customer now. Your Buyer Persona Profiles should guide you towards your ideal customer, the person you really want to work with, whether they're your main buyer *now* or not. "Sales people need to meet their quotas and if those quotas don't include the company's most valuable customer, sales will not be prospecting or acquiring the right customers. Marketing can help identify these customers, develop materials to do so, and service sales as it closes these deals," Moorman advises.

3. ORGANIZE AROUND THE CUSTOMER, NOT THE FUNCTION

If there are too many turf wars in your company between sales and marketing or even among members of your salesforce, consider reorganizing around customer types instead of product lines. A combined sales-marketing group focused on a Buyer Persona rather than a particular technology might work together more effectively to reach and cultivate that type of buyer. "The idea puts the function the employee represents into the background while bringing the activities and purpose of that function into the foreground," says Moorman.

4. INTEGRATE CUSTOMER INFORMATION

"When marketers and sales people know different things about the customer, strategy is weakened. Both functions have different customer experiences, so it is inevitable that they develop unique and varying insights," says Moorman. Can you encourage more water-cooler chat between the two departments? Casual, comfortable sharing of insights is always best. However, technology can also help. For example, share databases. Offer both sales and marketing staff access to the company's CRM, for example. Marketing automation suites like those from HubSpot, InfusionSoft, or Pardot offer integration with common CRMs such as Salesforce or SugarCRM.

So, host a Casual Friday late-afternoon bull session to exchange ideas and generate new approaches. Holding regular no-pressure creative brainstorming sessions, preferably with a little work perk like an in-office lunch on the firm, or end-of-week Happy Hour, can inspire a team sensibility while leaving it to the next day or next week for the ideas to marinate into new strategies and angles.

5. REQUIRE JOB ROTATIONS

Many of Moorman's marketing leadership students spend 6-12 months working as sales reps, to understand how sales works first hand. But you don't need to be in school to try different roles, if your company supports it. "Although less common in most companies, asking salespeople to spend time in marketing could also facilitate cross-fertilization and integration." Solar sales and marketing will only work well together if they understand what the other side does. And this is just one more reason for solar companies in particular to bring their marketing in-house. A fellow employee who you see every week at the office will be much more likely to understand what you do than a lead-generation vendor who may be located overseas but is certainly not on-site or even in your geographical market.

6. ESTABLISH INDIVIDUAL AND SHARED INCENTIVES

"Binding marketing and sales together with shared incentives can help pull the organization in one direction," says Moorman. Your company can draw up an agreement, mutually acceptable to both marketing and sales, to share incentives when a lead closes to a new customer, for example. Do be careful, however, not to tie marketing's compensation entirely to the performance of sales—or vice versa—as that loss of control can create its own kind of tension and stress.

To align marketing and sales, HubSpot goes even further and offers the concept of "SMarketing," as I mentioned earlier. Here's how they define it:

The term "smarketing" refers to alignment between your sales and marketing teams created through frequent and direct communication between the two.

The goal is to have measurable goals that each team agrees to hit so there's mutual accountability. For instance, Marketing might have a mutually agreed upon leads SLA (service level agreement) to hit, and Sales must agree to follow up with a certain amount of those leads.

Smarketing goals should be made together, and re-evaluated every month to identify opportunities for improvement on both teams.

Larger solar companies with a marketing team in-house can benefit from some of HubSpot's recommendations on how to align marketing and sales, for example, for a marketing staffer to meet with every new salesperson when they're hired; for the marketing department to plan new web content with the sales team; and to publish blog posts under the bylines of salespeople to help them build more authority.

Finally, even if your company is already doing some inbound marketing, you'll still need to reach out to solar buyers in traditional ways, by phone and email. Hopefully, your inbound marketing program will bring you enough sales leads that you won't have to cold call or cold email anybody. But you'll still need to follow up with people who've already expressed interest in your company. It's just that now those calls will be warm leads instead of cold ones.

Fortunately, a growing number of companies offer help in doing sales outreach "the inbound way," that is, in ways that may be different from old-school outbound selling but that still help move prospects along towards a sale. Methods include using email and phone calls together with social media strategically for the sales rep to become a trusted adviser of the buyer as he goes through the stages of his decision-making process on solar.

Resources for those who'd like to learn more about inbound sales include a training company called the Inbound Sales Academy as well as HubSpot's free Inbound Sales Certification.

Coming up next, the final section of this book will offer advice on how to get help with your marketing by hiring a marketing professional in-house or engaging a freelancer or an agency to help you on a consulting basis.

SWITCH ON THE LIGHT—GET MARKETING HELP

*If you think it's expensive to hire a professional,
wait until you hire an amateur.*

— Red Adair

*It doesn't make sense to hire smart people
and then tell them what to do; we hire smart
people so they can tell us what to do.*

— Steve Jobs

Chapter 42

IN-HOUSE OR AGENCY?

How any solar company handles marketing will mostly depend on the company's size.

Smaller solar companies tend to focus on making sales and leave the marketing to outside lead-generation vendors. As we've seen, that approach is attractive because most solar installers don't know much about marketing and don't feel comfortable trying to generate their own sales leads. But outsourcing your marketing also carries certain risks, primarily, that your company will become dependent on outside lead generators even if the leads they provide close at a low rate.

If you're unhappy with leads that you're buying, then your only options are to try to buy better leads somewhere else or to start to generate leads yourself. Either way, you'll lose valuable time in the transition that will cost you sales.

Getting control over your own marketing will give you an advantage over your competitors who are still buying leads. It will help you build your brand, create an audience of potential buyers for your pipeline, and start generating your own flow of leads. As long as you keep publishing good content and nurturing your audiences, this flow of leads will become a long-term asset for your company that will remain even if you decide to stop buying leads from vendors.

And if competitors get marketing help before you do, you'll be caught playing catch up once they start to build a brand for themselves and start cultivating the same solar buyers in the area that you want to reach.

How does a solar installer or commercial solar developer know when it's time for them to get help on marketing? If you answer "yes" to any of the questions below, then now may be the time to consider either retaining a marketing agency or bringing in a marketer to your office:

1. Do you generate more than $500,000 per year in revenue or have more than five employees?
2. Is the owner or company founder still buying ads, writing copy for direct mail pieces, setting up informational events, and overseeing the website himself?
3. Are you relying on your salespeople to do your marketing—that is, are they responsible for getting most or all of their own leads?
4. Are you 100% reliant on lead-generation vendors for your sales leads?

When you've reached the point where you need help with marketing, you'll find that the owner or sales reps are getting bogged down in marketing outreach that is not their speciality and that is taking them away from doing what they're really good at. That is, running the company and closing new customers. At that point, unless you get some professional marketing help, your sales will be damaged.

Deciding to take the plunge and get marketing help will offer an immediate sense of relief. But pretty quickly a new anxiety will come along. Should you bring in an in-house

staffer or hire an outside agency? There are advantages to either approach, as To the Point Marketing Agency explains.

Let's start with hiring an agency:

*   Lower cost overall—you can pay by the hour, the project or even a monthly retainer, but you'll never have to pay benefits or employee taxes.

* Access to marketing software and expertise to use it—Agencies have access to powerful but expensive software for everything from keyword research to web design that they already know how to use. It could cost you thousands of dollars alone to get and learn this software.
* Higher skilled personnel-to-cost-ratio—Agencies with different levels of staffers can assign higher paid managers only when necessary, say for planning and strategy. For daily tasks like posting to social media, they can bill you at a lower rate for junior staffers.
* Lowers internal investment and hassle in managing employees—agencies are responsible for managing their own employees, saving you the trouble.
* Brings agency-wide skill sets—Agencies offer specialists who can go deeper into different marketing disciplines, whether blogging, building landing pages, or analytics than a generalist employee working in-house could ever do.

But there are also key advantages to hiring a marketing staffer in-house:

* Staff control—An employee working in your office, or even telecommuting, has to follow your company's policies and report directly to one of your managers.
* Targeted product/service familiarity—Your own marketing staffer will develop deep knowledge of your offerings by all-day contact with your people and information.
* Accountability to upper management—Your company founder, owner or C-suite may feel more comfortable having a staffer in-house.
* Software control—If you need certain marketing software or even a whole software suite like those from HubSpot or InfusionSoft, you can license it yourself and build expertise in-house, which becomes an asset for your company.

* Skills specific to the individual—If you find the perfect solar marketer for your company, why share them with an agency's other solar clients?

Can't decide? Then here's a way to get the best of both worlds, hiring an agency and bringing on someone in-house.

A small solar company may decide to start out by hiring an agency to get their Internet marketing program started and then hire a marketer in-house once things are moving. An agency can develop a marketing plan, write a job description for your in-house marketing position, and even help you hire the right person for you, based on their own experience working with your company.

After a certain point, there's really no getting around it. If you want your solar company to continue to grow, especially in a competitive local market like California or the Northeast, you'll need both an in-house marketer and one or more marketing consultants, whether an agency or several freelancers. It's difficult for non-marketing managers, say the CEO or the sales director, to effectively manage a marketing agency because of lack of expertise in the discipline of marketing. The best person to manage outside marketing consultants is an inside marketer.

So, the next chapter will deal with hiring the right solar marketer in-house. After that, we'll talk about getting the right solar marketing agency.

Chapter 43

●   ●   ●

HIRING SOLAR MARKETING STAFF

These days, to be a qualified marketer, it's not enough to have staffed a few solar company booths at home shows or produced a few brochures for residential solar installers. The first qualification is that any marketer should be comfortable and experienced on the Internet—and that means more than posting photos of the home show booth or the new brochure to Facebook and Twitter.

First, a marketer these days needs to know how to buy pay-per-click ads on Google or Facebook. But she also needs to know when NOT to buy pay-per-click ads and when other types of online marketing might be more effective and less costly. Joanna Lord, vice president of marketing at home improvement network Porch.com, offers five things you should look for in a marketing hire. As I've done previously, I'll adapt these to the solar industry:

1. THERE'S NO SUCH THING AS A PERFECT MARKETING TEAM OR EVEN A PERFECT MARKETING HIRE

The best person for you will depend on your company culture and your goals. For most growing residential solar installers, their biggest need will be more customers. So, to help you kick the habit of buying leads from vendors, you'll want to hire an inbound marketer, the type of marketing professional focused on building website traffic and converting visitors to leads. But if you're a commercial solar developer that does bigger deals and thus needs fewer but more targeted leads to get bigger customers, then you may need someone who can do videos and professional graphics to upgrade your brand and make your company more credible to bigger customers.

2. INVEST IN PEOPLE WHO HAVE SHOWN THAT THEY LIKE TO LEARN NEW THINGS

Even when somebody has been out of school for a few years, she should still be interested in building her marketing toolbox and keeping up with new technology and the cultural changes it brings in buyer behavior. As Lord puts it, "The best marketers out there are called full-stack marketers, which means they have a working knowledge of all types of business marketing, not specializing in just social media or just search engine optimization (SEO)." To get all those skills and keep them up-to-date as things change, a marketer needs to be constantly learning. A tangible sign of this learning is to have achieved one or more certifications such as Basic SEO from Yoast or Inbound Marketing from HubSpot and to have kept them up to date.

And don't be too stuck on getting somebody who already has a lot of expertise in solar. Better to hire a marketer who knows about reaching buyers using today's technology than to promote one of your rooftop installers with who uses Facebook a lot and knows that volts times amps equals watts but doesn't know much about reaching your audience through blogging.

3. LOOK FOR MARKETERS WHO BALANCE STRATEGY AND TACTICS

While there are a few marketers out there who spend too much time in the clouds of grand plans, the problem of most marketing candidates, especially those early in their careers, is that they don't do enough strategy.

They're good on completing tasks and can program Hootsuite to post on Twitter three times daily for the next six months. But they can't say why they're posting on social media except to grow your followers or "create buzz." A marketer needs to be able to take your solar company's goals and build a strategy to reach them that includes the right tactics for each stage of your marketing program. So, for example, if you want to get more qualified leads from homeowners in a certain city, then your marketer should be able to come up with a full plan including customer research, SEO, content, promotion, and analytics to reach that goal.

4. ALWAYS HIRE FOR CULTURE FIT OVER SKILL

Avoid the temptation to hire the cocky hotshot from one of the national solar installers who used to hang out at TEDx Silicon Valley. And definitely avoid a fast-talker who promises results that sound too good to be true, such as getting you to the top of a Google search in a couple weeks by buying inbound links (as you'll remember, that approach would qualify as "black hat" SEO and it's likely to backfire). Instead, insist on a marketer with integrity who can explain how he'll help meet your goals in a way you can understand.

As Lord explains, "There is no candidate worth losing your culture over. Similarly, no marketing team can reach it's full potential if there's a culture mismatch. Culture clashes can lead to negativity, lack of respect for processes, turf wars, silos, and friction about the current plan. All these things can tear a marketing team apart—and stunt the company's success."

5. PLAN FOR THE NEXT BIG CHALLENGE

Don't wait until you're ready to roll out no-money-down PPAs or solar leases before hiring a marketer who can help get the word out of you new offering. And definitely don't wait until the day you announce that you've acquired a smaller competitor to find a freelancer to help with the news release. Instead, look ahead at the next 6-12 months in terms of product and service changes but also in terms of the national, state, and local solar market. Then, try to plan for anything big you might need to reach out to your audiences about. Once you know your plans, see if you need to add a marketer to properly spread the word so you'll be ready.

Chapter 44

● ● ●

FINDING A MARKETING AGENCY

Once you've got one or two marketing staffers in-house, then you've made good progress. But you'll also find that your in-house marketers can only do so much. It's not just a question of time. It's also that excellent marketing employees who are very good at several approaches may also lack other skills to plan and execute your solar inbound marketing program. An agency may be better able to help with areas from campaign strategy to data crunching that lets you know what works and what doesn't to writing copy for landing pages that converts visitors to leads at a high rate.

At this point, you may have already hired outside consultants here and there for various tasks, especially web design or SEO. But maybe your company has outgrown the collection of freelancers that you've assembled over the years and you now want a one-stop shop for all your outside marketing needs. Or maybe you've got an agency that does traditional solar marketing but you just aren't seeing the ROI from the expensive marketing tactics they recommend like trade shows, print ads, direct mail, or cold calling purchased lists of leads.

Whatever the reason, after reading this book, you now know about inbound marketing:

* You understand that traditional solar outbound marketing tactics are becoming less and less effective since the Internet enables prospects to do their own research and comparison shopping. You know that means your potential customer may have made more than half of her buying decision before she ever talks to one of your salespeople.

* You also know that your potential customers have less and less patience for interruptions in their lives like ads or sales calls, as marketing expert Seth Godin explains. You've heard that it's possible to actually create marketing that solar prospects want to receive.

* And you know that this new type of marketing involves producing content—blogs, social media posts, ebooks, and guides—that businesspeople and homeowners interested in a solar array would find helpful.

Finally, you've got a nice looking website but it isn't bringing in many qualified leads for your salespeople. You've heard that you're supposed to have an online marketing funnel that attracts new visitors to your website and then somehow converts some of those visitors into good leads.

But where to get started? A marketing agency that specializes in solar companies is a good place to begin. But knowing the solar industry well is not enough to do well on the web. Plenty of agencies with experience in trade shows and direct mail can list solar client logos and show case studies from big solar companies. That's a good start, but it's not enough if you want a digital-savvy agency that knows how to make your solar homepage into an active sales funnel rather than a passive online brochure.

You also need your agency to know the digital world.

So, to see if an agency is really a digital native or just a recent move-in from the world of print design and old-school marketing, look at what the agency says they can do—web design, blogging, social media, etc.—and then compare that to how well this agency does all those things for themselves on their own website.

1. HOMEPAGE LOOKS GOOD AND WORKS PROPERLY

It seems obvious that if an agency offers to build you a solar website that their own site should look impressive and function well. But unfortunately, you can't always take this for granted. Web design technology moves quickly, and an agency that had a good-enough website in 2008 may be way behind the curve today.

Put the agency's website to the test. Is their own website design up-to-date and professional with a good balance of text, pictures, and white space? Or is the agency's site cluttered? Do all the links work? Is there an easy way to contact them online through a professional-looking form rather than just a low-tech email link that leaves them vulnerable to spammers?

2. WEBSITE ADAPTS ELEGANTLY TO MOBILE DEVICES

An agency that offers to build solar websites and help with online solar marketing campaigns needs to be able to help your company reach the maximum number of visitors online. Today, that means users of phones and tablets, which can account for 50% or more of visits to your website. To please these users and to avoid SEO penalties from Google, your website must look good on smaller screens.

How do you know whether an agency can help you with that? The easiest way is to see if the agency's own site uses mobile-responsive design. Look at it on your iPhone. Or if you're on a laptop, just narrow down your browser screen and see if the agency's homepage starts to respond well to a smaller view. For, example, everything shouldn't just shrink (that's bad). Instead, columns should stack into one long column and text should rearrange itself so it's still big enough to easily read but doesn't get cut off on the right side.

3. WEBSITE FEATURES AN ACTIVE BLOG WITH NON-BORING POSTS

Inbound marketing is all about producing content that your potential solar customers want to read, to draw them into your website and convert some of them into qualified solar leads. The best way to do that is to publish a regular blog with articles that solar customers would find interesting. That doesn't mean company news releases about new hires and promotions, corporate acquisitions or new product announcements. Boring! A solar blog too focused on internal company concerns or too promotional is almost worse than no blog at all.

If solar buyers don't care about your HR news, they may not be ready for the hard sell either. What solar buyers do want is advice, tips, and news focused on their needs—for example, how financing is making residential solar more affordable in general.

A solar digital agency may offer to help you with blogging. But if they don't do it well themselves, then you have to wonder how good a job they'd do for your solar company. Check their blog for recent articles on stuff that the agency's own clients among solar installers and developers would care about such as how to convert visitors to leads, how to have a powerful solar homepage, or how inbound marketing can bring in solar leads.

4. ACTIVE ON SOCIAL MEDIA

More and more solar marketers are using Facebook, Twitter, LinkedIn and other services to get qualified leads at a very low cost. And many marketing agencies offer to help. But does an agency's own website seem well connected to social with a Facebook like box, Twitter feed (with recent posts), and buttons to easily share content?

Check out the agency's own social media accounts too. An agency that hasn't tweeted since 2012 or boasts only a few dozen Facebook fans may not be able to help you recruit the quantity and quality of audience on social media that you'll need to get qualified leads from these services.

5. WEBSITE USES CLEAR CALLS-TO-ACTION

To build business from your website, first you need visitors. Then you need to try to coax some of those visitors to convert into inquiries and leads. Finally, for those leads who qualify as interested in solar and potentially ready to buy in the next few months, you can nurture them along until they become your customers.

Lots of solar marketing agencies promise that they can make this happen. You don't just have to take their word for it, though. See if the agency does has a way to attract visitors and then funnel them into leads on their own website. Does the site feature clickable calls-to-action at the bottom of its blog posts and major sales pages, with an offer such as a free consultation or free ebook? To get the offer, does the visitor have to put in their contact information so that the company can follow up with them as a lead by email or phone?

ELIMINATE, AND THEN FOCUS ON THE REST

As we discussed, testing whether a marketing agency practices what they preach is the easiest way to tell if that agency really has expertise not just in solar marketing but also in web marketing. Applying this test is a quick way to eliminate agencies that may be great at staffing booths at trade shows or in designing print brochures but won't necessarily help you on turning your solar website into a solar lead generation tool.

Once you've narrowed down your focus to agencies that know the solar industry and can also make great solar websites optimized for today's Internet, then see how well those agencies connect their digital work to what you really need: not just a pretty website, but an online hub that brings in more and more visitors over time and turns more of those visitors into qualified leads.

Next, in the conclusion to this book, I answer the burning question for any solar marketer who's convinced that there's a better way to sell solar than door knocking and cold calls, but is so busy that he wonders if maybe he can get started on trying Internet marketing sometime soon or if it's really necessary to jump into it right now.

Conclusion

● ● ●

WHY NOW?

For an advanced energy source, it's ironic that solar power might be one of the last products in America that's still marketed using the nineteenth-century method of door-to-door sales. With the armies of solar door-knockers out there, you'd think that monocrystalline PV panels were competing against blackening polish for coal stoves or the latest wonder from the medicine show that just rolled into the fairgrounds at the edge of town, maybe Clark Stanley's Snake Oil Liniment or Dr. Rose's Arsenic Complexion Wafers.

Once the wagons of the medicine show are hitched up to their horses and roll out towards the next town, then it's the job of the commission salesmen to sell the boxes of product left behind. And at that point, it's whoever can knock on more doors and have a better pitch will make the most sales. At least that's how it worked in isolated little towns across the American frontier in the days after Custer made his last stand at Little Big Horn and before the arrival of the horseless carriage and the home radio changed the world of sales and marketing forever.

That also was how things worked during the age of the traveling salesman, into the Depression, and up to the classic suburban door-knocking era of the 1950s with its Fuller Brush men. But today, any company that relies on canvassing, or its cousin cold calling, as a main marketing technique, whether that company sells magazine subscriptions or solar panels, is setting itself up for failure. And as the solar growth cycle experiences its ups and downs, many solar companies across the US have already gone bust. Perhaps it was because their work was shoddy or they didn't have enough financing. But using outdated marketing tactics couldn't have helped.

If you knock on doors now, you may think that you're playing it safe, doing what solar companies have always done since the 1970s and what lots of them still do today. But that doesn't mean that door knocking or other old-school marketing tactics have a bright future. Past performance doesn't guarantee future results, as they say in the investment business.

LIKE A TURKEY BEFORE THANKSGIVING

Solar companies that want to survive in the future need to stop "thinking like a turkey before Thanksgiving."

No offense intended, of course. I just mean that, if you were a turkey living somewhere in America during the month of October, you might think that you had a pretty bright future based on a pretty happy past. For months, the farmer had come by to give you food. Life was good and you had no reason to think it wouldn't just keep on being good. And then, one day in early November, the farmer came by, put you in a truck, and then, as they say, the rest is history. Or as people call it, turkey with all the trimmings.

When it comes to marketing and sales, too many solar companies today are like that turkey in October: Living in the past and blissfully ignorant of change that's about to hit them hard.

Meanwhile, most other industries stopped knocking on doors decades ago, and the better ones stopped cold calling years ago. Moving past direct home sales into the new technology of the mid-twentieth century, mass media, allowed companies to do their marketing more efficiently by reaching a bigger audience all at once.

We discussed this kind of marketing, which we call outbound marketing, at the beginning of this book. It's traditional marketing using mass media and its main activity was buying advertising. So, outbound marketing consisted of companies buying ads in newspapers and magazines, on the radio and on TV, and on billboards. This marketing revolution had a huge impact on American business, helping to replace local economies and their mom-and-pop stores with a national economy driven by mass retailers who could afford to buy ads that reached consumers all across the country such as P&G, Budweiser, and McDonald's. And it was the Madison Avenue advertisers who helped these companies to become the multinational giants they've become today.

The outbound marketing revolution has lasted for more than half a century. But today, the era of mass advertising is winding down as the Internet replaces older media.

Now, American business is witnessing a second marketing revolution as consumers become more overwhelmed by information and more able to dodge marketing messages that would interrupt their day by using caller ID on their phones and ad blockers on their web browsers. The decline of mass advertising and the rise of the Internet is creating a new type of marketing that doesn't depend on interrupting people but instead tries to attract buyers with content that they want to see—inbound marketing.

As Brian Halligan and Dharmesh Shah explain in their book *Inbound Marketing,* the new medium of the Internet calls for a new approach that's different from what worked in the old media of print, broadcast, and outdoor advertising:

> Just as the rules from door-to-door didn't translate to outbound mass marketing, the rules from outbound marketing do not apply to inbound marketing. You can't simply move your advertising budget and 30-second spot online—it won't work. Pushing a message at a potential customer when that message has not been requested will fail as a major source of new customers, and by extension, revenue, for most companies.

Halligan and Shah argue that this marketing revolution, the transition from old mass media to the Internet, has also brought big changes to the business landscape.

Just as the transition from door-knocking to mass advertising allowed big national companies to replace local mom-and-pop shops, so today's transition from mass advertising to Internet marketing is already shaking up big companies and creating a space for new types of businesses to take their place. That's why half of the brands listed in the Fortune 500 in 1995 were gone by 2009. Household names including Toys "R" Us, Ace Hardware, and Polaroid dropped out—and newcomers including Amazon, eBay, and Google came in.

Even if your ambition is not to create a solar company that grows large enough to join the Fortune 500 someday, there's a lesson for you here. A revolution in marketing is creating a revolution in business. People in the solar industry are already familiar with the energy revolution that their industry is helping to lead. Solar accounted for 64% of new generating capacity at the beginning of 2016 and the Solar Energy Industries Association projects that solar would soon rise to more than 90% of new generation.

Despite the efforts of electric utilities and fossil fuel interests to slow it down, solar is winning. Only a few years back, the idea that America could run on 100% clean energy seemed unrealistic. But now, this goal is starting to sound more and more achievable. And when it happens, perhaps the biggest thanks will be due to the solar industry.

No one can say whether most of that solar power will come from large arrays run by electric utilities or from small solar systems installed on millions of rooftops of homes, businesses, and government buildings in cities across America. Personally, I hope that our clean energy future is distributed. After all, you don't need to put solar in big power plants the way you did with coal, gas, or nuclear. Putting small solar arrays all over the place will save on transmission lines, free up the visual landscape, increase national security, and give people more control over their own energy—while creating more opportunities for local solar installers, which means more local jobs.

And I'm counting on residential and commercial solar contractors to make that dream come true. With marketing that's as advanced as the clean energy the industry provides, I'm confident that solar installers from San Diego to Savannah, and from Portland, Oregon to Portland, Maine can find more customers and delight those customers for decades to come.

But even if you're convinced that solar needs to make the move from 1970s-style marketing into the 21st century, it may take some work to convert your colleagues. And that will require persistence, patience, and good arguments.

As Seth Godin explains, "The flip is elusive...For a generation after people realized that smoking would kill them, many smart, informed people still smoked. Then, many of them stopped. [Likewise] after a technology breakthrough makes it clear that a new approach is faster, cheaper and more reliable, many people stick with the old way. Until they don't."

His words will give you inspiration to keep working for a better way to sell solar, even while it seems that so many others are still stuck on old-school marketing and sales tactics that are less and less effective over time. As Godin explains about this better approach,

Computers don't work this way. Cats don't have a relationship like this with hot stoves. Imaginary logical detectives always get the message the first time.

For the rest of us, though, the flip isn't something that happens at the first glance or encounter with new evidence.

This doesn't mean the evidence doesn't matter.
It means that we're bad at admitting we were wrong.

Bad at giving up one view of the world to embrace the other.

Mostly, we're bad at abandoning our peers, our habits and our view of ourselves.

If you want to change people's minds, you need more than evidence. You need persistence. And empathy. And mostly, you need the resources to keep showing up, peeling off one person after another, surrounding a cultural problem with a cultural solution.

Americans already know that the solar industry is awesome. Now let's show them that the solar industry's marketing and sales can be just as great. That's how we can cover every available rooftop in America with solar arrays. That's how solar companies can thrive. And that's how families, businesses, and local communities from California to the Carolinas can take control of their energy and join the fight against climate change.

Appendix A

●　　●　　●

THE VALUE OF AN INBOUND SALES LEAD

"**B**est-in-class organizations distinguish inquiries that come from inbound and outbound sources," advises Sirius Decisions, a company that consults on generating demand for businesses across industries. This makes sense for the solar industry just as it does for such industries as real estate or financial services. Potential buyers who have expressed an interest in getting solar are much more likely to buy than those who haven't. Therefore, inbound leads are certainly more valuable than outbound ones.

People who work in sales and marketing across industries have been debating how to determine the value of a sales lead for more than half a century. We won't come to a definitive answer here. But we will examine a few ideas and facts that will help marketers and salespeople at solar contractors make an apples-to-apples comparison between leads that they buy and leads that they generate themselves.

But first, it's necessary to understand what a sales leads actually is. According to Investopedia,

A sales lead is a prospective consumer of a product or service that is created when an individual or business shows interest and provides his or her contact information. Businesses gain access to sales leads through advertising, trade shows, direct mailings, and other marketing efforts.

A couple things here to note. First, businesses get leads through marketing. The solar industry generally tends to outsource most of its marketing to other businesses that do the marketing for them and get the leads. Those businesses, of course, are lead generation vendors. So, it's fair to say that for the vast majority of solar installers, marketing and sales are handled by different companies. Most solar installers who purchase leads do only sales in-house but do little if no marketing themselves. That wouldn't be a problem—if it worked to make sales.

Which leads to the second issue. Namely, that buying leads risks putting you into a state of mind that's not just mistaken but also, unhelpful to make sales.

The mistake is to think of leads as a thing to be bought and sold just like solar power equipment or office supplies. But it's more accurate and more helpful to remember that leads are not like a PV panel or a stapler, but that sales leads are people. Really, a lead is a relationship between a company and a potential customer. In the case of leads you buy, the relationship begins with one company—the lead generation vendor—and is then transferred to another company or companies, namely one or more solar installers who buy leads.

Transferring relationships happens all the time in life, for example, when you meet someone and that person introduces you to a second person. Without introductions, it would be hard for anybody to make trusted connections with new people. But the challenge comes in how the introduction is made and by whom. The problem with sales leads that you buy is that these leads represent a relationship with potential customers started by a telemarketer. And any relationship begun by cold-callers has already started off on a shaky footing.

As we discussed in Chapter 6, sales coach Steli Efti is an experienced phone salesman who recommends cold calling and other outbound sales tactics on a regular basis. Yet, even he doesn't want to be cold called and he recognizes that potential customers hate telemarketing and other outbound sales tactics. Efti sees other risks in outbound sales. For example, in today's Age of Information Overload prospects have less patience for interruptions. Also, with a general loss of trust in advertising over the last few decades, prospects are put off by high-pressure sales pitches.

Yet, Efti still recommends outbound sales in certain situations, especially, if you're getting good results. "Outbound is probably the least trendy, hip, cool, awesome, amazing thing a startup can do to grow the business. But you're not in business to get admiration from your peers and the press; it's not a popularity contest. Business is about the bottom line. The only thing that matters is: Does outbound sales make your business more successful or not?"

So, if traditional solar sales work for your company, and is showing reliable upward growth well into the future, then by all means, keep knocking on doors and buying leads. But to determine whether those tactics really are working, and working efficiently for a strong profit margin, you need to be able to compare the value of an outbound lead with the value of an inbound lead.

Rather than doing a lot of math here, I'll just share a few points that will help you make your own calculations.

First, the advantages of outbound leads:

* They're ready to buy solar now (at least in theory) and so they can bring in business quickly, which is key to maintaining cash flow.
* If you buy all your leads, you don't have to do any marketing yourself to get them; you just pay your lead generation vendor to do all the marketing work to bring leads in.
* You already have a process to work outbound leads, so it's comfortable for everybody, both the sales team and company management.
* You can target who you want, how you want, and when you want. If you want to reach a particular person, you can just call them up. As Steli puts it, "Want to reach the VP of Marketing at Citigroup?

Good luck trying to get his attention with inbound tactics." This might be more relevant for commercial than residential solar, since it's probably not worth putting in the same effort to reach a single homeowner for a $20,000 home solar installation as it would be to reach a corporate energy manager to sell a $10 million dollar array.

Then, the value of inbound leads generated online:

* They give you a sales flow for the future, as you nurture early-stage buyers into people who are ready to purchase.
* Since you've had to do some marketing to get inbound leads, each lead carries more value than just a single potential sale—it also represents branding value such as search engine optimization, word-of-mouth, and goodwill that will translate into interest from other people besides the single initial lead.
* If your marketing team is good at keeping initial inquiries for nurturing over time and passing only qualified leads onto the sales group, then they'll find the potential buyer much friendlier and more receptive than a lead purchased from a vendor.
* If you've done your homework—research and development of buyer persona profiles and search engine keywords—then your inbound leads will also be targeted to people who are good candidates for solar from your company.

And actually, if you want to reach that CEO at Citibank, online marketing can help. Generate enough buzz about his company on social media, and you may just get a call from his office. Is that easy to do? Of course not. But it's not easy to get a big CEO on the phone either. There are no magic shortcuts in either outbound or inbound marketing and sales.

In the end, I don't expect solar companies that are having success with buying leads to abandon outbound tactics altogether. I just hope they'll honestly investigate the value of the leads they're buying in terms of how many of them convert into sales. Then, I'm confident that the numbers will speak for themselves, that the return on investment in buying leads is low. At that point, it makes sense to try something else. Given the success of companies in other industries in marketing online, solar companies would be well advised to try adding some inbound marketing to what they're already doing.

Of all the marketing tactics reported by companies across industries in research done by HubSpot over the last few years, inbound marketing online—including SEO, social media, and blogging—has proven to be the most cost-effective way to get new sales leads.

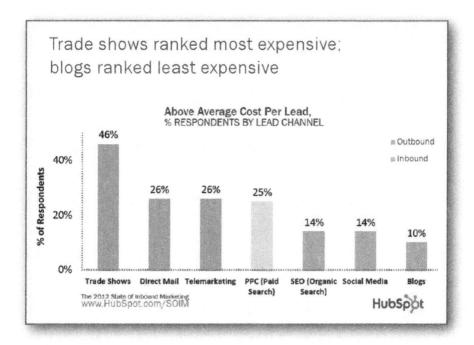

I know it may seem risky to try something new. But it can also be risky to keep doing what you've always been doing when the market is starting to change. As Tim Ferriss, author of *The 4-Hour Workweek*, says, "If you define risk as 'the likelihood of an irreversible negative outcome,' inaction is the greatest risk of all." Or, consider the words of JFK: "There are risks and costs to action. But they are far less than the long-range risks of comfortable inaction."

Today, perhaps the biggest risk in business is that technology will leave you behind. And if your business is stuck doing things the old way while competitors are getting online and leveraging the powerful tools of the digital world, you can be almost certain that your business won't be around in five years.

With the dominance of the Internet over nearly every aspect of modern life, solar companies that begin inbound marketing are likely to see a significant competitive advantage over those that don't.

Appendix B

● ● ●

RESOURCES AND TOOLS

The resources here will help you become a smarter online marketer and better sales rep. They'll help you keep up with news and trends in the solar industry, educate yourself on the latest online marketing techniques, and do more effective research to make better decisions on your marketing and sales, both online and offline.

SOLAR POWER AND RENEWABLE ENERGY NEWS

RENEWABLE ENERGY WORLD

With an uncluttered and minimalist design, the site bills itself as "The World's #1 Renewable Energy Network for News, Information, and Companies." Daily, *Renewable Energy World* puts out stories on areas of renewables from wind, geothermal, hydro, and storage to jobs and finance. And of course solar. To avoid having to sift through all their content on other areas, you can subscribe to their newsletter on solar alone. Each day, you'll receive about half a dozen stories on solar news and analysis around the world, but mostly focused on the US. The site also allows members to publish their own blogs, making it a good place to reach an audience of clean-energy industry peers.

SOLAR POWER WORLD

Solar Power World posts articles daily online and also publishes a print magazine every other month. Their description: "*Solar Power World* is the leading online and print resource for news and information regarding solar installation, development, and technology. Since 2011, SPW has helped solar contractors—including installers, developers and EPCs in all markets—grow their businesses and do their jobs better."

Their website offers two features worth checking out. First, each year they update their extensive list of Top 500 Solar Contractors in nearly a dozen categories ranging from contractors for utility, residential, and commercial markets, to solar construction firms and solar EPCs. Second, the site offers well done short videos across the range of technical and non-technical topics in solar, from new products to reports from events to coverage of industry milestones such as the one millionth solar installation in the US.

GREENTECH MEDIA

This attractive and modern website offers a nice balance of easy-to-skim news along with longer articles based on research from analysts at *Greentech Media*'s partner company GTM Research. Though they cover many topics in clean energy and technology, they offer a strong focus on solar, as they explain: "*Greentech Media* delivers business-to-business news, market analysis, and conferences that inform and connect players in the global clean energy market. Our coverage extends across the clean energy industry with a focus on solar power and the electric utility market's evolution."

Along with videos and other multimedia, the site is the home of the entertaining and informative *Energy Gang* podcast. Each week, the show's three hosts—Stephen Lacey, senior editor of *Greentech Media*; public policy advisor Katherine Hamilton of 38 North Solutions in Washington, DC; and Jigar Shah, author and clean-energy investor—summarize and analyze the latest clean technology news. They've covered such topics as Tesla's purchase of SolarCity, rethinking energy subsidies, and defection of big corporate power users from electric utilities.

ONLINE MARKETING RESOURCES AND EDUCATION

HUBSPOT

This company makes online marketing software and their founders invented the term "inbound marketing." As you'll remember, in contrast to "outbound" marketing where you try to reach your buyer with sales messages by interrupting whatever they happen to be doing at the time with your cold call or your ad, "inbound" marketing is where you attract buyers on their own time to visit your website by posting educational content online.

As you can tell from the amount of times I quote them in this book, I'm a fan of HubSpot. Their paid software suite is impressive. And they also offer many free resources to help you do both marketing and sales "the inbound way." Free offerings include software, especially their user-friendly customer relationship management system (CRM), as well as half a dozen skills certifications. I recommend both their Inbound Marketing Certification and their new Sales Certification. Both of these courses, which involve watching a dozen or more videos online and then taking a test, will help solar marketers apply inbound marketing to generate more solar leads themselves and convert more of those leads into customers for residential and commercial solar installations.

I also highly recommend subscribing to one or both of HubSpot's blogs. My favorite is their marketing blog, which covers such topics as myths about marketing, how to use various social media services such as Snapchat more effectively, and the best new tools for researching competitors. I also enjoy their sales blog, which talks about subjects like how to use LinkedIn more effectively to connect with prospects, habits of effective negotiators, and how to turn negative thinking patterns into positive ones. Even if you use none of HubSpot's other resources, reading their blog posts will give you an education in sales and marketing that will keep your skills sharp and give you an advantage over competitors.

Finally, HubSpot also offers dozens of free ebooks, checklists, and PowerPoint decks that will give you a deeper understanding of such topics as how to create an effective landing page, how to create a social media marketing plan, or how to do modern search engine optimization that works for the latest Google algorithm updates.

COPYBLOGGER

Like HubSpot, *Copyblogger* offers a variety of paid and free resources for marketers in general that can be useful to people who do marketing and sales in the solar industry. *Copyblogger*'s parent company, Rainmaker Digital, offers paid products including hosted WordPress websites along with WordPress themes you can use to build your own site.

But *Copyblogger* itself is mostly a blog with posts, ebooks, podcasts, and videos that you can get for free. Paid offerings include a membership site called Authority where you can get advice from digital entrepreneurs and other experts in online marketing and connect with other content marketers as well as a paid credential course, the Certified Content Marketer program.

The free *Copyblogger* blog offers hundreds of articles on website design and online marketing. They're big on lists. Popular articles at the time I wrote this book included "The #1 Conversion Killer in Your Copy (and How to Beat it)," "The 7 Essential Elements of Social

Media Marketing," and "13 Simple Questions to Help You Draft A Winning Content Strategy [Worksheet]."

At partner site Rainmaker.fm, you'll find a dozen lively and informative podcast shows hosted by *Copyblogger*'s likable company leaders and their friends. Several of the shows are targeted specifically at entrepreneurs. These include *Unemployable*, hosted by *Copyblogger* founder Brian Clark and *Youpreneur* hosted by serial entrepreneur and author Chris Ducker. Both shows cover the challenges of starting your own company. Meanwhile, you can find more general online marketing advice and keep up with trends in online marketing with *Copyblogger FM* hosted by Sonia Simone and *Technology Translated* with Scott Ellis. Finally, you can get tips for using LinkedIn more effective on *The Missing Link* with Sean Jackson.

For marketers who want to go deeper, *Copyblogger* offers four free email courses covering the basic areas that are essential to building and running a website that generates sales leads online: Design, Content, Traffic, and Conversion.

SETH GODIN'S BLOG

Seth Godin has become perhaps the world's most famous authority on modern marketing and his bald head has become an kind of lovable icon around the Internet. Godin was founder and CEO of Yoyodyne, the industry's leading interactive direct marketing company, which Yahoo! acquired in late 1998. Godin worked as VP of Direct Marketing at Yahoo before leaving to become a full time speaker, writer and blogger. Since then he's authored 18 books including *Linchpin, Tribes, The Dip,* and *Purple Cow.* He also wrote *Permission Marketing: Turning Strangers into Friends, and Friends into Customers,* whose title pretty much sums up the approach of inbound marketing, the method that I've recommended in this book.

Aside from his books and his entertaining talks available on video (and live, if you're lucky enough to catch him at a conference), Godin publishes a daily blog with short snippets of advice, analysis, and musings on marketing and business intended to make marketers and businesspeople question their assumptions about things like how to price their products, how to protect yourself from a scammer, and the benefits of growing your company vs. keeping it small. You can get his blog by email for free and I recommend that you do.

GETTING MORE OUT OF GOOGLE

Google is one of those tech companies that has already conquered the world but obviously isn't satisfied until it conquers the universe. You probably use Google everyday for web search, and as we discussed, Google is the most popular search engine by far in the United States and around the world. You may also have used Google AdWords to place pay-per-click ads alongside search results for certain keywords. But in their mission to go beyond conquering the world to own the whole universe, Google has created many more products besides search. Some of the more popular ones include Gmail, Google Docs, and Google Maps.

If we stick only to the area of web search and analytics, several of Google's products can be useful to solar marketers aiming to be more effective online. These include:

Google Advanced Search—Allows you to refine a search by including or excluding certain kinds of results. For example, you can search for "solar installers" and then indicate that you want results only in English and from the United States and also specify that you want only files posted in Microsoft PowerPoint format (.ppt). This would be a way for you to quickly get to presentations made by American solar companies without having to wade through lots of other search results that will include ordinary web pages that mention the term "PowerPoint."

Google Custom Search—A way to add Google as the search engine on your own website. By installing their search box on your site, your visitors will be able to search your site more effectively, using the power of Google's software, rather than with the low-powered default search that comes bundled in with WordPress or most other website building systems.

Google Alerts—A service that will send you an email every day or whenever there's news on a topic that you choose. For example, if you create an alert for your company name, you'll get an email whenever somebody online mentions your company. You should set up alerts not only for your own company name but also for your main competitors, so you can keep tabs on what they're doing.

Google Analytics—The most popular software to keep track of traffic to your website. It measures how many people visit your site each day and also what pages they look at and even if they convert to a sales lead. It's so full of features that it can be intimidating and hard to use. But it's worth getting some help to understand at least the basic information about your website such as how many visitors you get per day and how they're finding your website (for example, from a Google search for certain keywords or from Facebook).

Google Trends—Shows the popularity of particular keywords over time. For example, you may be surprised to learn that, even as solar installations were growing at a rapid rate in the US, over the last few years searches for the word "solar power" actually declined from a high in July 2008 until they hit their low point in December of 2014, making a recovery since then. This is useful information because it ties interest in solar power to prices for fossil fuels. You'll remember that July 2008 was the peak of gasoline prices in the US, which passed $4 per gallon in some areas.

GOOGLE FOR SOLAR: PROJECT SUNROOF

Like many Silicon Valley tech companies, Google has its roots in software but it also takes an interest in clean energy. Aside from trying to source renewables for its data centers, Google has even created a product for the solar industry in particular, Project Sunroof. Targeted at consumers, Project Sunroof is Google's way of helping make it easier for homeowners in selected US cities to get rooftop solar.

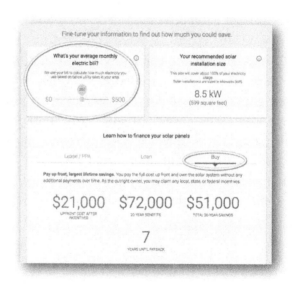

As the site explains, "Project Sunroof puts Google's expansive data in mapping and computing resources to use, helping calculate the best solar plan for you. When you enter your address, Project Sunroof looks up your home in Google Maps and combines that information with other databases to create your personalized roof analysis."

The visitor who types their address into the initial page of Project Sunroof gets an attractive report on whether their property is suitable for solar, how much they could fit there, and how much energy that would likely produce as shown in the screenshot. The user can then make adjustments to information circled. The process is fun and it's easy to go through. After entering all of his or her information, the user receives a list on screen of solar companies that have partnered with Google and do installations in the area, which Google can put in touch with the user if that person wants.

As of the time I wrote this book, all the partner installers seemed to be large national companies. But perhaps Project Sunroof will include local installers in the future. If you're interested in getting on Google's list of installers, you can contact Project Sunroof through the website. Also, Project Sunroof initially only covered certain cities in the United States, including the San Francisco Bay Area and Boston but it has already expended to offer service around the US

As a result, more and more often, if you search Google for solar in a certain local area, after some ads, the first thing to come up in the results is a little box from Project Sunroof. See an example from a search for "solar panels Indianapolis."

Solar savings estimator

Estimate how much you can save on your electric bill with rooftop solar.

Enter home address

©2016 Google · Map data ©2016 Google · Terms of Use

Shady ▬▬▬▬▬▬ Sunny

Average home in Indianapolis
Based on your query

Estimated savings
Over 20-year solar lease;
no upfront cost

-$5,000

Source: Project Sunroof

Feedback

This means, of course, that Google is now going to be directly competing with the solar installers that have done the SEO to appear in its search listings. That's going to represent both a challenge and an opportunity for solar companies to continue to get web traffic from Google searches. I recommend that you keep an eye on Project Sunroof, as they are likely to set the bar high for the industry to use solar calculators online to acquire new solar customers.

CPSIA information can be obtained
at www.ICGtesting.com
Printed in the USA
LVOW13s1620301116
515170LV00011B/264/P